Better Safe Than Sorry

Better Safe Than Sorry

HOW CONSUMERS NAVIGATE EXPOSURE
TO EVERYDAY TOXICS

Norah MacKendrick

UNIVERSITY OF CALIFORNIA PRESS

University of California Press, one of the most distinguished university presses in the United States, enriches lives around the world by advancing scholarship in the humanities, social sciences, and natural sciences. Its activities are supported by the UC Press Foundation and by philanthropic contributions from individuals and institutions. For more information, visit www.ucpress.edu.

University of California Press
Oakland, California

Library of Congress Cataloging-in-Publication Data

Names: MacKendrick, Norah, author.
Title: Better safe than sorry : how consumers navigate exposure to everyday
    toxics / Norah MacKendrick.
Description: Oakland, California : University of California Press, [2018] |
    Includes bibliographical references and index. |
Identifiers: LCCN 2017049895 (print) | LCCN 2017054558 (ebook) |
    ISBN 9780520969070 (Epub) | ISBN 9780520296688 (cloth : alk. paper) |
    ISBN 9780520296695 (pbk : alk. paper)
Subjects: LCSH: Consumer behavior—United States. | Women consumers—
    United States—Psychology. | Product safety—United States. | Consumer
    goods—United States—Safety measures.
Classification: LCC HF5415.33.U6 (ebook) | LCC HF5415.33.U6 M33 2018
    (print) | DDC 306.30973—dc23
LC record available at https://lccn.loc.gov/2017049895

Manufactured in the United States of America

26 25 24 23 22 21 20 19 18
10 9 8 7 6 5 4 3 2 1

For William and Martin

CONTENTS

LIST OF ILLUSTRATIONS

FIGURE

TABLES

ACKNOWLEDGMENTS

This book is the culmination of research and writing that took place in Canada and the United States, and its very existence speaks to the network of supportive colleagues, family members, and friends who helped along the way.

Josée Johnston, at the University of Toronto, convinced me that precautionary consumption was an idea worth exploring, and she supported me in writing a dissertation about women's foodwork and chemical avoidance. I am deeply indebted to her for her mentorship and friendship. I am also grateful to Kate Cairns, who helped me think through some of the core ideas in this book. Josée and Kate put the fun in research and writing, and that is no small accomplishment.

Susan Markens and Miranda Waggoner provided the scaffolding that I needed to move this project from vague idea to coherent words on a page. They read many drafts of the book and consistently offered incisive critique and encouragement. Their own research was instrumental to my thinking about precautionary consumption, gender, and embodiment. I don't know if I will ever be able thank them enough for all they have done to help me complete this book.

At Rutgers, I am fortunate to be surrounded by supportive colleagues. Tom Rudel and Karen Cerulo encouraged me to write a book and then read early drafts of this work. They devoted many hours of their time to providing me with helpful advice over coffee, lunch, and dinner. In a stroke of good luck and great timing, Steve Brechin joined our department midway through this project, and he has become a trusted mentor. Catherine Lee, a dear friend and unofficial faculty advisor, counseled me on our train trips to and from campus. She also helped me find a writing group. Hana Shepherd,

Joanna Kempner, and Sharon Bzostek provided much needed doses of distraction and humor that put this project in perspective. I am grateful to Deborah Carr and Paul McLean for making the department a truly supportive environment for a junior faculty member. I am thankful to have colleagues like Laurie Krivo, Pat Roos, Judy Gerson, Eviatar Zerubavel, Julie Phillips, Kristen Springer, Rachael Shwom-Everlich, Chip Clarke, and Arlene Stein, who provided advice and ample encouragement as I was writing this book. Lisa Iorillo and Amy Shockley provided valuable logistical support that helped move this project along. Teja Pristavec, Lindsay Stevens, and Elizabeth Kushnereit assisted with the many necessary aspects of putting together a book. They also provided smart critique and helped me think through some of the ideas that went into the book. I am lucky that they agreed to work with me. Noa Rabin assisted with data collection for chapter 3, and her help is much appreciated.

I am especially grateful to the thirty women who generously volunteered to be interviewed for this project. Funding to support these interviews was provided by a School of Arts and Sciences Research Council Grant.

I owe a great deal to Sarah Bowen, Keith Brown, Phil Brown, and Jennifer Reich, who all read drafts of the book and offered suggestions that helped strengthen my arguments. They, along with Rebecca Altman, Joslyn Brenton, Sinikka Elliott, Rene Almeling, Dayna Nadine Scott, Anne Rochon Ford, Rachel Schwartz, Caroline Dimitri, Nadine Blumer, Leah DeSole, K. A. Dilday, Julia Brody, and John Myles, helped inspire various ideas and arguments throughout the book.

At University of California Press, I had the good fortune of working with Kate Marshall and Bradley Depew. I thank them for moving this project along so quickly and expertly. I am also grateful to Dore Brown, Genevieve Thurston, Janine Baer, and Victoria Baker for helping prepare the manuscript for production.

I thank Miriam Diamond, Clifford Weisel, Robert Laumbach, and the late Paul Lioy for teaching me a bit about toxicology and exposure science and for showing an interest in my research.

Sometimes a book needs a cheerleading section, and I was fortunate to have one made up of friends and neighbors from near and far who inquired about the book, connected me to interview subjects, and provided constant encouragement. Codesha and Bridgette helped me juggle work and family, and I am forever thankful for them. I owe a debt of gratitude to my parents,

Judy and Harry, as well as Lois Field, Mo MacKendrick, and the late Ruth MacKendrick for offering an abundance of love and support while I wrote this book. Closer to home, Robert made it possible for me to have time to write, and he never stopped encouraging me to finish this book. William and Martin, it was the early days with you that inspired the ideas for this book. Thank you for being patient with me all the way through this project. And if you are reading this, then, yes, the book is finished now.

LIST OF ABBREVIATIONS

ACC	American Chemistry Council
BPA	bisphenol A
CAA	Clean Air Act
CCOF	California Certified Organic Farmers
CDC	United States Centers for Disease Control and Prevention
CPSC	Consumer Product Safety Commission
CWA	Clean Water Act
DBP	dibutyl phthalate
DDT	dichloro-diphenyl-trichloroethane
DEHP	di-2-ethylhexyl phthalate
DES	diethylstilbestrol
DOHaD	Developmental origins of health and disease
EDCs	endocrine disrupting compounds
EPA	United States Environmental Protection Agency
EWG	Environmental Working Group
FAA	Food Additives Amendment
FDA	United States Food and Drug Administration
FDCA	Food, Drug and Cosmetic Act
FIFRA	Federal Insecticide, Fungicide and Rodenticide Act
FQPA	Food Quality Protection Act

GAO	United States Government Accountability Office
GMOs	genetically modified organisms
GRAS	generally recognized as safe
HCHW	Healthy Child Healthy World
HFCS	high fructose corn syrup
LDDI	Learning and Developmental Disabilities Initiative
NEPA	National Environmental Policy Act
NIEHS	National Institute for Environmental Health Sciences
NLEA	Nutrition Labeling and Education Act
NRDC	Natural Resources Defense Fund
PBBs	polybrominated biphenyls
PBDEs	polybrominated diphenyl ethers
PCBs	polychlorinated biphenyls
PFCs	perfluorinated compounds
PFOA	perfluorooctanoic acid
POPs	persistent organic pollutants
PVC	polyvinyl chloride
REACH	registration, evaluation, authorization, and restriction of chemicals
rBGH	recombinant bovine growth hormone
SDWA	Safe Drinking Water Act
SNAP	Supplemental Nutrition Assistance Program
TDCPP	tris(1,3-dichloro-2-propyl)phosphate
TSCA	Toxic Substances Control Act
UNEP	United Nations Environment Programme
USDA	United States Department of Agriculture
VOCs	volatile organic compounds
WHO	World Health Organization
WIC	Women, Infant, and Children

ONE

Introduction

> Chaz Dean believes in a natural, healthy lifestyle, so it's no wonder his approach to hairstyling follows suit. . . . Chaz's own hair care line is made with natural ingredients. . . . So dedicated is he to this philosophy that his WEN® product line does not include a shampoo. Rather, his cleansing conditioner is a single product that both cleanses and conditions, without the use of sodium laurel sulfate or other damaging detergents found in shampoos.
>
> From the website of Chaz Dean, entrepreneur and celebrity hairstylist

> Regulatory and scientific authorities worldwide, such as the United States Environmental Protection Agency and European Commission, have concluded that glyphosate, when used according to label directions, does not pose an unreasonable risk to human health, the environment, or pets.
>
> From "What Is Glyphosate?" published online by
> Monsanto, manufacturer of Roundup

When Chaz Dean, a celebrity hairstylist based in Los Angeles, launched the product WEN Sweet Almond Mint Cleansing Conditioner, he pledged to change the world of hair care. He explained that his cleansing conditioners were inspired by his garden, and he claimed that they were made from natural ingredients and were healthier for hair than conventional shampoos.[1] By 2014, however, Dean's company had received over 21,000 complaints from customers who had experienced hair loss, hair breakage, and scalp rashes after using WEN hair products.[2] As permitted by law, none of the ingredients in Dean's products underwent formal safety testing. Despite numerous consumer grievances, and notwithstanding an advisory issued by the Food and Drug Administration (FDA), WEN products are still for sale, and Dean maintains that they are safe.[3] Although the FDA has no power to recall the products, warnings distributed via social media caused sales to drop, and in 2017, Dean settled a class action lawsuit launched by affected customers.[4]

In 2017, a judge in Fresno, California, ruled that, in accordance with California's chemical safety labeling law Proposition 65, the herbicide Roundup, produced by Monsanto, must carry a warning label stating that the active ingredient glyphosate is "known to the state to cause cancer."[5] But Roundup must only carry this warning in California, where chemical safety rules are considerably stricter than those in the rest of the country. In a separate ruling that same year, Monsanto was ordered to turn over emails it exchanged with government regulators and scientists about the safety of this herbicide. This correspondence revealed a close relationship between the company and the United States Environmental Protection Agency (EPA), which is responsible for ensuring the safety of agricultural pesticides, and a deliberate effort on the part of key EPA officials and Monsanto to downplay results from studies showing that glyphosate caused tumors in some animals.[6] Glyphosate is the world's most widely applied pesticide, and, not surprisingly, glyphosate residues can be found in most foods containing soybeans, oats, and corn—food crops typically treated with glyphosate.[7] The International Agency for Research on Cancer—part of the World Health Organization—has classified glyphosate as "probably carcinogenic to humans" and as positively associated with non-Hodgkin lymphoma.[8]

Stories like these reflect a disturbing but familiar pattern in the U.S. retail landscape: a food or product is assumed to be safe, evidence emerges that associates it with health problems, this evidence is disputed, and the product is left on the market, leaving consumers to figure out what to do. In fact, the marketplace has evolved to capitalize on widespread concern and uncertainty over such matters by promising safety. Shoppers walking into a major supermarket, like Target, Kroger, or Safeway, will encounter a number of labels telling them about the "bad" things that are *not* in products and all the "good" things that are. As illustrated by the case of WEN, the proliferation of promotional materials and labels emphasize the natural quality of the products being sold.

As a result, everyday decisions about what to buy have become exceedingly complicated for shoppers concerned about environmental contaminants in their food and consumer products. Many plastic water bottles, for instance, have labels stating that they are "bisphenol A–free," while stainless steel bottles claim to be "plastic-free." How do shoppers know which bottle is best? In the produce aisle, choosing an apple is just as complex. Customers are likely to find a pricey certified-organic apple, an imported conventional apple (grown with pesticides), and, possibly, a locally grown but conventional variety. Which one should they choose? When they get to the dairy section of the store, they might wonder about the difference between "rBGH-free" yogurt and certified-organic yogurt. Perhaps the most perplexing choice they will encounter is whether the instant macaroni and cheese made with organic milk from grass-fed cows is healthier than the instant macaroni and cheese made with organic milk from cows fed something other than grass. Of course, both products are highly processed, high in sodium, and, as it turns out, likely contain traces of toxic substances that can interfere with the human reproductive system.[9]

These decisions seem small because, after all, they are about food and consumer goods, and they take place in a grocery store. But in actual practice, they are complex. Consumers must decipher seemingly infinite warnings plastered on product packages—suggesting that one bad shopping choice could imperil their health (or the health of their children)—while trying to balance the household budget and buy the right foods and products to suit every family member's tastes. All of this reading and decision-making could prompt shoppers to drop their baskets in the middle of the aisle, walk out of the store, and vow never to read a label again.

Such experiences are not limited to the grocery aisle. Messages to avoid toxic chemicals abound.[10] Popular books about the dangerous chemical substances in foods and consumer products feature such titles as *No More Dirty Looks: The Truth about Your Beauty Products—and the Ultimate Guide to Safe and Clean Cosmetics, Plastic: A Toxic Love Story, The Body Toxic: How the Hazardous Chemistry of Everyday Things Threatens Our Health and Well-being,* and *The Non-toxic Avenger: What You Don't Know Can Hurt You.*[11] The Environmental Working Group (EWG)—one of the largest environmental health advocacy groups in the United States—offers readers multiple safe-shopping guides, including the popular *Dirty Dozen* guide to pesticide residues in fresh produce, and the *Skin Deep Guide to Cosmetics.*

Sales of certified-organic food and so-called natural foods, cosmetics, and cleaning products are higher than ever in the United States, and growth in this sector outstrips growth in the conventional grocery sector.[12] Whole Foods Market, a global natural and organic food retailer, reported record profits from 2008 to 2014 and opened hundreds of new stores across the United States during that period.[13] Conventional retailers now compete with the company by offering their own low-cost, generic, eco-friendly, or certified-organic brands. According to figures from the Organic Trade Association, more middle-class shoppers than ever before, including middle-class African

American and Latino consumers, are choosing organic items when they shop.[14] The food industry projects that natural and organic food sales will continue to outpace other sectors of the grocery market.[15]

I call this trend toward "green" or nontoxic shopping "precautionary consumption." Precautionary consumption is a kind of "looking before you leap" that takes place in grocery stores.[16] It can involve, for example, reading a product label to identify potentially harmful additives, checking for an organic certification seal, or using the EWG's Skin Deep database to find cosmetics that don't contain carcinogenic ingredients. Precautionary consumption is about deploying a *personal* standard of safety, a standard that shifts depending on what a person is concerned about at a particular moment, where they are shopping, their disposable income, how busy they are, and other demands on their attention. The sheer expansion of precautionary consumer spaces and advice means that the individual consumer angle is now a dominant way of thinking about and framing chemical exposure. This approach, in so much as it hinges on suggesting that better label reading at the supermarket will address and mitigate chemical pollution, obscures the larger systemic context that has resulted in a marketplace awash in untested chemicals. By focusing on consumer practices, individualized precautionary consumption directs attention away from the responsibility of government and chemical companies to enforce and enact responsible testing and manufacturing protocols.[17]

Put another way, precautionary consumption is a product of broader social, economic, and political transformations, whereby collective risks—that is, risks that affect large numbers of people—are increasingly addressed as individual-level problems with individual-level fixes. Precautionary consumption requires individuals to make subtle calculations, such as deciding whether it is better to save a dollar by choosing a conventional apple with pesticide residues that could cause cancer later in life or to spend the extra money to buy an organic apple and avoid such chemicals—at least momentarily.[18] Most significantly, precautionary consumption often falls to *mothers,* as they are the primary shoppers in most households. Middle-class women in particular become aware of the dangers of synthetic chemicals in their food and consumer product during the transition to motherhood—either before conception, during pregnancy, while breastfeeding, or when preparing to offer an infant its first solid foods.[19]

This book engages these issues and other pressing questions: How and why has precautionary consumption become a major component of consumer culture? More to the point, why are mothers taking on the responsibility for precautionary consumption? How do they approach the task of chemical avoidance through shopping? Do they embrace it as a marker of their commitment to motherhood, or do they resist it as another job they have to incorporate into their busy lives? Finally, what are the larger social and political implications of approaching contamination as a matter of consumer choice? This book traces the rise of precautionary consumption to understand why consumers are so concerned about chemical substances in their food and consumer products. More specifically, it explores the gendered labor of precautionary consumption to show that it is not the practice of paranoid, affluent mothers; rather, it is a response to social and medical discourses that hold women responsible for producing healthy children. These discourses have been mobilized in powerful ways in response to advances in science and technology, revealing the remarkable permeability of the human body to ubiquitous environmental chemicals that have never been properly evaluated for their impacts on human health.

The rise of precautionary consumption corresponds to the poor regulation of the American food system and chemical production at a cultural moment when Americans are preoccupied about what they eat and put into their bodies and even more apprehensive about what they feed their children. In this milieu, it is overwhelmingly women who are working to bypass the legacy of widespread chemical pollution. Not only does precautionary consumption place a large and unfair burden on women, I argue, but it is also a temporary and piecemeal response to the widespread problem of environmental chemicals.

A TOXIC LEGACY

Many Americans believe that the federal government keeps a close eye on the chemicals used in food and consumer products.[20] However, the majority of synthetic chemicals used in processed foods, cleaning products, personal care products, furniture, and electronics have entered into production without any rigorous testing or federal government review, and most of the chemicals used in cosmetics require no premarket review. The EPA has the authority to regulate commercial and industrial chemicals, but between 1976 and 2016 it took action on less than 10 percent of the eighty-five thousand chemicals that were registered for use in the United States.[21] The FDA is responsible for regulating chemicals used in cosmetics, but it only reviews coloring additives and maintains a short list of chemicals that are prohibited or restricted.

Outside the jurisdiction of the U.S. federal government, major reforms to chemical legislation have been enacted. Starting in 2007, the European Union adopted an explicit precautionary approach to chemical regulation, much to the disappointment of U.S. chemical producers, who lobbied extensively to stall or derail these regulatory efforts.[22] In the case of cosmetics, the European Union has banned or restricted the use of over 1,300 chemicals because of concerns about health effects, while the FDA has banned or restricted only 11 chemicals.[23] More action is occurring at the state level in the United States. California, Maine, and Washington, for example, have all enacted legislation to restrict compounds such as certain brominated flame retardants, bisphenol A (BPA), and triclosan—restrictions that are not present at the federal level.

Reading about the cocktail of chemicals flooding the consumer landscape and the myriad commodities promising that they are "safe," many observers will inevitably wonder if they should be worried about synthetic chemicals in their food and homes. The short answer is yes. It would be a mistake to dismiss this phenomenon as consumer paranoia or the consequence of bad information distributed through the Internet, the approach taken by books like *Scared to Death: How Chemophobia Threatens Public Health.*[24] Concern about low-dose exposure to environmental chemicals is supported by published, peer-reviewed toxicology and environmental health research— research that has compelled organizations such as the Endocrine Society, the American College of Obstetricians and Gynecologists, the American Society for Reproductive Medicine, and the American Academy of Pediatrics to issue policy statements urging government action to restrict the use of many synthetic chemicals currently being used in food and consumer products.[25] The International Federation of Gynecology and Obstetrics released its opinion on this issue:

> Widespread exposure to toxic environmental chemicals threatens healthy human reproduction. Industrial chemicals are used and discarded in every aspect of daily life and are ubiquitous in food, water, air, and consumer products. Exposure to environmental chemicals and metals permeates all parts of life across the globe. Toxic chemicals enter the environment through food and energy production, industrial emissions and accidents, waste, transportation, and the making, use, and disposal of consumer and personal care products.[26]

In the rest of this chapter and throughout this book, I outline the scope and significance of human environmental chemical exposure. I demonstrate how the distribution of toxic substances in the environment and human bodies, and the attribution of responsibility for addressing toxic exposures, are not random. Exposure and responsibility are culturally and socially determined.

THE CHEMICAL BODY BURDEN

Owing to massive investments in industrial research during World War II, the manufacturing of synthetic chemicals increased three-fold after the war and is now a trillion-dollar industry.[27] In the United States, 85,000 synthetic chemicals are registered for use, and just under 2,500 new substances are introduced into the U.S. market each year.[28] These substances must be registered with the EPA, and yet, until very recently, there was no requirement that they be tested for their potential environmental impact and human health consequences.

The adult human body contains hundreds of these chemicals, accumulated during a lifetime of exposure. This internal load of synthetic chemicals is referred to as a chemical dose or body burden.[29] By breathing outdoor and indoor air, drinking, eating, using a computer, and sitting on a couch, the human body continually absorbs multiple chemicals, often at low concentrations. Some of them, like BPA (used to line food cans and produce some types of plastic), are excreted from the body, while others, like brominated flame retardants and pesticides, accumulate in tissues and fat deposits. Pregnancy mobilizes some of these chemicals, and many of the chemicals that pass through a mother's body (e.g., air pollutants, BPA, parabens) enter the placenta, where they are absorbed by the fetus.[30] Breastfeeding mobilizes maternal fat stores and the fat-soluble chemicals that they contain. Thus, through breastfeeding, a mother transfers to her infant some of the environmental chemicals stored in her body.[31]

Chemical body burdens can be detected through biomonitoring, a technology first developed in the early twentieth century that uses analytical chemistry to measure chemical biomarkers of exposure in human tissues and fluids.[32] Because of improvements to this technology in the late 1990s and early 2000s, scientists can now identify chemicals that are present even at very low levels in the human body (as low as parts per quadrillion)—levels that were previously undetectable.[33] Every five years, the United States Centers for Disease Control and Prevention (CDC) publishes its national biomonitoring survey, which documents the multitude of environmental chemicals found in the typical adult American.[34] As the technology improves, the agency is able to measure additional chemicals.[35] The most recent full report was published in 2009, and the agency published updated tables in 2015 and 2017. In a 2017 update, the CDC reported data for 308 chemicals. These compounds include acrylamide (from the combustion of organic matter during cooking), arsenic metabolites, environmental phenols (such as BPA), and triclosan.[36] The biomonitoring data from the CDC and the National Institute for Environmental Health Sciences (NIEHS) confirm that *all* individuals have synthetic chemicals in their bodies, whether they live next to a factory or toxic waste dump, in a suburban home, or in a log cabin in the Appalachians. In the words of Linda Birnbaum, director of the NIEHS, "It is now impossible to examine an unexposed population anywhere on Earth."[37] For instance, the body burdens of Inuit living in the far north, thousands of miles away from the central hubs of chemical production and toxic emissions, are significantly higher than individuals living in the south. Studies of Inuit women's breast milk reveal exceedingly high body burdens of persistent organic pollutants, such as polychlorinated biphenyls (PCBs), dichloro-diphenyl-trichloroethane (DDT), and brominated flame retardants.[38] This surprising finding is explained by global air and water currents, which transport these and other persistent organic pollutants from industrial regions to the poles. In the far north, they settle in the bodies of the fish and mammals that constitute a major staple of the indigenous peoples living in this region.

Indeed, while all bodies contain synthetic chemicals, body burdens differ in crucial ways that reflect the social and political organization of risk, gender, and social inequalities. There are major differences in how bodies become exposed to chemicals, whose exposures become noticed, and how these exposures are addressed. In the United States, low-income households, communities of color, and indigenous communities are exposed to toxic chemicals at levels that exceed those of white, middle-class households and communities. These exposures come from multiple environmental and outdoor sources, such as proximity to heavy industry, highways and busy roadways, and landfills and toxic waste disposal sites.[39] The locations of low-income neighborhoods, indigenous communities, and communities of color are no coincidence. They are the consequences of siting decisions that target these areas, the lack of political power these communities have to oppose polluting industry and to encourage the creation of parks and environmentally friendly spaces, and racist zoning ordinances and covenants that have prevented non-whites from settling in "desirable" neighborhoods and have thus limited housing options for particular population groups.[40] Finally, occupation affects exposure to toxics. Workers employed in automobile manufacturing, coal mining, transportation, farming, food manufacturing, and nail and hair salons are exposed to endocrine disruptors and carcinogens at levels that are much higher than those of the general public owing to the requirements of their jobs. These workers are at greater risk of developing reproductive health problems and certain forms of cancer.[41] Occupational chemical exposures disproportionately affect immigrant and minority workers, as they are more likely to be assigned jobs that require close contact with hazardous substances.[42]

The indoor environment also contains toxic compounds due to the presence of building materials like flooring and carpets, as well as furniture, electronics, cleaning products, and air fresheners that release an array of chemicals, from volatile organic compounds such as benzene, formaldehyde, and plasticizers, to dust comprised of flame retardant polybrominated diphenyl ethers (PBDEs).[43] All individuals who work, live, or spend any time indoors are exposed to toxic indoor air. However, exposures are classed and racialized.[44] Low-income families and families of color are more likely to live in older homes with peeling lead paint and aging water pipes that leach lead into household water.[45] Low-income homes are more likely to have higher levels of PBDEs in household dust because of the presence of older, crumbling foam furniture that releases these compounds into air.[46] PBDEs make their way into people's bodies, and exposures are considerably higher in young children, who play and crawl on the floor and mouth objects that have come into contact with dust.[47] When California implemented stringent new flame retardant standards that restricted certain classes of PBDEs from furniture, some households replaced older couches with newer ones that did not contain these chemicals, but the old couches were destined for thrift stores, donation centers, and curbside giveaways, thereby increasing the risk of exposure for low-income households.[48] After this phaseout in California, researchers found that house dust levels of PBDEs began to drop, but they also detected a corresponding increase in the chemicals used to replace PBDEs. Their research suggests that swapping one chemical for another will not lower the human chemical burden.[49]

Social scientists readily acknowledge the environmental justice implications of toxic exposures from air, water, soil, occupation, and home environment, but there is comparatively less research exploring unequal toxic exposures from food and consumer products.[50] Like exposures from the outdoor environment, consumer-based exposures are stratified by race, gender, and class. Women who use beauty products, for example, are exposed to a toxic cosmetic cocktail of heavy metals and endocrine disruptors (synthetic substances that interfere with the synthesis and secretion of the body's hormones and affect the regulation of the endocrine system), and this is borne out in biomonitoring studies.[51] Women's exposure is higher than men's because they participate in more intensive forms of beauty work that require an array of cosmetics, hair products, and creams and lotions as part of meeting the cultural expectations of normative femininity.[52] Black women have higher levels of parabens and phthalates in their bodies than do white women, as the beauty products marketed to Black women, such as skin lightening products, chemical relaxers to straighten hair, and vaginal douches, contain these toxic compounds.[53] Such products are connected to beauty practices rooted in the sociocultural devaluation of Black bodies and hair, and Black women's bodies in particular.[54]

Yet exposure to some environmental contaminants increases with household income. One study found that higher socioeconomic status households have higher body burdens of mercury, arsenic, perfluorinated compounds (PFCs), and benzophenone-3, among other compounds.[55] Exposure to mercury, PFCs, and arsenic, the researchers speculate, arises from dietary exposure to fish and shellfish, dairy, and meat—relatively expensive foods that are consumed in greater quantities by affluent households.[56] Benzophenone-3 is associated with using conventional sunscreen, and wealthier individuals are more likely to use sunscreen. For these specific pathways of exposure, precautionary consumption can likely make a difference. Households can switch to eco-friendly sunscreens, choose fish and shellfish that contain less mercury, and avoid high-fat dairy and meat products—advice that is, in fact, recommended by environmental health advocacy groups. Of course, these solutions protect only one consumer at a time and work only if individuals know what to do, have access to alternative products, and can afford them.

A significant body of research indicates that exposure to toxics in foods and everyday consumer products is a cause for serious concern. Chemicals such as lead (found in some older toys and water and paint in older homes) and other heavy metals, BPA, phthalates (found in flexible plastics and scented products), parabens, and PBDEs, along with dozens of other classes of chemicals, can affect the human reproductive system, metabolism, and thyroid function, as well as neurological development and cognition.[57] Even low-level exposures to these compounds have been linked to reproductive disorders, neurological disorders, obesity, and cancer, with early life exposures during fetal development and infancy being of greatest concern.[58] Researchers attribute increases in incidences of obesity, diabetes, genital abnormalities at birth, breast cancer, thyroid cancer, infertility, testicular cancer, asthma, and attention deficit hyperactivity disorder to chronic exposure to environmental chemicals.[59]

The chemical industry has long tried to discredit these concerns and fought to restrict the power of state and federal governments to regulate suspected endocrine disruptors and carcinogens.[60] Between 2005 and 2014, the American Chemistry Council (ACC)—the main lobbying arm of the chemical industry—doubled its lobbying budget to $64.9 million, making it the twenty-fifth highest spender on federal lobbying that year.[61] These were critical years during which pressure to reform the nation's regulatory framework for chemicals was building. The ACC insisted that the legislation at the time—the Toxic Substances Control Act of 1976—was robust and that its "members go to great lengths to ensure products are safe for their intended uses."[62] The council rejected the proposition that there were significant health consequences from low-dose exposure to endocrine disruptors.[63] The ACC has a strong influence over the EPA, which makes decisions about chemical safety. Within the EPA, the council is able to promote the results of industry-funded studies that show no evidence of harm from chemicals of concern, thus giving the EPA little formal grounds to request more comprehensive risk assessments. The ACC and its members are, not surprisingly, opposed to regulatory restrictions on the chemical industry.[64] In 2016, the TSCA was amended to institute modest precautionary measures. This reform was heralded as a new era for chemical regulation, but it was quickly undermined by the Trump administration.

LOOKING AT PRECAUTIONARY CONSUMPTION THROUGH A SOCIOLOGICAL LENS

While it is related to the precautionary principle, precautionary consumption is much narrower in its perspective and is enacted in the here and now. The precautionary principle is a policy ethic urging the universal protection of human and environmental well-being. This principle arose in the 1970s, at a time of growing public concern about environmental degradation, especially surrounding the global circulation of persistent organic chemicals, such as DDT. The precautionary principle has been a guiding logic behind several major environmental initiatives, including the Montreal Protocol on Substances that Deplete the Ozone Layer of 1987, the Rio Declaration (or Earth Summit) of 1992, and the Stockholm Convention on Persistent Organic Pollutants of 2001. The U.S. federal government supported all of these agreements, but, domestically, it has systematically rejected the application of the precautionary principle in environmental and chemical legislation.

Precautionary consumption is related to, but distinct from, the concept of the inverted quarantine identified by sociologist Andrew Szasz.[65] Szasz describes the inverted quarantine as a kind of commodity bubble that quarantines the "clean" individual from the toxic environment. He warns that as individuals cocoon themselves from toxic threats, they are less likely to demand regulatory action to prevent toxic materials from being released into the environment and retail landscape. Precautionary consumption builds on Szasz's work to reveal how the underlying logic behind consumer-based self-protection is an individualized deployment of the precautionary principle. Whereas the global diffusion of the precautionary principle represented a major turn in environmental politics that focused on improving worldwide environmental quality, precautionary consumption represents the individualization of a universal risk. Chemicals in the food supply and in consumer and household products affect everyone living in industrial society, not just those who shop. The exposures from contaminants lurking on a plate of conventional food cannot compare to the chronic, high-level exposures experienced by people living in communities in close proximity to or downstream from chemical manufacturing plants, who are constantly being exposed to polluted air, water, and soil, or factory workers who handle toxic materials as part of their job. Communities close to farming operations contend with pesticide drift, and farm laborers are exposed to pesticides at much higher concentrations than are urban dwellers who eat a diet of conventional fruits and vegetables.[66]

So-called green companies and eco-brands, as well as stores like Whole Foods Market, have expanded the possibilities for precautionary consumption, promising to empower individuals by giving them an escape from chemical risk. But this expansion of safe shopping spaces merely obscures the larger systemic problems that have led to toxic chemicals being used in food production and manufacturing in the first place. There are deeper structural explanations at the root of what amounts to a two-tiered marketplace, where organic grapes are for sale alongside conventional ones, and phthalate-free shampoo is sold on the same shelf as varieties containing phthalates. Under precautionary consumption, the problem of undesirable chemicals in food and consumer products is not understood as a government problem or corporate problem but rather as an individual consumer problem, and even more precisely—insofar as children's health is a predominant concern—a problem that implicates women's preconception, pregnant, and breastfeeding bodies, and domestic labor.

In this book, I trace the political, economic, and social forces that gave rise to precautionary consumption. I show how this consumer practice is a personalized endeavor—and one that is also typically gendered. I show how women practice precautionary consumption and experience it in their everyday lives, and I explore how it is classed, while not being entirely out of reach for low-income women.

One the one hand, sociologists like Andrew Szasz express concern that these individualized behaviors represent a kind of political apathy such that the public no longer pressures political institutions to improve environmental health but seeks instead to build private commodity bubbles.[67] On the other hand, sociologists like Thomas Rudel take a slightly more optimistic look at this kind of behavior, seeing it as a kind of defensive environmentalism.[68] Rudel suggests that small acts of individual protection can become more altruistic and collective when there are "focusing events" that draw attention to the linked, common fate of groups touched by the same environmental problem. The concept of precautionary consumption helps to crystallize these overlapping but distinct interpretations of the rise of eco-friendly products and chemical avoidance practices. Increasing consumer concern—and action—about chemicals represents a calculated strategy of self-protection vis-à-vis distrust toward manufacturers and government regulators. [Precautionary consumption is powered by deep skepticism that food and products for sale have been thoroughly tested using standards that prioritize public health over industry profit] Precautionary consumers are not naïvely confident that they can sequester their bodies from harmful chemicals.[69] Rather, they seek to piece together small moments of precautionary action that they hope will stem some of the harm of a lifetime of chemical exposure. In other words, precautionary consumption is accomplished in the moment—while an individual is shopping, making a shopping list, or planning a meal—

and it becomes routinized over time. It is an effort to do something to protect oneself, even if that protection is only temporary.

The presence of harmful chemicals in human bodies and in everyday foods and products reflects political failures on a large scale and over an extended time frame. The environmental health movement has already called government to account for failing to carefully regulate chemicals and monitor their effects on human health,[70] and in some cases, it has successfully pushed government to adopt stronger regulations or forced companies to change their manufacturing practices. While these wins are noteworthy (some of them are discussed in this book), ever more environmental chemicals—whose safety has not been established— continue to be released into the environment and retail landscape. Precautionary consumption provides an immediate response to widespread chemical pollution, particularly when the answer to the question of how to hold government and industry accountable is elusive. Is it possible to launch a lawsuit against the government for a lifetime of accumulated chemicals? Can a mother sue the EPA after learning that her newborn contains a body burden of more than two hundred compounds?[71] Can she sue the chemists who invented these compounds, the companies that manufactured them, or the companies that put them in her consumer products? Or does she blame herself for failing to read the ingredient label on her face lotion or for eating conventional, rather than certified-organic, food?

Responsibility for the harm created by chemical production is not only challenging to define but also nearly impossible to track, as chemicals come from many points of origin, move across jurisdictions and borders, and are difficult to detect in human bodies. Their impact on human health is not immediate but rather unfolds over time. In the words of historian and technoscience scholar Michelle Murphy, "Chemical injury is not just displaced spatially with super stacks, toxic trading, and selective plant placement. Chemical injury is displaced temporally, such that accountabilities exceed the scope of individual lives, bioaccumulating or persisting over time, beyond regulatory regimes, into the long future."[72] The footprint of regulatory inaction is expansive, and individuals are on their own when it comes to managing the consequences of environmental risk.

Defining Risk and Responsibility

Chronic chemical exposure reflects major social, economic, political, and scientific shifts during the past seventy years. The sheer ubiquity of tens of thousands of substances that move in and out of human bodies and across the globe speaks to an era of rapid industrialization where the speed of innovation and industrial production has outpaced social and political responses to it and is moving faster than the science that tries to understand its consequences on human and environmental health. Following the end of World War II, the acceleration of industrialization ushered in a level of unprecedented progress in the Western world, in the form of better food security, vaccines and medical technologies, and policy instruments that could offset economic risk—including old-age pension programs, unemployment benefits, and strong workers unions.

Yet, as sociologist Ulrich Beck argues, this period also marked the beginning of a "risk society," where such progress generated risks that were global, high-consequence, incalculable, and unpredictable.[73] By the 1960s and 1970s, postwar industrial development had brought transnational pollution and the kind of environmental and technological failures that produced global consequences. The globe witnessed examples of these failures multiple times, such as the nuclear accident in Chernobyl in 1986, the outbreak of mad cow disease (bovine spongiform encephalopathy) in England in 1996, and, of course, climate change.

Chemical production, in particular, is emblematic of the risk society. Chemical innovation took off in the postwar period, leading to major technological advances that helped propel population and economic growth, such as highly effective pesticides that were used for agricultural production (e.g., DDT), substances that could resist heat and flame (e.g., PCBs), and oil-repelling compounds like polytetrafluoroethylene (PFTE) that could be used for domestic and industrial purposes, including nonstick frying pans and cosmetic foundations. Such developments led to unprecedented growth and prosperity for some sectors of society while bringing about adverse consequences for the natural world and other segments of humanity—from the thinning eggshells that nearly eradicated the peregrine falcon to soil, water, and air pollution in Louisiana's "Cancer Alley" and the accumulation of PCBs in the breast milk of Inuit women. These unforeseen hazards affected the well-being of people across the globe and shook the public's confidence in science, technology, and political systems. Many began to recognize that the very mechanisms that brought wealth and prosperity were also poisoning the planet and its inhabitants.

British sociologist Anthony Giddens writes about society's declining faith in institutions like government, science, and technology to steer or control modernity[74] and about the considerable uncertainty that individuals experience as the future becomes more unpredictable.[75] According to Giddens, the current risk society is not more risk averse than previous eras, but it is preoccupied with making risk calculable and predictable. Because individuals must negotiate widespread, high-consequence risks on their own, they invest time and energy into learning how to calculate risk. By virtue of how risk is managed—by experts who make risk calculations and put systems into place to manage risk—individuals must put trust in expert systems that have little visible presence in their everyday lives.

Evidence of chemical body burdens reveals that human bodies are porous and therefore part of the environment, and this revelation creates deep fissures in the public's trust of technological innovation, which created these chemicals in the first place. This disruption is contradictory. One area of science and technology—biomonitoring—helps render body burdens visible and thus increases the public's trust in science.[76] Yet it can simultaneously erode confidence in other sectors of science (namely chemical innovation), recasting the basic acts of eating, drinking, or applying a face cream as potentially hazardous activities.

Meanwhile, what constitutes a technological hazard is socially defined, meaning that risk is shaped by organizational and institutional contexts that, by virtue of acting or failing to act, produce and mediate technological hazards.[77] The simple question of whether environmental chemicals are hazardous to human and environmental health depends on these contexts. Government agencies, like the EPA, assert that compounds such as triclosan are safe, but they also state that they will re-evaluate this decision over time.[78] Advocacy groups like the EWG and Beyond Pesticides disagree, arguing that there is already sufficient data to consider triclosan hazardous.[79] Companies such as the global personal care products company Johnson & Johnson have pledged to take the compound out of their products, but they nevertheless declare that it is safe and frame a phaseout as a conscious choice to bring "peace of mind" to consumers.[80] In 2016, a class action lawsuit was brought against Johnson & Johnson because its baby powder was found to contain a compound associated with cancer. For years, the company denied any causal relationship between its baby powder and disease, but recent investigations have pointed to a link between regular use of this product and ovarian cancer.[81] A sociology of precautionary consumption examines how individuals define these hazards, respond to them, and try to manage their exposure to them. Such an analytic approach must thus equally attend to how chemical hazards are defined by different organizations and how these definitions influence whether a compound is introduced onto the market or removed from production.

Central to this examination are the questions of what constitutes acceptable scientific uncertainty and who gets to define hazard and safety. Social scientists argue that we are now in an age of "post-normal" science and "post-normal" risk, where scientific uncertainty in risk analysis depends, ultimately, on value judgments of what constitutes acceptable uncertainty.[82] The process of deciding whether science is solid or uncertain—which is so central to determining the safety of environmental chemicals—is a symbolic and temporal process shaped by competing interests. Representing these interests are industry, health, and environmental advocacy groups who seek to define acceptable levels of uncertainty. Crucially, in the United States, arguments over this definition happen *after* chemicals have been released into the marketplace. Risk assessment is left to experts, with little opportunity for public input. Precautionary risk assessments debate acceptable uncertainty *before* production begins and consider the process of defining acceptable risk to be a value-laden exercise that should include lay perspectives, not just expert views.[83]

Given their role in evaluating and mitigating these hazards, legislative and regulatory bodies are key actors in the landscape of chemical hazards. Science in regulatory decision-making employs a model of risk assessment that assumes hazards can be fully known and measured and that any uncertainty about the severity of a hazard is a problem requiring more science.[84] The standard of proof for determining that something is hazardous is high in regulatory science in the United States, and evaluations of that standard contain value judgments that are vulnerable to the influence of powerful corporate interests that frame risk mitigation as a threat to economic growth.[85] There are numerous examples in the United States where public definitions of acceptable proof have been at odds with those of corporate actors. Prominent examples are found in Woburn, Massachusetts, where residents suspected that childhood leukemia was linked to the dumping of chemicals that seeped into local waterways; in California, where pesticide drift was affecting the health of farmworkers; and in Michigan, where meat was contaminated after livestock feed was accidentally mixed with polybrominated biphenyls (PBBs).[86]

Risk and Power: The Case of Lead

In the United States, definitions of risk are tied to power dynamics; powerful actors can delay regulation by raising questions of scientific uncertainty. The effort to remove lead from paint and gasoline is an important example.[87] According to Harold Markowitz and David Wosner, experts on the history of lead regulation, lead was identified as a neurotoxin in the nineteenth century.[88] As early as 1909, restrictions on lead in paint were put in place overseas, in France, Belgium, and Austria. Throughout the twentieth century, local and state governments in the United States, as well as advocacy groups, urged the paint and gasoline industries to stop using this substance in their products. Yet the claim that exposure to specific products containing lead— namely paint and gasoline—was responsible for cognitive delays and other health problems in children was highly contested, with public health advocates on one side and industry and government on the other. The paint and gasoline industries would not accept that there was sufficient proof of this relationship, while medical and health advocacy groups insisted the existing proof was strong enough. These industries resisted even voluntary measures that would require modest decreases in the use of lead in common substances. In 1955, the lead and paint industries caved to pressure from state governments and the American Medical Association by agreeing to put labels on paint cans warning parents not to use the paint on children's toys and furniture. The American Medical Association pushed for a label reading: "WARNING: This paint contains an amount of lead which may be POISONOUS and should not be used to paint children's toys or furniture or interior surfaces in dwelling units which might be chewed by children." However, the lead industry rejected this warning and deployed a softer language that did not include any references to poison.[89]

The battle over lead lasted fifty years, from the mid-1920s to the mid-1970s. Meanwhile, millions of children continued to be exposed to lead in early childhood, and many of them suffered from high-dose exposures that resulted in irreversible cognitive damage and, in some cases, death.[90] Disputes over scientific proof in lead science nearly devastated the career of respected environmental health scientist Herbert Needleman, who was accused of scientific misconduct by supporters of the lead industry. Needleman's research suggested that health effects from lead occur even with low-level exposures. His conclusions were eventually supported by other research in environmental toxicology, and his name was cleared.[91]

Between 1970 and 1980, the United States began phasing out the use of lead in gasoline and paint. The burdens of lead in American children's bodies dropped 37 percent between 1976 and 1980, and they have continued to decline.[92] The implementation of strong regulation lowered the burden of lead in children's bodies—something voluntary labeling did not accomplish. Strong regulation resulted in a collective, population-level decline in lead burdens. Presumably, some individuals—those with the power to choose what paint went on the walls of their homes and on their furniture—had been able to take advantage of voluntary labels and likely had lower burdens before regulations were enacted. Nevertheless, delays in regulation resulted in immeasurable damage to children's health but advantaged industries that used lead in their products. Despite regulatory change, lead is still found in paint in older homes, in older water pipes, in decorative paints on imported products, and in some cosmetics in the United States. Some places in the U.S., like Flint, Michigan, have experienced tragic levels of lead poisoning from old water pipe infrastructure. Exposure to lead paint continues to be a problem throughout Africa, Asia, and South America.[93]

Shifting Political Ideologies

As the case of lead demonstrates, government regulation of toxics can serve as a robust mechanism for protecting environmental health. But as regulations to ban lead were unfolding, political ideologies had started to shift, fundamentally undermining the principle that government has a legitimate role in protecting environmental health.

In late 1970s and early 1980s, the United States, Canada, and the United Kingdom, under the political leaders Ronald Reagan, Brian Mulroney, and Margaret Thatcher, respectively, touted the free market as the most efficient and effective system for distributing goods and services.[94] Promoting the ideology of neoliberalism, these leaders cut environmental protection agency budgets and reduced welfare and unemployment benefits, claiming that these programs entrenched, rather than improved, social and environmental problems.[95]

Neoliberalism in this sense refers to a political project that strives for smaller government and relies on market-based, voluntary mechanisms to encourage industries to operate in the best interest of society. The neoliberal state views individuals as autonomous and responsible consumers or clients who must learn to look out for themselves rather than become too dependent on government.[96] It views the market as able to correct itself without the interference of government regulations, and reasons that companies can police themselves in the interest of keeping consumers happy.

In the United States, neoliberalism came into force as the political ethos of the "Reagan Revolution," or what Jacob Hacker calls the great risk shift.[97]

As part of the great risk shift, economic risks typically borne by corporations and the state were transferred to families, resulting in greater social and economic insecurity.[98] With the 2016 election of Donald Trump and Republican majorities in the Congress, the United States is witnessing a new, more intense, era of neoliberal reforms that are gutting federal environmental and social programs.

In the case of chemical production, the neoliberal state refrains from interfering in chemical innovation and manufacturing (as was the case for lead) so as to avoid slowing entrepreneurship and economic growth. The neoliberal state rejects the precautionary principle, as it requires government to take a leading role in arbitrating competing definitions of risk. The neoliberal state prefers tools like precautionary consumption and tools that encourage industry self-monitoring.[99] Examples include the Toxic Release Inventory, which requires industry to publicly disclose chemical emissions and waste disposal of toxics, and education campaigns that encourage households to switch to energy-efficient appliances and light bulbs to lower carbon emissions that contribute to climate change. Since the rise of neoliberalism, the United States has seen a growth of eco and "green" labels (e.g., labels indicating energy efficiency and organic certification standards).[100] Voluntary tools such as these are thought to put pressure on highly polluting industries to reduce their contribution to environmental degradation and reward environmentally friendly companies.[101] Ecologically minded citizens, the reasoning goes, can vote with their dollars to encourage new social and economic arrangements focused on quality of life and environmental improvement.[102] As I discuss later in the book, under neoliberal regimes, eco-labels have proliferated for all kinds of consumer goods. These labels are most common for goods with poor regulatory oversight, like food, personal care products, and cleaning products.

Individuals view these labels as an empowering option for protecting their health, and parents look for them as part of protecting their children's health. Sociologist Jennifer Reich observes how this neoliberal approach to health requires parents to invest their free time and energy into personalizing and optimizing how they care for their children through individualist parenting. This approach to raising children, Reich finds, reflects a deep distrust of medical institutions, science, and corporations.[103] Precautionary consumption is testament to this distrust and to profound social, political, and economic shifts that have influenced the environmental movement, the marketplace, and, ultimately, our everyday lives and experiences.

Precautionary consumption is not just the product of neoliberal shifts in economic, political, and social arrangements that alter the relationships between the individual, the family, the state, and society. It is also a reflection of poststructural changes in discourses about risk, gender, and reproduction. Risk, in this sense, is a discourse that produces self-regulating subjects who learn to manage their exposure to hazards by using rational calculations. These calculations are often subtle, such as reading an ingredient label and deciding whether a listed ingredient is safe to consume.[104]

This poststructuralist interpretation of precautionary consumption draws on Michel Foucault's concept of governmentality, or, as he called it, "technologies of the self."[105] Foucault argues that populations are governed through the production of knowledge and discourses, which influence how individuals conduct their physical behavior and manage their bodies. In the case of precautionary consumption, formal and collective mechanisms to manage collective risk exposure (such as more stringent regulation to mandate fewer chemical releases) fade, and tools for personal risk assessment and commodities of self-protection (like safe shopping guides and toxic-free shampoo) abound. This approach to risk also reflects biopolitics—a term drawn from Foucault but extended and elaborated on by sociologist Nikolas Rose. Rose suggests that political life is regulated less through formal institutions and organizations and more through interventions into human biology and bodies, particularly at the molecular level.[106] According to sociologist Sara Shostak, biomonitoring is a form of biopolitics, as measurement of chemical biomarkers in individuals has become increasingly important to environmental epidemiology and, correspondingly, to the prevention of disease.[107] Such concern about chemical exposure and future health is visible in the science and medical practices surrounding fetal and early infant exposure to chemicals. Geographer Becky Mansfield links safe consumption advisories for fish (related to concerns about mercury) to the biopolitics of reproduction, since women's biological bodies become sites for managing health risks to future populations.[108]

Maternal bodies, more than other bodies, are presented as pathways of contamination owing to their ability to birth and breastfeed children, who are presented as vulnerable recipients of women's contamination. This attention to maternal bodies is evident in the groundbreaking report from the President's Cancer Panel of 2010, which states, "While all Americans now carry many foreign chemicals in their bodies, women often have higher levels of many toxic and hormone-disrupting substances than do men. Some of these chemicals have been found in maternal blood, placental tissue, and breast milk samples from pregnant women and mothers who recently gave birth. Thus, chemical contaminants are being passed on to the next generation, both prenatally and during breastfeeding."[109] The panel furthermore observes that, "to a disturbing extent, babies are born 'pre-polluted.'"[110] This report references a large body of environmental epidemiology and toxicology research on fetal and infant exposure to chemicals and the impact on future health outcomes.[111] Much of the research on health effects from environmental chemical exposure views the maternal body as a conduit that transfers chemicals to the developing fetus and breastfeeding infant. Men's bodies and men's domestic labor are rarely mentioned in such discussions. Public health promotion materials focus on women's preconception, pregnancy, and breastfeeding behaviors to safeguard children's environmental health. These materials urge women to reduce their exposure to pesticides, potential carcinogens, endocrine disruptors, and mercury in fish when planning to conceive, while pregnant, and when breastfeeding.[112] Like other medical interpretations of reproduction, environmental health promotion directs most attention to women's bodies and ignores men's contributions to the reproductive process.[113]

Precautionary consumption implicates women's domestic labor as well as their bodies. Industry estimates that two-thirds of U.S. women do the grocery and pharmacy shopping for their households, as well as the shopping for other family needs.[114] Women begin thinking about their child's health during pregnancy, and some even begin planning for a healthy child before conception.[115] After forming a family, women still do most of the cooking and shopping for their children, such that most studies investigating how families feed their children look primarily at the demographic characteristics and behaviors of mothers.[116] In previous studies of mothers' foodwork, researchers have found that mothers use foodwork to safeguard their children's health.[117]

Upper- and middle-class women are highly aware of their biological role in transferring chemicals to children. This consideration can sometimes begin before conception.[118] These mothers are especially concerned with raising children on diets of certified-organic, local, and ethically sourced food.[119] More than this, mothers now also think about other commodities for children, including natural or nontoxic personal care products, furniture, and toys. This kind of consumption is integral to the classed performance of middle-class motherhood.

To understand how precautionary consumption has emerged and how it impacts everyday life in the twenty-first century, I examine four interrelated contexts where precautionary consumption emerges and is practiced. The first is the regulatory system for chemical substances and the political and economic dynamics that have shaped this system. The second context is the campaigns of major environmental health social movement groups, which raise awareness of the hazards of chemical body burdens and provide advice on how to avoid chemicals. The third is the marketplace where green and nontoxic items are sold. The fourth is mothers' lived experience of precautionary consumption, since the work and responsibility of precautionary consumption is connected to maternal bodies and family feeding.

To study these contexts, I collected and analyzed data from multiple sources, starting with extensive background research on chemical regulation to understand the history behind the regulatory system for chemicals in food and consumer products.[120] I then turned my attention to major environmental health movement organization campaigns that raise awareness of health threats from environmental chemicals, and encourage individuals (particularly women and mothers) to practice precautionary consumption. I studied campaign materials from major groups such as the EWG, which publishes advocacy biomonitoring reports and numerous safe shopping guides. I then conducted a case study of the health food giant Whole Foods Market, collecting information on the retail culture of precautionary consumption created by the company and the many brands it sells. Finally, I undertook in-depth interviews with thirty mothers to understand how women contend with the pressure to become better consumers as part of protecting their current or future children from harmful chemicals. I explored if and how mothers practice precautionary consumption or if they resist this practice, and I identified the many contradictions inherent to it.

The book is organized as follows: In chapter 2, I provide a history of the U.S. regulatory system for chemicals up to the present day. I pay close attention to the power dynamics that shape corporate-government relations, as well as to the power of certain actors to define chemical risk. The chapter chronicles the uneasy relationship the United States has with the precautionary principle, from the Pure Food Act of 1906 to the amended Toxic Control Substances Act of 2016. In chapter 3, I turn to the environmental health movement, which has politicized precautionary consumption. This movement uses human biomonitoring as a provocative tool for raising public awareness of chemical body burdens, but it has focused much of its attention on women's reproductive bodies. Groups present the safe shopping tips that are so central to precautionary consumption as easy and effective steps that anyone can take. This movement, I argue, has been critical to the gendering of precautionary consumption and to the framing of precautionary consumption as a legitimate strategy for addressing chemical pollution. In chapter 4, I focus on Whole Foods Market, the ultimate precautionary consumer retail space. My case study of the company and its stores spans the years when Whole Foods Market was at the peak of its success, prior to its acquisition by Amazon. The company aims for radical transparency of ingredients and production processes, and it imbues consumers with a sense of agency, making them feel that their precautionary choices are making a difference to their health.

In chapter 5, I turn to the lived experience of precautionary consumption by talking to those most likely to practice it: mothers living in large urban centers.[121] I interview thirty mothers to understand how they practice precautionary consumption and the extent to which they believe it is making a difference to their health and their children's health. Most of the women I interviewed spoke of becoming aware of chemicals in early adulthood, when they were pursuing the thin ideal and began to read product labels as part of maintaining their weight. Entry into motherhood intensified their preoccupation with "good" eating but also brought on feelings of anxiety and guilt that they were not doing enough to protect their children from potentially toxic ingredients. This chapter reveals a collective, cultural moment where feeding and shopping for children is considered high stakes work, and this work becomes women's work by virtue of the social expectations of who will invest in children's futures. No matter what kind of precautionary consumption routine these mothers practice, what we learn from them is that the gold standard of good mothering is to have a healthy child who loves vegetables, eats a varied diet, and has few pesticide residues and other synthetic chemicals in their body. Feeding children necessarily becomes a personal project for these women, and the work it involves is sequestered from other labor that might be shared with a spouse or partner. In chapter 6, I dig deeper into my interview data to show how precautionary consumption is a classed practice. Precautionary consumption requires tremendous resources, beyond the extra money needed to afford more expensive food and consumer products. It takes time and consumer literacy to sift through the overwhelming amount of information about safe shopping and chemical dangers. By profiling women who lacked money, time, and sometimes the support of a partner to help with other domestic labor while they took care of precautionary consumption, I show how these women leveraged multiple resources to make at least some changes to their consumption routines. Their stories reveal that precautionary consumption is a concern shared by lower-income and wealthy women. The fewer resources a woman has at her disposal, the harder she must work to practice precautionary consumption.

In chapter 7, I discuss the implications of precautionary consumption as individualized self-protection. If precautionary consumption has become a dominant approach to dealing with environmental contamination, what does this mean for environmental justice? While precautionary consumption celebrates consumer agency, there are limits to self-protection. Precautionary consumption, I suggest, represents a million temporary commodity bubbles situated in a polluted landscape.[122] This approach to dealing with toxics does little, I conclude, to protect people whose bodies are at greatest risk of harm from chemical exposures, such as blue-collar workers, the poor, and residents of polluted communities. The following pages document how precautionary consumption may reduce risk but ultimately leaves behind the already vulnerable, doing little to advance population health or environmental protection.

TWO

——————

Safe until Sorry

CHEMICAL REGULATION IN THE
UNITED STATES

> American lawmakers primarily look to cost-benefit analysis,
> which holds that the benefit of imposing regulation should out-
> weigh its cost. European nations have more readily embraced
> what is called the precautionary principle. Essentially, Europe-
> ans emphasize the cost of inaction, while Americans tend to
> focus on the cost of action.
>
> **OTTO POHL**, *New York Times*

> People believe when they go to the grocery store and go to the
> hardware store and they get a product, that product's been tested
> and that product's safe. Well, that isn't the case.
>
> **TOM UDALL**, Democratic senator from New Mexico

Precaution is an old concept. It is demonstrated in the adage "it is better to
be safe than sorry" and in the Hippocratic oath, which dictates, "do no
harm." This concept can be informal and guide individual action (e.g., "I will
take an umbrella with me today even though the sky is clear"), or it can be
codified as law or policy that supports restricting industrial activities and
technologies until they are proven to be safe, even when the scientific evidence of harm is uncertain or inconclusive. The precautionary principle has
shaped European Union (E.U.) environmental policy since the 1970s.
American environmental policy has unevenly embraced and rejected precautionary logics, from as far back as the Pure Food and Drug Act of 1906 and
as recently as the Clean Air Act Amendments of 1990. At the global level, the
United States has signed on to several global precautionary agreements but
has never formally adopted the precautionary principle as a guiding principle
for domestic environmental, food, and chemical policy. The chemical
industry and its representatives reject policy premised on the precautionary

principle, considering it unscientific and bad for business, as I demonstrate throughout this chapter. Over time, the most consistent aspect of U.S. policy in these areas is the application of the "safe-until-sorry" model—that is, first wait for proof of harm to accumulate and then institute restrictions.

In this chapter, I outline the United States' uneven and contradictory relationship with the precautionary principle as a policy ethic and more specifically point to how the safe-until-sorry model at the regulatory level helps explain why precaution has flourished as an individualized consumer principle. In outlining this relationship, I document the serious gaps in regulatory oversight in what is a vast, fractured, and, frankly, mind-boggling policy framework that oversees chemicals used in agriculture and food production and in the manufacturing of cosmetics, personal care products, and consumer goods.

THE PRECAUTIONARY PRINCIPLE AS CONTROVERSIAL

As a policy ideal or ethic, the precautionary principle refers to a duty to prevent damage to human and environmental health even when evidence of harm is inconclusive. The principle traces back to the global cultural ecological movement of the 1970s, which proposed fundamental changes to industrial capitalism to promote environmental protection and global, democratic deliberation.[1] The precautionary principle was proposed as a key mechanism to achieve these ambitious goals.

Germany was the first country to incorporate the precautionary principle into law, as the foresight principle, or *Vorsorgeprinzip,* in the German Clean Air Act of 1974.[2] In Europe, this principle guided several environmental policies in the 1970s and 1980s, notably those addressing pollution in the North Sea and acid rain.[3] In 2000, the European Union codified its commitment to this principle in the European Commission's Communication on the Precautionary Principle.[4] Internationally, the precautionary principle was the founding principle for agreements related to ozone depletion, environmental sustainability, and transboundary chemical pollution.[5] The precautionary principle became synonymous with sustainability at the Rio Convention (or Earth Summit) of 1992.[6] At this meeting, the United Nations Conference on Environment and Development delegates agreed that, "in order to protect the environment, the precautionary approach shall be widely applied by States according to their capabilities," and that, "where there are threats of serious or irreversible damage, the lack of full scientific certainty shall not be used as a reason for postponing cost-effective measures to prevent environmental degradation."[7] It was here that countries, including the United States, signed the United Nations Framework Convention on Climate Change, the first global commitment to reduce greenhouse gas emissions.[8]

As these statements attest, under the precautionary principle, governments act to protect the environment and human health even under conditions of scientific uncertainty, and the burden of proof of safety is the responsibility of *industry*. Industry must convince regulators (and the public) that a compound or product is safe before it can be released into the market. Adopting the precautionary principle requires broad social and political consensus that government should intervene in the market and industrial activities in the name of reducing harm to the environment and human health. Institutionalizing the precautionary principle requires parties to agree that scientific uncertainty can rarely be completely eliminated, and therefore the threshold of acceptable uncertainty must be subject to transparent and democratic debate.

In addition to the United Nations Framework Convention on Climate Change, the United States has signed several other major international agreements premised on the precautionary principle, such as the Great Lakes Water Quality Agreement (1972, amended in 1978), the Montreal Protocol on Ozone Depleting Substances (1987), and the Stockholm Convention on Persistent Organic Pollutants (2001).[9] Signing these agreements gives the impression that the United States supports the precautionary principle, at least in global environmental agreements. However, to protect the domestic market, U.S. officials and lobbyists have repeatedly undermined key precautionary provisions of these agreements. Sociologist Brian Gareau's investigation into the Montreal Protocol, for example, reveals that the United States supported the protocol only as long as it would not affect domestic strawberry production, which depends on the ozone-depleting substance methyl bromide and stalled on its commitment to phase out use of this substance.[10] Furthermore, although the United States signed the Stockholm Convention, an agreement to reduce the manufacturing and release of persistent organic pollutants (including compounds such as DDT, which take decades to break down, circulate the globe, and bioaccumulate in animal tissues), it never ratified it, making the country one of the few signatories to fail to do so, effectively releasing the federal government from following through on the agreement's commitments.[11]

As it relates to food, the environment, and consumer products, the United States takes a hostile approach to the precautionary principle as a policy ethic. American businesses and lobbyists present precautionary policy as governmental overreach and a threat to innovation and economic growth. American hostility to the precautionary principle is felt by one of its major trading partners, the European Union. In the years leading up to the implementation of the European Union's flagship precautionary chemical legislation, called REACH, American regulators and lobbyists visited Brussels to discourage the European Union from adopting this policy.[12] REACH represented a major overhaul of European chemical regulation to align it with the precautionary principle, as REACH places the burden of proof of safety on the chemical industry. Under this legislation, chemicals can be removed from production if manufacturers do not supply data demonstrating that compounds are safe for humans and the environment. REACH was implemented in 2007, despite steady U.S. campaigns to undermine its adoption. Because of REACH, European regulators have banned or restricted the use of chemicals such as the pesticide atrazine, potassium bromate (a dough conditioner used in baked products), di-2-ethylhexyl phthalate (DEHP) (used in plastic tubing), certain artificial food colorings, and coal tar in hair dyes.[13]

E.U. regulators are now turning their attention to endocrine disruptors. The toxicity of endocrine disruptors cannot be assessed using the traditional dose-response measures that are used to evaluate most other chemicals. The dose-response model identifies a threshold where an increase in dose causes an adverse response in an organism.[14] Doses below the identified threshold are generally considered to be safe, and doses above the threshold are considered toxic. The FDA, EPA, and European Food Safety Authority all rely on this model.[15] According to the dose-response model, BPA has a high acceptable daily intake dose of 50 µg/kg per day—an amount that is well above typical everyday exposure.[16] Animal studies, however, have discovered that very small doses of BPA elicit responses from the endocrine system (such as stimulating the pancreas to release insulin) while high doses do *not* elicit a response.[17] Moreover, timing of exposure in the life course matters, as exposure to endocrine disruptors in utero, during puberty, or at other sensitive moments of development can lead to illness or other disorders, such as cancer, attention deficit hyperactivity disorder, infertility, and diabetes, and these effects may not appear until later in life.[18] Because of the unique toxicity profile of endocrine disruptors, evaluating their health risks requires novel approaches beyond what the dose-response model can offer. Research showing that low doses of certain synthetic chemicals, like BPA, can affect the endocrine system has led to calls to reform the models for assessing toxicity so as to capture the hazards of low-dose exposures.

A precautionary approach to regulating endocrine disruptors, advanced by the Endocrine Society (a global professional organization representing endocrinologists) and multiple environmental groups, demands that these compounds be restricted until proof of safety is established. Because so many compounds (e.g., many plastics, pesticides, and ingredients in cosmetics) are considered endocrine disruptors, a precautionary approach would require a tremendous expansion of regulatory approvals, a move that industry fears will hurt their bottom line. And the U.S. chemical industry is powerful because of its value to domestic and global economies. In 2016, products from American chemical companies accounted for 14 percent of all U.S. goods exports, valued at $174 billion.[19] Not surprisingly, the American Chemistry Council—a large organization that represents the interests of the U.S. chemical industry—downplays the risks of these compounds, calling endocrine disruption a "still-unproven hypothesis."[20]

American companies and trade officials (including those from the ACC) have been working behind the scenes to discourage the European Union from adopting stringent criteria for evaluating the risks of endocrine disruptors, threatening severe trade repercussions should such a policy be implemented.[21] This pressure appears to be working. In 2013, the directorate-general of the Environment at the European Commission missed the deadline to develop an endocrine disruptor policy, a failure the General Court in Luxemburg attributed to American influence.[22] In 2015, the European Union decided against banning the use of thirty-one endocrine-disrupting pesticides in European agriculture—pesticides produced by American and European companies.[23]

Certainly, E.U. regulatory bodies are susceptible to corporate influence—and not just from American chemical producers. European chemical manufacturers also lobby for looser regulatory oversight over their products.[24] Under REACH, industry must provide the data to inform chemical safety reviews. This gives them the opportunity to design experiments and data-gathering exercises that will garner favorable results.[25] In other words, while REACH is precautionary, it is not immune to industry influence, as industry provides the data that will be used to determine safety. Consequently, REACH has not achieved everything the E.U. environmental movement had hoped for when the policy was first proposed.[26] Even so, across the

Atlantic, consumer and environmental health advocacy groups look to the European Union as a shining example of precautionary policy in action.

The U.S. federal government consistently rejects the precautionary principle in national environmental, cosmetic product, and food regulation. Opposition to the precautionary principle is especially strong inside the EPA. Formed in 1970, the EPA is responsible for monitoring the country's air and water quality, preventing pollution, and cleaning up toxic waste, and it is in charge of regulating pesticides and chemical substances used for commercial and industrial purposes. It has, for the past forty years, used a proof-of-harm model to evaluate chemical risks. This model is very much the opposite of the precautionary principle. It seeks to establish scientific certainty of a *threat* before launching into regulatory action.[27] Under the proof-of-harm model, the EPA has to demonstrate that it has sufficient evidence before it can place a restriction on a chemical, and the agency must also provide the data to make this evaluation, data that rely on voluntary disclosures of information by industry. The proof-of-harm model makes it exceedingly difficult to restrict new chemicals, particularly when the EPA is underfunded and understaffed, so it cannot keep up with the pace of chemical innovation and the introduction of new compounds onto the market.[28]

Disagreements over what constitutes reasonable evidence of harm consist of, for example, determining whether results from experimental studies on lab animals accurately reflect potential health effects on humans, deciding whether a study's methodology is sufficiently rigorous, and questioning whether findings from a key study are replicable. The chemical industry is adept at amplifying the uncertainty of harm, and has successfully delayed restrictions on lead, polyvinyl chloride (PVC), and PCBs—all compounds that are now known to be extremely harmful to human health and the environment.[29] It took years, and in some cases even decades, for the EPA to ban or restrict these substances.

The EPA's inability to protect the public from harmful chemicals has not escaped external scrutiny. In 2005 and 2007, the United States Government Accountability Office (GAO) offered a scathing audit of the EPA's approach to chemical regulation, and it pointed to the European Union's precautionary approach as a model for reform. The GAO is a government watchdog agency that audits and investigates government programs that spend tax dollars.[30] In 2005, GAO auditors concluded that the EPA "does not routinely assess the human health and environmental risks of existing chemicals and faces challenges in obtaining the information necessary to do so," such that only a fraction of chemicals authorized for use in the United States have been flagged for further testing for their environmental or human health effects.[31]

In June 2016, under the authority of President Barack Obama, the federal government introduced new rules to overhaul the regulatory system for commercial and industrial chemicals. The new regulations offered some precautionary mechanisms to allow the EPA to evaluate new chemicals before they were introduced to the market and established a process to evaluate the risks of those already in use.[32] These changes applied to chemicals under the EPA's authority—such as paint remover and compounds used to make food packaging—but did not apply to additives used in food processing, or compounds used in cosmetics, which are the responsibility of other government agencies. These precautionary provisions did not have a chance to become formally institutionalized, as they were swiftly revised by EPA Director Scott Pruitt, appointed in early 2017 by President Donald J. Trump. With a guidance issued in June 2017, Pruitt paved the way for less precautionary regulatory approvals for new and existing chemical substances.[33]

In the remainder of the chapter, I map out key moments in the history of chemical policy and detail the reluctance of American regulators to adopt a precautionary approach and the longstanding conflicts and debates that have helped give rise to precautionary consumption. I start by tracing the history of the regulatory framework for chemicals in the United States, from the early 1900s, when there was little to no government oversight or regulation of chemicals or the safety of the food supply, to late 2017, when precautionary consumption became a dominant approach for addressing toxics. For the contemporary period, from the 1990s through to late 2017, I navigate the convoluted maze of regulation and policy that determines what chemicals are allowed in our food, cosmetics, and other consumer products. This regulatory framework involves multiple federal government bureaucracies that govern human exposure to synthetic compounds via the environment, food, consumer products, and agriculture. This framework is utterly complicated owing to shared regulatory oversight across multiple agencies in addition to numerous revisions and amendments to policy and legislation.

In general, the history of chemical regulation in the United States reflects a larger struggle to define the role of government vis-à-vis corporate actors. In rare cases, the federal government has introduced regulation to carefully review what chemical, food, and consumer products corporations can introduce to the market, but most of the time, government has allowed corporations to call the shots. Industry has been especially successful at convincing regulators that testing for chemical safety is costly and burdensome and thereby threatens innovation and, by extension, economic growth. With few exceptions, corporations have controlled the balance of power over regulators, from the days before a regulatory system for food and environmental chemicals was first put in place to the formation of the agencies charged with watching over industry practices. As this chapter makes clear, consumer self-protection has long been a default position under the safe-until-sorry regulatory system. As I show in chapter 4, once untested substances started flooding the retail landscape, there was a corresponding expansion of products that purported to be "safe," labeled as "green," and labeled as eco-friendly, or non-toxic. In short, under the safe-until-sorry model, the retail landscape expanded in two directions. First, there was an expansion of goods made with untested chemicals but with nifty functions (such as repelling flames or moisture or being shatterproof), and this was followed by a rise in eco-friendly goods that promised *not* to contain unsafe chemicals. As this history makes clear, the regulatory system has failed to keep consumers and the environment safe. The burden of living with this failure has been handed to consumers, and women and mothers in particular, as I demonstrate later in this book.

EARLY DEBATES ABOUT CHEMICAL SAFETY

Public concern about chemicals is not new. In the nineteenth century, the American public began calling for formal mechanisms of government oversight of food and medicines.[34] At that time, the number of novel foods and drugs was expanding rapidly, largely as a result of unprecedented advances in chemistry, and a growing advertising industry that marketed (often with false claims) these new commodities to consumers.[35] Although the term "precautionary principle" did not enter policy discourse in the United States until the 1990s, scientists, consumer movement groups, doctors, and individual consumers (particularly mothers) spoke of the need to place limits on the expansion of new foods and medicines for the sake of public health. Women's consumer groups, like the General Federation of Women's Clubs, pushed for pure and unadulterated foods, and these organizations published lists of "pure" foods and provided tips on safe shopping—much like the Environmental Working Group (EWG) does today.[36] Women's groups used their leverage as shoppers to pressure the government to introduce strong regulation to protect consumers. The federal government found itself caught in between a movement of consumers that were angry about accidental poisonings and illnesses caused by adulterated foods and medicines and the farming, chemical, and processed food sectors, which pushed back against government interference in their industries.[37]

In 1906, Congress heeded the call for government action by passing the Pure Food and Drug Act (PFDA). The PFDA required manufacturers to provide evidence to support any claims they placed on product packages or used in product advertising. Harvey Wiley, the chief chemist of the Bureau of Chemistry in the Department of Agriculture, headed the enforcement of this law. As environmental historian Nancy Langston writes, "Wiley believed passionately in a form of the precautionary principle. Only precaution could protect the public from harm; waiting to see whether a particular chemical contaminant in food might be harmful was unethical, for it would turn America into a nation of guinea pigs. . . . Wiley's precautionary principle held that a foreign substance should be presumed guilty until proven innocent; the industry believed the opposite."[38]

Yet the PFDA fell short of Wiley's dream. In particular, it failed to provide clear, consistent, and enforceable standards of "purity, potency, and wholesomeness."[39] Testing for safety was often shoddily conducted or neglected altogether, and the government virtually never penalized companies that used poor production practices, used fraudulent advertising, or failed to pull toxic products from the market.[40] In the 1920s, some scientists expressed concern about the circulation of chemicals in the environment and in the food supply. In one article published 1928 in the *American Journal of Medical Sciences,* scientist Karl Vogel sounded the alarm about arsenic, a toxic compound used in pesticides at the time:

> A little investigation reveals the fact that the world we inhabit is permeated by this subtle poison so that the possibilities for its accidental absorption are countless. . . . It is an uncanny thought to realize that this lurking poison is everywhere about us, ready to gain unsuspected entrance to our bodies from the food we eat, the water we drink, and the other beverages we may take to cheer us, the clothes we wear, and even the air we breathe.[41]

Vogel's warning about the ubiquity of chemicals and the vulnerability of the human body to exposure is strikingly similar to today's concerns about chemical body burdens.

In 1930, the government formed the FDA to enforce the PFDA. During the Great Depression, the agency was tasked with monitoring drug production, pesticide residues in food, and the safety of food additives. Consumer groups and the news media sounded the alarm over the dangers of the industrial food supply. The book *Eat, Drink and Be Wary,* published in 1935, advises readers to "follow your grandmother's instincts" and go "back to the ... pre-Crisco days" by rejecting "artificial, preserved, stabilized, canned, ethylene-ripened, dyed and over-processed foods too far removed, in growing and marketing, from sun and air and the realities of woodland, farm and field."[42] Public support for FDA intervention reached a tipping point in 1937, when a drug prescribed to treat streptococcus infections, Elixir Sulfanilimide, killed ninety-three people, including many children. This drug was tested for its effectiveness against streptococcus but was not tested for toxicity. The tragedy spurred Congress to pass the federal Food, Drug and Cosmetic Act (FDCA) of 1938.[43] The FDCA introduced some precautionary measures in the form of better testing of drugs for impacts on human health before they could go to market. Under the FDCA, before manufacturers can introduce a drug to the market or begin marketing a drug, they must present evidence to the FDA that the drug is safe for human use and that the benefits of taking the drug outweigh the risks. After the drug is on the market, the FDA monitors unexpected health effects.[44] Despite the provisions of the FDCA, drug companies applied pressure on the FDA and doctors to administer drugs that were suspected carcinogens. The FDA sometimes ceded to this pressure. One well-known case of the FDA ignoring evidence of harm is estrogen diethylstilbestrol (DES), a synthetic hormone prescribed to pregnant women starting in the late 1930s through to the early 1970s. Even when faced with mounting evidence that DES caused vaginal cancer in the daughters of women who took the drug during pregnancy, the FDA kept the drug on the market to prevent financial losses to pharmaceutical companies.[45]

The modest (and imperfect) precautionary measures of the FDCA may have helped improve the regulation of drugs, but they did not apply to other substances, like household chemicals and pesticides. Instead, Congress passed the burden of safety on to consumers through the Federal Insecticide, Fungicide and Rodenticide Act (FIFRA) of 1947, which required pesticide manufacturers to add dyes to their products to prevent accidental mixing with food, to put warning labels on poisonous substances, and to include detailed instructions for proper application and directions for preventing direct contact with skin or inhalation.[46] This emphasis on educating the *users* of these products about the dangers of chemicals reduced instances of accidental poisoning and direct exposure, but it did not stem the production of harmful chemicals. This is an early example of the government's failure to put limits on industry in favor of putting the onus on consumer self-protection. This is one of many instances where the U.S. government has encouraged precautionary consumption.

THE POSTWAR PERIOD TO THE MID-1990s

While the first half of the twentieth century was a time of worry about adulterated foods and medicines, the beginning of the 1950s marked a period of rising public concern over carcinogens in food. Carcinogenic food additives came under scrutiny during formal hearings before Congress from 1951 to 1952, called the House Select Committee to Investigate the Use of Chemicals in Food Products. The transcripts from these hearings document industry leaders and the FDA defending their passive approach to chemical safety, which had failed to protect the health of Americans.[47] Public health advocates, doctors, and health scientists challenged the agency to adopt more rigorous and scientific evaluations of chemical safety *before* substances were introduced into the food supply.[48] In 1958, Congress added the Food Additives Amendment (FAA) to the FDCA (section 409).[49] This clause stipulated a precautionary approach to the regulation of food additives, placing the burden of proof of safety on the manufacturer and requiring companies to furnish this proof before submitting their product or packaging for FDA approval. The FAA also banned select food additives and colorings. Even so, many suspected carcinogens continued to enter the market, as the FDA could choose to regulate additives under more permissive clauses of the FDCA, allowing carcinogenic food additives to continue to enter the food supply.[50] For instance, in 1962, livestock producers lobbied Congress to pass a DES proviso that would amend the FAA to permit DES in livestock production. Producers argued that DES was a powerful growth promoter and therefore good for business. The proviso passed despite evidence that DES was carcinogenic, and over the next several years, the FDA and USDA continued to ignore evidence that the compound was carcinogenic. In 1971, following the publication of a major study that revealed DES to cause vaginal cancer, the FDA was forced to withdraw its approval of DES during pregnancy. The FDA and USDA nevertheless maintained that the synthetic hormone was safe for livestock production because, they claimed, DES residues were not detectable in the meat of treated animals. When the Natural

Resources Defense Council asked a U.S. district court to declare DES illegal, the court uncovered that the FDA and USDA had, in fact, detected high residues in some samples of meat. However, these departments had not disclosed their discovery, as they believed the science surrounding DES was too uncertain to risk harming the financial interests of livestock producers.[51] In 1972, the FDA began a long, arduous process of banning DES in livestock production. The ban eventually came into effect in 1979.[52] Events surrounding the DES proviso showcase the federal government's permissive stance toward industry in the face of mounting evidence of harm to public health. Rather than acknowledge this evidence, government officials ignored it, believing that the evidence was not solid enough to risk hurting industry.

In 1976, Congress passed the Toxic Substances Control Act (TSCA), which charged the EPA with controlling commercial and industrial chemicals that posed an "unreasonable risk of injury to health or the environment."[53] This act came about toward the end of a brief flurry of regulatory environmentalism, when multiple acts and policies with precautionary logics (though not explicitly referencing the precautionary principle) were passed in quick succession. They included the National Environmental Policy Act (1970), the Clean Air Act (1970), the Clean Water Act (1972), the Endangered Species Act (1973), the Safe Drinking Water Act (1974), and the 1994 phase-out of aerosols containing fluorocarbons.[54] In contrast to these acts, which resulted in measurable improvements in air and water quality and the protection of some species of wildlife, the TSCA was toothless from the moment it came into force. It grandfathered an estimated sixty-two thousand chemical substances that were in use prior to the bill being signed into law, thus rendering existing chemicals exempt from safety assessments.[55] Put another way, the TSCA effectively presumed that these sixty-two thousand chemicals were safe, and put the onus on the EPA to prove otherwise. To test the safety of a chemical already in commercial use, the EPA had to provide evidence that the compound posed an *unreasonable* risk and had to apply the "least burdensome requirements" on the chemical industry.[56] In the event that the agency wanted to restrict a chemical, it had to prove that the potential harm from the compound was higher than the potential cost to industry from complying with a new rule. In short, the burden on industry to contend with regulation, not the burden on public health from exposure to potentially harmful chemicals, had to be the EPA's primary consideration.

The EPA had neither the resources nor the ability to prove whether the thousands of grandfathered chemicals posed an unreasonable risk to human health or the environment. More often than not, it relied on information supplied voluntarily by industry.[57] The agency nevertheless had some success reviewing new chemicals by evaluating them against data it had for analogous compounds.[58] Even so, the EPA reviewed only 2 percent of the grandfathered chemicals, and it requested additional data for only 10 percent of the thirty-two thousand new chemicals industry presented to the agency after the TSCA came into force.[59] By 2005 eighty-two thousand chemicals were registered for use in the United States, and the EPA had restricted only *five* of them.[60] A much larger number were restricted in the European Union under REACH.[61] As of 2016, the EPA must adhere to an amended TSCA, which gives the agency the power to more carefully evaluate all new chemicals before they are introduced to market. This amendment has been weakened under the Trump administration, as I discuss later in the chapter.

THE 1990s TO TODAY

In the early 1990s, the federal government introduced some modest precautionary reforms to food and environmental legislation. President George W. Bush, for instance, signed the Clean Air Act amendment in 1990, which set standards for urban air quality and aimed to reduce emissions that contributed to ozone depletion and acid rain.[62] The Clean Air Act amendment was more of an anomaly than a trend. The 1990s marked a major turning point in the American regulatory landscape, establishing consumer self-protection as the standard response to government inaction and introducing even greater complexity to the regulatory landscape for food, personal care products, consumer products, and chemicals used for industrial or commercial purposes. Below, I give a brief overview of how chemicals in each of these categories are regulated. The complexity of this regulatory landscape is staggering. By mapping this complex landscape, I show how precautionary consumption has become a necessary default response to a regulatory system that consistently puts industry profit ahead of public health.

Food

The regulatory system overseeing chemicals in food—from compounds used in agricultural production to chemicals employed in food processing—is bewildering. The responsibility of enforcing and monitoring chemical safety is split between the EPA, the FDA, and the USDA. Chemicals used in agriculture, for instance, are the purview of the EPA, while those used in food processing and packaging fall under the authority of the FDA. The USDA regulates the country's meat, dairy, and egg supply; it also collects data on pesticide residues, although regulating these residues is the authority of the EPA. The USDA also oversees organic food certification, runs the National Organic Program, and oversees the labeling of genetically modified organisms.

The 1990s was a key period during which the major legislation shaping today's foodscape was formed or amended. What follows is just a snapshot of this decade, but it reveals multiple regulatory statutes, the splitting of regulatory monitoring and enforcement, and industry's considerable freedom to exploit loopholes in regulation. It makes visible the guiding logic of the safe-until-sorry model.

Conventional Fruits and Vegetables. Agricultural pesticides (insecticides, fungicides, and herbicides) fall under FIFRA, which is enforced by the EPA. FIFRA requires that pesticides undergo toxicological and environmental testing before being brought to market. Under this act, all pesticides must be registered with the EPA, and the agency has the power to remove dangerous pesticides. In practice, however, this power is limited, as industry frequently challenges proposed EPA limitations via the courts.[63] The EPA also sets tolerances for pesticide residues—standards for acceptable pesticide residues remaining on an agricultural product after harvesting. Residues fall under the Food Quality Protection Act (FQPA) of 1996 and the FDCA (amended in 2002). The FQPA is precautionary, as it mandates "reasonable certainty of no harm" from exposure to pesticide residues, and so residues are a consideration when the EPA decides whether to approve a pesticide for agricultural use.[64] President Bill Clinton signed the FQPA into law after environmental advocacy groups raised concerns about children's exposures to pesticide residues in food. Significantly, the FQPA was written with express consideration of children's health, given their lower tolerance for pesticide residues. The FQPA requires the EPA to consider aggregate exposure to pesticides from food and other pathways (e.g., use in the home, presence in the air or water). Testing and monitoring of pesticide residues is split across agencies and divisions within agencies, and only a small percentage of foods are actually tested for residue levels.[65] The USDA's Food Safety and Inspection Service (FSIS), for instance, monitors pesticide residues in meat and processed eggs, while the FDA monitors residues on domestic and imported fruits and vegetables. The USDA's Agricultural Marketing Service collects residue data for fruit and vegetables, but it does not have authority to use these data for regulatory purposes. In fact, the FDA and the FSIS are not required by law to test for all the pesticides that have tolerances set by the EPA.[66] While in theory, the FQPA enforces proper use of pesticides to prevent overspraying, in practice, the implementation and enforcement of this law is weak, and tolerances set by the EPA are higher than what is allowed under E.U. law.[67] In 2014, the GAO published a report concluding that testing methodologies used by the FDA and the USDA are insufficient for safeguarding public health.[68]

For well over a decade, environmental groups have voiced concerns about the lax implementation of the FQPA and have stepped in to raise public awareness of inadequate monitoring and testing of pesticide residues on fresh fruits and vegetables. In 2004, the EWG began analyzing USDA and FDA data to rank fruits and vegetables by level of residue and number of detectable pesticides, and it publishes the information as the *Dirty Dozen* guide, which is updated every year. This resource was widely known among the women I interviewed for this book. In 2017, the guide ranked strawberries as the most contaminated, followed by spinach, nectarines, apples, peaches, pears, cherries, grapes, celery, tomatoes, sweet bell peppers, and potatoes.[69] The group found that strawberries contain more than seven pesticides per sample, on average, including carbendazim, a pesticide banned in the European Union because of its toxicity and effects on reproductive health.[70]

Processed Foods: Buyer Beware. The FDA governs processed foods under the FDCA, and chemical additives used in processed foods fall under the FAA. The FAA requires premarket approval for chemical additives, and it was passed to protect consumers from carcinogenic food additives.[71] By the 1970s, the FDA, as part of fulfilling its mandate under the FAA, had developed sophisticated and rigorous methods for testing food additives.[72] By the late 1990s, however, the FDA had loosened its oversight of food additives, such that approval is no longer precautionary in practice.

Furthermore, in 1997, the FDA intentionally created a major loophole to allow food processors to use nearly any new food additive they wished without notifying the FDA.[73] At the time, the FDA was drowning in a backlog of applications from companies wanting to introduce new chemical additives—including substances that could extend a product's shelf life, add flavor, or improve texture—to processed foods. Food processors argued that the FDA backlog interfered with growth and profitability, and they pressured the agency to find a solution the problem.[74] The FDA, underfunded and understaffed, elected to expand what could be allowed under its generally recognized as safe (GRAS) category—a classification originally created for benign food additives that are known to be safe in small amounts, such as salt, sugar, and commonly used herbs. By loosening the rules, the FDA gave food processors the possibility to call nearly any new food additive a GRAS substance, allowing them to bypass formal FDA review and get their products onto the market more quickly. The one exception was artificial colors, which still had to undergo premarket approval. These changes to GRAS made it so that companies could choose whether to register new food additives with the FDA. The FDA does not actually require notification from food processors, nor does it review industry tests or conduct its own tests on new additives. In rare cases, manufacturers will voluntarily register a compound with the FDA. In effect, industry has the power to decide whether to notify the FDA of new food additives, and the majority of new additives go to market without notifying the agency.[75] The FDA asks companies to do their own safety evaluations and recommends that they use the most up-to-date and rigorous scientific procedures when making these evaluations. However, the definition of scientific expertise to determine safety remains vague, and there are no clear rules as to what happens when a company fails to appropriately test for safety. In practice, the public has little view of the data, methods and procedures that are used to determine food additive safety. For example, if a company develops a new compound to replace some of the fat to make a low-calorie chocolate bar, it can use its own testing protocols to determine whether the compound is safe. If it is satisfied with the safety of the ingredient, the company can declare it a GRAS substance and not notify the FDA of the results of the tests or of its decision to categorize the substance as GRAS.[76] The company must still list the substance in the ingredient list on the product package.

According to one count, around one thousand food additives have never been carefully studied for their impacts on human health.[77] The GAO and Pew Charitable Trusts have both called attention to GRAS as a major regulatory failure. This is a shocking regulatory loophole that defies both the FAA and the principles on which the FDA was founded.

Even when formal precautionary measures have been put into place, there is no guarantee that these rules will be followed or properly enforced. Rather, the safe-until-sorry approach dominates, in large part owing to a combination of industry pressure on government and the poor funding and staffing of government agencies.

One consequence of the safe-until-sorry approach is that food industry watchdogs are not located within the FDA; instead, they are external or extragovernmental forces, like consumer advocates and environmental health organizations that do background research on food additives. In 2017, environmental and health groups, including the Environmental Working Group, Center for Science in the Public Interest, and Breast Cancer Prevention Partners, sued the FDA for delegating authority to determine the safety of food additives to industry.[78]

Certified Organic: The Bread and Butter of Precautionary Consumption. While most consumers are not aware of the intricacies of food regulation, they have a general sense that certified-organic food is produced with fewer chemical inputs than conventional food.[79] In this sense, I consider organic certification to be the "bread and butter" of precautionary consumption. All of the mothers I interviewed for this book—including those who practiced very little precautionary consumption—considered eating certified-organic food to be a reasonable option for reducing personal exposure to pesticides.

One reason consumers turn to certified-organic foods is that there are clear rules governing whether a food can be certified organic, and these rules aim to minimize the use of synthetic chemicals in agricultural production. The United States' standardized system for certifying organic foods can be traced back to the Alar scare of 1989. That year, the CBS News show *60 Minutes* aired a segment on Alar (a ripening agent used in apple production), flagging it as a possible carcinogen and raising the alarm about its impact on children's health. The public backlash was profound. Apple sales dropped overnight, leading some producers to falsely label their apples sprayed with Alar as organic.[80] The federal government responded in 1990 with the Organic Food Production Act to address consumer confusion and protect legitimate organic producers. This inaugurated the National Organic Program within the USDA Agricultural Marketing Service, which became responsible for developing national standards for four categories of agricultural products: crops, livestock, multi-ingredient processed foods, and wild crops.[81] In 2002, the USDA adopted national standards for certified-organic food, although developing them involved much controversy between members of the organic farming movement, the USDA, and industrial farmers. Some of these parties wanted the organic program to reflect the original goals of the organic movement, while others wanted the organic sector to move away from small-scale agriculture and adopt some of the practices of industrial agriculture.[82]

To be certified organic by the USDA, food cannot be grown with synthetic pesticides and herbicides typically used in conventional food production. Some synthetic substances that do not contaminate the soil or water are allowed.[83] The USDA requires farms and food producers to pass a comprehensive audit before they are allowed to use the green and white USDA certified-organic seal. Like other labeling provisions, the onus is on the consumer to look for the USDA certified-organic label if they want to avoid pesticide residues in their food.

Processed foods that have some organic ingredients must meet specific criteria if they want to carry the USDA certified-organic seal, and the agency designates four categories. A food is "100 percent organic" if all ingredients and processing aids are certified organic. It is "organic" if at least 95 percent of its ingredients are certified organic. A product with only 70 percent organic ingredients may say that it is "made with organic [name of ingredient(s)]." Foods with less than 70 percent organic ingredients cannot have a prominent organic claim on their label, but they can indicate on the ingredient label which ingredients are certified organic.[84] The USDA has no regulatory authority over cosmetic products (I will discuss this later in this chapter); however, a cosmetic or personal care product can list ingredients as certified organic if those ingredients meet USDA certification standards.[85]

Genetically Modified Organisms in Food. Genetic modification is a process of directly manipulating an organism's genes by, for example, transplanting DNA (deoxyribonucleic acid) from one organism to another. This is distinct from the centuries-old practice of selectively breeding plants and animals to get desired traits. In 1994, the Flavr Savr tomato, engineered to prevent over-ripening by the time the tomatoes arrived at the grocery store, was the first genetically modified food to be sold in the United States.[86]

Although genetically modified organisms (GMOs) are not synthetic chemical substances, I cover them here, as many consumers consider them to be a hazardous food and apply precautionary consumption to avoid buying them.[87] Genetically modified plants and plant-based ingredients are allowed for sale in the United States, and the most common GMOs used in food are canola, corn, soy, and sugar beets.[88] Applying the precautionary principle, the European Union began restricting the use of GMOs in European agriculture in 2001, and it expanded these regulations in 2003 to cover imported and domestic animal feed and food products.[89] Looking to the European Union, American consumers and environmental advocacy groups began to demand labels on food to allow them to apply their own precautionary standards to avoid GMO foods, which some refer to as "frankenfoods."

U.S. food producers have two options for labeling GMOs: they can label the *absence* of GMOs or label the *presence* of GMOs. The first is a voluntary action, and is prevalent in the market for "natural" foods, particularly among organic food manufacturers, which are already prohibited from using GMOs due to USDA organic certification standards. To increase consumer trust in GMO-free claims, several nonprofit groups have formed to certify food as GMO-free. The nonprofit group the Non-GMO Project runs the most popular program. For a fee, the Non-GMO Project will test a crop or food product for the presence of GMOs. If GMOs are absent, the grower or manufacturer can use the colorful Non-GMO Project seal and logo on its packaging and advertising. As of 2017, the organization had verified over forty-three thousand products, accounting for about $19.2 billion in sales.[90]

The second approach, mandatory labeling, has long been controversial and has faced vigorous opposition from agribusiness groups, such as the Grocery Manufacturers Association, the Snack Food Association, the International Dairy Foods Association, and the National Association of Manufacturers.[91] Advocacy groups like the Center for Food Safety, Greenpeace International, and U.S. Right to Know, among others, and have lobbied for decades for a federal, mandatory labeling system for GMOs. This has been vehemently opposed by the processed food industry, which fears that such a system will cause undue anxiety among consumers and turn them away from foods containing GMOs. However, once the states of Connecticut, Maine, and Vermont proposed mandatory GMO labels, food processors could see the writing on the wall and asked the federal government to introduce a nationwide standard. The result was the National Bioengineered Food Disclosure Law, signed into law in July 2016, which supersedes any state-level labeling requirements. The law is friendly to industry; it requires manufacturers to label GMO products, but they have the choice to use text (e.g., "partially produced with genetic engineering") or a QR code that can be scanned by a smartphone, leading customers to a website with more product information. The law has been criticized as awkward and nontransparent, particularly since the QR code effectively hides the GMO label from shoppers. The USDA is charged with administering this law and, as of late 2017, had not prepared the final labeling rules. Industry does not expect the USDA to impose severe penalties for noncompliance with the law.[92] Aware of public support for labeling and opposition to the QR code approach, a handful of major food processors, such as Campbell's and Frito Lay, have chosen to clearly label when their food products contain GMO ingredients.

Food Labels. In addition to carrying organic certification seals and QR codes with information about genetically modified ingredients, today's food commodities are plastered with images and text that make claims about health ("good for heart health"), nutrition ("zero calories"), ingredients ("low fat," "no refined sugars"), and chemical-free status ("rBGH-free," "no artificial colors"). In the absence of strong government oversight of the food system, these labels attempt to guide consumers on their precautionary journey through the grocery store, making it easier (in theory) to work around a regulatory system that does not protect them. Labels themselves are subject to regulation, but they are governed under a different set of laws from the ones reviewed above, making the already complex regulatory system for food even more bewildering.

The labels on packaged, conventional foods are regulated by the FDA, and the agency has the authority to introduce new labeling provisions.[93] The FDA tracks misleading statements on food packaging, a vital task, as manufacturers often put *more* information on packages than the FDA requires (see chapter 4); regulations say that information can be included as long as it is truthful. One particularly sticky issue is the claim that food is "natural," as there are no guidelines on what constitute a natural product, yet this label exists on thousands of items. The FDA does not provide a definition of natural foods, but it will ask companies to remove the claim if their product uses synthetic colors, flavors, or other synthetic substances.[94] In early 2016, the agency began considering how to revise its rules to more clearly define what constitutes a natural food.

The FDA also oversees basic nutritional labeling provisions and regulates all health messages on packaging. The Nutrition Labeling and Education Act (NLEA) of 1990 demands comprehensive and standardized nutrition labeling for packaged foods.[95] For example, if a beverage claims to contain fruit juice, the label must specify what percentage of the product is actually fruit juice. Companies must also list any added colors, flag the presence of allergens (e.g., wheat, milk, soy, or nuts), and list grams of trans fats. The FDA regulates the design, layout, and content of the nutrition label and makes periodic updates to the rules.[96]

Labeling regulations are meant to protect consumers from misleading claims and allow them to identify permissible but potentially harmful ingredients.[97] One such ingredient is sugar, and in May 2016, the FDA announced changes that will require manufacturers to disclose how many grams of added sugar are in all foods. This is scheduled to come into effect by 2020.[98] Ultimately, the purpose of food labels is to allow consumers to make informed decisions. Key here is that the responsibility to read the label and interpret it correctly lies with consumers.

This approach of informed choice necessarily depends on consumer literacy—that is, the ability to read a label and understand what it means. The nutrition facts label, for example, assumes that consumers can quickly identify the grams of fat, sodium, and sugar content in foods and also make sense of what constitutes "too much" of any of these ingredients. About 75 percent of food shoppers indicate that they consult these labels while shopping, and women are significantly more likely to do so than men.[99] Individuals with low incomes and low levels of educational attainment are less likely to use nutrition labels while shopping, meaning that this strategy of buyer-beware mostly benefits upper- and middle-class shoppers.[100] More to the point, reading labels falls to the bottom of a person's priority list if they are juggling multiple pressures while grocery shopping, such as keeping an eye on children they may have with them, feeling pressed for time, or trying to shop on a limited budget, when price matters far more than the ingredient list.

Advocacy groups challenge industry to prove the truthfulness of claims on a label, and they put pressure on the FDA to monitor industry more carefully. In 2015, the EWG tested 7,500 foods with partially hydrogenated oils in their ingredient lists and found that nearly 90 percent of them did not disclose the presence of trans fats on the nutrition label, choosing instead to round the low trans fat content of the products to zero grams. A few months after the group's report was released, the FDA announced that it was giving industry three years to completely phase out trans fats from foods.[101] In 2011, Kashi, a food brand owned by Kellogg's, was sued in California for using the terms "natural" and "nothing artificial" on some of its products that contain synthetic ingredients. It eventually agreed to settle out of court and remove these claims from certain products.[102] In 2012, the yogurt manufacturer Chobani was hit with a lawsuit for advertising its yogurt as having "no added sugar" although it listed "evaporated cane juice"—a form of sugar that is less processed than white sugar—on its ingredient label. The lawsuit was eventually dismissed. The Chobani case is just one of two hundred lawsuits filed against companies using the term "natural."[103]

In a regulatory system that prioritizes consumer information and loose monitoring of industry, consumers feel very much on their own—an issue I explore in interviews with mothers in chapter 5.

Personal Care Products: Precaution Recommended

Most cosmetics, like perfumes, lotions, eye shadows, and soaps, fall under the jurisdiction of the FDA and are regulated under the safe-until-sorry approach.[104] The FDA maintains that manufacturers "have a legal responsibility to ensure the safety of their products. Neither the law nor FDA regulations require specific [safety] tests," and it also states that the law "does not require cosmetic companies to share their safety information with FDA."[105] Key here is that the agency does not impose premarket approval, and thus allows unreviewed chemicals to be used in products that are often applied directly to human skin or hair. The FDA maintains a short list of prohibited ingredients and depends on industry to collect its own data about the safety of ingredients used in its products and notify the agency if it suspects a product is harmful to health.[106]

Companies must, nevertheless, list all ingredients a product contains on its packaging. However, to protect trade secrets, when labeling products with fragrance—from perfumes to scented lotions—companies can use the general description "fragrance" and are not required to disclose the multiple compounds that make up a fragrance. This is troubling because many synthetic fragrances are made up of endocrine-disrupting ingredients, such as phthalates, and these compounds enter the body via the skin or inhalation.[107]

There are few regulations for cosmetics, and the FDA often fails to punish companies who break the rules that do exist. As just one example, in 2011, hair salon workers in California and Oregon began complaining of nosebleeds, dizziness, respiratory difficulties, and headaches tied to the use of a product called Brazilian Blowout—a treatment that renders hair straight and smooth. The FDA determined that Brazilian Blowout products contained methylene glycol, a compound released as formaldehyde when it is heated during the flat-ironing and blow-drying stage of hair straightening. As a known carcinogen, methylene glycol should have been listed on the product's ingredient label, along with a warning to consumers and salon workers that the product contains formaldehyde. The FDA issued a warning to salon workers and recommended a voluntary recall of the product. In response, the company that produced Brazilian Blowout promised to remove the ingredient, and soon falsely labeled their product as formaldehyde-free. The company eventually settled a $4.5 million class action lawsuit with California's attorney general, but it was still allowed to sell its product as long as it labeled the presence of formaldehyde and warned consumers of the health risks. In other words, even though the FDA lists formaldehyde as a carcinogen, the agency could not force the company to change the formula or stop selling its product. Instead, the FDA issued letters asking the company to put a warning label on its product and created a website with safety tips for consumers of hair-straightening products.[108] The case of Brazilian Blowout reveals that consumers, as well as workers, have to take responsibility for their own safety by taking precautionary action.

Consumer Products: The Year of the Recall

The Consumer Product Safety Commission (CPSC) maintains safety standards for over fifteen thousand consumer products, including children's toys, clothing, and furniture. The CPSC is regulated under the Consumer Product Safety Act, which was passed in 1972 to introduce uniform standards for consumer products and protect the public "against unreasonable risks of injuries associated with consumer products."[109] The agency also issues recalls for consumer products that do not meet its safety criteria.

The CPSC and the federal government's safe-until-sorry approach came under intense scrutiny in 2007, often called the Year of the Recall. That year, twenty million children's toys and jewelry items were recalled from retail locations across the country—from dollar stores to high-end boutiques—because they posed a choking hazard or had a high content of heavy metals, such as lead, nickel, or cadmium.[110] One particularly shocking incident involved the popular toy Aqua Dots. Aqua Dots were colorful beads that, when combined with water, allowed children to make designs on paper. The dots, however, were coated with a compound that metabolized into gamma-hydroxy butyrate—a so-called date rape drug—when swallowed.[111] Thus, if ingested (as they were in at least two cases), the dots posed a serious health hazard.[112] The case of Aqua Dots and other toxic toys received widespread media attention.

Most of the recalled toys were manufactured in China, bringing attention to the massive imports of commodities from a country with different safety standards and poor monitoring of industry. Caving to public outrage, Congress passed the Consumer Product Safety Improvement Act of 2008. This was an update to the Consumer Product Safety Act of 1972, and it outlined stricter provisions for children's toys (including regular testing for lead) and banned three types of phthalates that had already been phased out by European regulators.[113] It also introduced more stringent certification standards for imports and gave more power to the CPSC to recall products found to violate the act's provisions.[114]

The CPSC continues to review the safety of consumer products and materials. In 2017, the agency issued a recommendation for furniture manufacturers to stop using organohalogen flame retardants, and it expanded the list of phthalates that are not allowed in children's toys and children's care products. The CPSC website lists all active recall notices, and there continue to be numerous recalls of products like car seats, child swings, dressers, and children's toys and apparel.

The website also notifies the public of all safety reviews in progress. The agency, along with the EPA and the CDC, are currently reviewing the safety of tire crumb materials—a popular material for artificial turf fields and playgrounds. These materials contain volatile organic compounds and heavy metals, known toxics, but it remains unclear whether children and athletes are exposed at levels high enough to warrant concern.[115] While government agencies review the safety of this material, the CPSC offers advice for concerned consumers that consists entirely of individualized, precautionary measures. This includes wiping a child's hands after they touch the rubber material at the playground, carefully washing any clothing that has come into contact with rubber crumb material, and avoiding surfaces made of tire crumb material during very hot days.[116]

Chemical Regulation in the Post-TSCA Era

After the introduction of the TSCA in 1976, the EPA was under tremendous public pressure to improve the safety of commercial and industrial chemicals, but its hands were tied by the weak legislation. In the early 1990s, as part of a creative move that captured the green consumerism zeitgeist of the time, the agency developed the Design for the Environment program to encourage companies to substitute potentially harmful technologies, chemicals, and production processes with environmentally friendly alternatives.[117] Through this program, a product could get a seal indicating that it was endorsed by the

EPA and recognized for "safer chemistry." Employees in the Design for the Environment division of the EPA identified alternatives by applying more precautionary forms of risk assessment than were required elsewhere in the EPA.[118] In 2015, the EPA changed the name of the program to the Safer Choices Label, allowing eligible companies to place the bright green and blue Safer Choices logo on their product packaging. As the agency wrote on its website, "Finding cleaning and other products that are safer for you, your family, and the environment should be easy—that's why we developed our new Safer Choice label. We all play a role in protecting our families' health and the environment. Products with the Safer Choice label help consumers and commercial buyers identify and select products with safer chemical ingredients, without sacrificing quality or performance."[119]

As of 2017, the agency has more than two thousand products that are qualified to carry the label, from dish soap to car cleaners to personal care products. The EPA reassured the public that "every ingredient must meet strict safety criteria for both human health and the environment, including carcinogenicity, reproductive/developmental toxicity, toxicity to aquatic life, and persistence in the environment."[120]

Products that do not meet the agency's Safer Choice criteria are assumed to be less safe, but they are not considered unsafe, as they are still allowed under the TSCA. Ironically, with the Safer Choices program, the EPA developed a market-based branding strategy to encourage precautionary consumption, the need for which was directly related to the poor chemical regulation under the agency's own authority.

In June 2016, in an unusual show of bipartisan cooperation under a Republican-controlled Congress, the TSCA was amended under the Frank R. Lautenberg Chemical Safety for the 21st Century Act. This amendment to the TSCA authorizes the EPA to institute a more precautionary approach to chemical regulation—although the legislation does not use the language of precaution or the precautionary principle. In contrast to the old TSCA, the new TSCA requires new chemicals to undergo review by the agency, and the criteria for review no longer take into account the burden of regulation on industry, effectively freeing the agency to review a compound for its health and safety impacts, independent of the impact on industry. Six months after the amendments were signed into law, the chemical industry complained that EPA reviews of new chemicals were "mired in inefficiencies, causing significant delay for manufacturers," signaling that industry is lobbying government for faster approvals.[121] Under the new TSCA, existing chemicals must also be screened by the agency using industry-approved risk-assessment models, separating chemicals into high or low priority for additional safety review. High-priority chemicals are considered persistent, bioaccumulative, and toxic—in other words, these are compounds that take a long time to break down in the environment, can accumulate in animal tissues, and have properties that make them likely toxins. These high-priority substances must undergo additional risk assessment, with some or all of the cost of assessment borne by industry. Most positively, the new TSCA provides guidelines for premarket review, meaning that the EPA must assess new chemicals before they are allowed onto the market. There are specific guidelines on how many chemicals must be reviewed each year, but the bar is set very low, with ten ongoing risk evaluations within the first year of implementing the act and twenty set to take place within the first three and a half years. The timelines for assessment are long. Recall that there are approximately eighty-five thousand compounds that have not been thoroughly tested by the EPA. Even if the agency determines that a compound poses a risk to health, it could still take several more years before restrictions are actually put in place.

While the new TSCA is promising, there are several reasons why it may have very little impact on the existing chemical landscape. First, it prohibits states from enacting their own chemical regulations after the agency has made a decision regarding a chemical or when it is reviewing a chemical. Restricting state laws in this way prevents states from initiating pressure that might scale up to the federal level, a tactic that has been very successful at pressuring industry to eliminate toxic substances. For the forty years the original TSCA was in place, state laws "served as the only cop on the chemical beat," to use the words of the EWG.[122] Massachusetts, for instance, was an early adopter of precautionary chemical regulation. In 1989, the state passed the Toxic Use Reduction Act, which requires manufacturers and businesses to reduce their use of toxic chemicals if they use them in large volumes. In 2007, California established a Toxic Information Clearinghouse "for the collection, maintenance, and distribution of specific chemical hazard traits and environmental and toxicological end-point data."[123] This clearinghouse is an essential step for reviewing the toxicity of chemicals that have never undergone comprehensive safety reviews. Since establishing the clearinghouse, the state has banned BPA in food containers and toys for children and banned certain classes of brominated flame retardants.

Second, and most critically, in early 2017, the Trump administration and EPA director Scott Pruitt proposed historically massive funding cuts to EPA programs that would seriously undermine the agency's ability to fulfill the mandate of the new TSCA. Around the same time, Congress proposed legislation, called the HONEST Act, to limit the kinds of scientific studies that the EPA can use to make decisions—a move that has been decried as an antiscience action and as a backhanded approach to deregulation.[124] If Congress is successful in pushing through the act, the EPA could find that it is not authorized to use all of the available published and independent research required to make an informed risk evaluation, thereby allowing the safe-until-sorry approach to creep back into chemical regulation. Furthermore, in April 2017, Congress appointed an American Chemistry Council official as the head of its Office of Chemical Safety and Pollution Prevention, the person who will have the power to revise how the EPA reviews chemical safety and risk under the new TSCA.[125] Finally, Pruitt appears set to adjudicate EPA decisions that are unfriendly to the chemical industry. Citing the need for "sound science," in March 2017, he reversed an EPA decision to permanently ban the pesticide chlorpyrifos in American agriculture, effectively going against the advice of his own agency scientists.[126] This decision will mean that farmworkers and their children, who are exposed to the chemical at high doses, will continue to suffer the ill effects of exposure to this compound, which include memory problems and learning disabilities. At the time of writing, attorneys general in seven states have applied to sue the EPA for failing to follow its own safety recommendations for chlorpyrifos.[127]

FRACTURED RESPONSIBILITIES, SAFETY GAPS, AND INDUSTRY INFLUENCE

This chapter has outlined the complex policy frameworks that govern chemicals used to make our food, cosmetics, and other consumer products. In this long history of chemical production and expansion of industrial capitalism, there have been only brief moments when chemicals were carefully evaluated for their impact on human health and the environment. The most consistent pattern is that of government inaction to environmental health threats that inspires precautionary consumption.

During the first century of the industrialization of the food system, numerous manufacturers deliberately misled consumers about the ingredients in their products, from foods to pharmaceuticals. Some of these ingredients led to death, illness, or disability. The most egregious cases of industry misconduct date back to the early years of chemical innovation, and at that time, there was little to no government regulation to monitor and punish dishonest manufacturers. When the federal government finally instituted modest precautionary measures, they were applied unevenly and could not withstand industry pressure to loosen government oversight. When agencies like the FDA and EPA were established to enforce regulations, they followed a proof-of-harm model of risk assessment that waited for evidence of harm to accumulate before instituting restrictions. Today, as a result of decades of lawsuits, amendments, compromises, scrapped laws, and brief moments of consumer outrage, the United States has a fractured regulatory framework for synthetic chemicals that prioritizes industry innovation and profit over public health and environmental protection. Some promising regulatory improvements, namely the new TSCA, have recently been implemented, but these are being scaled back at an astonishing pace under the Trump administration.

Figure 1 gives a timeline of this regulatory history, marking key moments in policy and the regulation of synthetic chemicals used in food production, consumer products, cosmetics, and chemical pollutants released into the environment. The timeline marks major policies, revealing a shift over time from weak precautionary policy toward a mandate of consumer self-protection, starting in the 1990s. As the figure shows, a precautionary logic was applied to policies such as the FAA of 1958 and the 1994 agreement to phase out fluorocarbons. In the 1990s, legislation was largely focused on creating mechanisms of consumer self-protection, such as the Nutritional Labeling and Education Act and the National Organic Production Act. Legislation and policy with a strong precautionary logic are few and far between. Significantly, even when precautionary legislation is in place, there is no guarantee that the precautionary principle will be enacted and enforced. The FDA's implementation of the FAA is a perfect example of how agencies can revise how they carry out a mandate and thereby undermine the original purpose of precautionary legislation.

The regulatory history outlined in this chapter reflects the strong influence industry has had from the very beginning of food and chemical legislation. From concern about arsenic residues on fruits and vegetables to debates about endocrine-disrupting plastics, industry has framed environmental and health risks from chemicals as small compared to the potential costs to the U.S. economy from close government scrutiny of industrial operations. The precautionary principle as a policy ethic is viewed as the enemy of economic

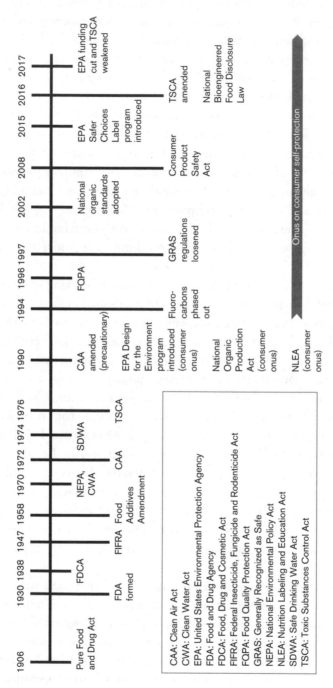

FIGURE 1. Key moments in U.S. federal food, chemical, and environmental health policy

1906 — Pure Food and Drug Act

1930 1938 — FDCA — FDA formed

1947 — FIFRA

1958 — Food Additives Amendment

1970 — NEPA, CWA

1972 — CAA Amendment

1974 — SDWA

1976 — TSCA

1990 — CAA amended (precautionary); EPA Design for the Environment program introduced (consumer onus); National Organic Production Act (consumer onus); NLEA (consumer onus)

1994 — Fluorocarbons phased out

1996 — FQPA

1997 — GRAS regulations loosened

2002 — National organic standards adopted

2008 — Consumer Product Safety Act

2015 — EPA Safer Choices Label program introduced

2016 — TSCA amended; National Bioengineered Food Disclosure Law

2017 — EPA funding cut and TSCA weakened

Onus on consumer self-protection

CAA: Clean Air Act
CWA: Clean Water Act
EPA: United States Environmental Protection Agency
FDA: Food and Drug Agency
FDCA: Food, Drug and Cosmetic Act
FIFRA: Federal Insecticide, Fungicide and Rodenticide Act
FQPA: Food Quality Protection Act
GRAS: Generally Recognized as Safe
NEPA: National Environmental Policy Act
NLEA: Nutrition Labeling and Education Act
SDWA: Safe Drinking Water Act
TSCA: Toxic Substances Control Act

growth and as an opportunity for environmental interests to disrupt industrial progress. Industry has long had the upper hand in shaping the regulatory landscape. It took forty years for the TSCA to be revised. During this time, new classes of chemicals were being introduced into foods, consumer products, and the environment and health science suggested that chemical exposures early in life could set the course for future diseases and disorders (which will be discussed in the next chapter).

Given the spotty and often lax regulation of chemicals, consumers have been left to puzzle out for themselves what foods and consumer products are safe. To do this, they must use their own standards of precaution by consulting product labels or ingredient lists to determine if products contain unwanted chemicals or by looking for a seal of approval from the USDA organic program or the Non-GMO Project. The next chapter looks at how the environmental health movement has responded to the lack of institutionalized precaution in the United States and played a key role in promoting precautionary consumption.

THREE

Personalizing Pollution

THE ENVIRONMENTAL HEALTH MOVEMENT

> Go fresh instead of canned—many food cans have BPA in their linings—or research which companies don't use BPA or similar chemicals in their products. Say no to receipts, since thermal paper is often coated with BPA. Avoid plastics marked with "PC," for polycarbonate, or recycling label #7. Not all of these plastics contain BPA, but many do—and it's better [to be] safe than sorry when it comes to keeping synthetic hormones out of your body.
>
> Keep a Breast Foundation and Environmental Working Group, *Dirty Dozen: List of Endocrine Disruptors*

> In recent years, public health advocates have rallied around an idea known as the Precautionary Principle. This philosophy says that whenever there is any suspicion that an activity or product may cause harm to human health or the environment, it should be set aside until its safety can be proven. The Precautionary Principle is about looking very carefully before we leap. It's a great philosophy to bring to your pregnancy and eventually your parenting, too. If there's any question that an activity or product may cause harm to you or your baby, set it aside until you can be absolutely sure it won't. You won't miss it.
>
> Healthy Child, Healthy World, *Easy Steps to a Safer Pregnancy*

While the federal government rejects the precautionary principle, organizations within the environmental health movement have embraced it by acting as alternatives to the FDA, EPA, CDC, and CPSC. These organizations test cosmetic products to evaluate the safety of their ingredients—the domain of the FDA. They measure pesticide residues on fruits and vegetables to determine what varieties have unreasonably high levels—the responsibility of the EPA. They test children's art supplies and jewelry for lead and chromium—the responsibility of the CPSC. They study the human body burden by testing human tissues for environmental chemicals—the role of the CDC. When did environmental health movement groups begin taking on these roles, and what has been their influence more generally in supporting the rise of precautionary consumption?

As I show in this chapter, the environmental health movement came together to call for a broad application of a strong precautionary principle in environmental regulation and worked hard to lobby for global and domestic policy change. As the movement presented a disturbing portrait of widespread human exposure to environmental chemicals, it faced the question of how to push for policy change while also raising awareness of the scope of chemical pollution. It settled on advocacy biomonitoring to personalize pollution, and on precautionary consumption as a way of teaching the public how to avoid some forms of chemical exposure. Moreover, organizations within the movement circulated a message about environmental pollution threatening human reproduction and the future of the human species, with a strong focus on how women's reproductive bodies transmit environmental chemicals to the bodies of the very young. This understanding of women's bodies as the primary pathway through which contamination enters fetal and infant bodies is closely linked to recommendations that target women's domestic labor, particularly shopping, foodwork, and cleaning the home. In an effort to protect human reproductive fitness and fetal, infant, and child health, organizations within the movement have become dominant producers of precautionary advice.

In this chapter, I tell the story of a movement that shifted away from demanding the institutionalization of the precautionary principle in domestic policy and toward an approach that embraced regulatory reform in tandem with precautionary consumption. To piece together this history and the key messages advanced by the movement, I analyzed reports, fact sheets, brochures, and studies published between 1992 and 2015 by major American environmental health movement groups.[1]

MOVING TOWARD THE STRONG PRECAUTIONARY PRINCIPLE

Groups within the environmental health movement apply the precautionary principle as a public paradigm to challenge regulatory failures that have led to widespread contamination of human bodies and the environment.[2] This paradigm, according to sociologist Phil Brown, "leads people to alter fundamentally how they view the world, poses deep levels of criticism as a route to an alternative model of social life, and occurs as a result of large-scale public participation."[3] The environmental health movement is said to have started in 1978 at Love Canal, New York, when a group of white, working-class residents, led by mother Lois Gibbs, brought national attention to an abandoned toxic waste site that was contaminating the community's soil and water.[4] Gibbs founded the Citizens Clearinghouse for Hazardous Waste in 1981, launching a populist antitoxics movement that channeled public outrage over the routine regulatory failure to prevent the illegal dumping of toxic waste into community waterways, soil, and airsheds.[5] Today's environmental health movement is more than the antitoxics movement. Groups use biomedical technologies to challenge existing explanations of how toxics end up in human bodies, to raise awareness about the pervasiveness of environmental pollution, and to dispute dominant explanations for the causation of disease.[6] They fight environmental injustices, such as the siting of major roadways and toxic facilities next to urban communities and neighborhoods that lack the political voice to oppose such projects. Some focus on the link between toxic exposures, occupation, and disease.[7] All organizations in this movement hope for better regulation to reduce toxic pollution, and many, though not all, teach the public how to become better precautionary consumers.[8]

In the early 1990s, the environmental health movement began mobilizing around what it called the strong precautionary principle in response to growing concern about the health effects of endocrine disruptors. At that time, endocrine disruptors had not received much attention in the health sciences, and regulatory agencies did not regard these substances as hazardous.[9] Theo Colborn, a zoologist and environmental activist, was instrumental in putting endocrine disruptors on the environmental health advocacy agenda. Colborn, who worked for the World Wildlife Fund, had reviewed hundreds of studies in toxicology and wildlife biology. She found that reproductive abnormalities in fish, birds, and reptiles were increasing in the Great Lakes region and theorized that these abnormalities were caused by pollutants that interfered with organisms' endocrine systems. Colborn is credited with setting in motion the theory of endocrine disruption.[10]

In 1991, members of the environmental health movement, including Colborn, along with other scientists, activists, and public health specialists, met in Racine, Wisconsin, at what was to be the first of two pivotal

Wingspread conferences. Endocrine disruptors featured prominently on the agenda, and the meeting culminated in a consensus statement on the hazards of these compounds: "Unless the environmental load of synthetic hormone disruptors is abated and controlled, large-scale dysfunction at the population level is possible. The scope and potential hazard to wildlife and humans are great because of the probability of repeated and/or constant exposure to numerous synthetic chemicals that are known to be endocrine disruptors."[11]

This statement was published in an edited volume, in which Colborn, along with other biologists, endocrinologists, and toxicologists drew parallels between reproductive abnormalities in wildlife and human reproductive disorders.[12] This book drew attention to the idea of the "fragile fetus"—an entity that is highly susceptible to low-dose exposures to endocrine disruptors.[13] As I address later in this chapter, this biological and ecological perspective coincided with biomedical views of the fragile human fetus that is vulnerable to a mother's exposure to endocrine disruptors.

In 1996, Theo Colborn, Diane Dumanoski, and Pete Myers published *Our Stolen Future,* a book that made a scientific case for the dangers of low-dose exposures to endocrine-disrupting pesticides, industrial chemicals, and plastics.[14] In the preface, the then vice president Al Gore heralded the book as the new *Silent Spring.* The book received coverage in national newspapers, became a bestseller, and was translated into eighteen languages.

Regulators, toxicologists, and the chemical industry vehemently pushed back against the movement's concern about endocrine disruptors. Arguing that the science around endocrine disruptors was highly flawed and undeveloped, they maintained that "the dose makes the poison," rejecting the possibility that low-dose exposures could harm human health.[15] The issue of low-dose exposures required a fundamental rethinking of how to evaluate toxicity. However, regulators and chemical manufacturers simply refused to adapt their models, and this inflexibility continues today.[16]

When faced with strong opposition from government and industry to recognize endocrine disruptors as potentially harmful to animals and humans, key members of the environmental health movement reasoned that institutionalizing a stronger version of the precautionary principle was the first step toward transforming the country's chemical and environmental laws.[17] This version would have to be more specific than the one articulated at the 1992 Earth Summit in Rio de Janeiro, Brazil, that made a general commitment to prioritizing environmental protection when faced with the lack of full scientific certainty of harm (see chapter 2).

In 1998, members of the environmental health movement met for a second Wingspread Conference, again held in Racine, Wisconsin, to ratify a consensus statement on the precautionary principle. Called the Wingspread Statement on the Precautionary Principle, it is considered to be the cornerstone of the American environmental health movement:

> When an activity raises threats of harm to the environment or human health, precautionary measures should be taken even if some cause and effect relationships are not fully established scientifically. In this context the proponent of an activity, rather than the public, bears the burden of proof. The process of applying the Precautionary Principle must be open, informed and democratic, and must include potentially affected parties. It must also involve an examination of the full range of alternatives, including no action.[18]

The strong precautionary principle became the common ground uniting multiple environmental health movement groups that were all fighting for structural reform to protect public health, the environment, or both.[19] Organizations like the Alliance for a Healthy Tomorrow, West Harlem for Environmental Justice (WE ACT), the Massachusetts Precautionary Principle Project, the Silent Spring Institute, the Breast Cancer Fund, the Campaign for Safe Cosmetics, Health Care without Harm, and Physicians for Social Responsibility, among dozens of others, consider the precautionary principle a pathway to better public health.[20] These groups point to examples of policies and laws built on the strong precautionary principle that restricted the production of compounds and led to clear declines in human body burdens. For instance, data from Sweden revealed remarkable declines in concentrations of dioxins, PCBs, and DDT in human breast milk once regulation was in place to restrict or ban these substances altogether.[21] When Swedish scientists detected a dramatic increase in concentrations of the flame retardant polybrominated diphenyl ethers (PBDEs) in samples of Swedish women's breast milk, the Swedish government quickly instituted precautionary restrictions on PBDEs, and concentrations soon declined.[22] Breast milk samples from women in America (where no restrictions were in place), meanwhile, revealed PBDE concentrations that were approximately twenty times higher than the concentration in Swedes.[23]

Although U.S. regulators have consistently rejected the strong precautionary principle, the movement has never given up its demand for policy reform. But as time has passed, it has looked to other mechanisms to raise public awareness of endocrine disruptors and to prevent environmental harm. In particular, the movement turned to the powerful strategy of "advocacy bio-monitoring" to make the case for regulatory reform and greener markets.

MAKING POLLUTION PERSONAL

To raise awareness of the dangers of everyday toxics, like endocrine disruptors, environmental groups launched highly effective public awareness campaigns to show that pollution was not just something "out there" in the general environment coming out of a smokestack. It was also "in here," meaning in the human body and the home.[24] They used biomonitoring technology to raise awareness of chemical body burdens, recruiting volunteers to donate samples of their blood, urine, or breast milk to be tested for traces of synthetic chemicals. Using this technology, they raised awareness of the permeability of the human body to synthetic chemicals and most especially to endocrine disruptors that were present in common foods and everyday objects.[25]

Environmentalists and biologists have long known that chemicals bioaccumulate in human tissues. In *Silent Spring,* the groundbreaking book that is said to have launched the modern environmental movement, Rachel Carson sounded the alarm that "virtually every human being is subjected to contact with dangerous chemicals from birth to death" and that "these chemicals are now stored in the bodies of the vast majority of human beings, regardless of their age. They occur in mother's milk, and probably in the tissues of the unborn child."[26] Advocacy biomonitoring has since come of age owing to improvements in technology that allow for the detection of compounds at much lower concentrations in the human body.[27] These technological improvements have helped transform the chemical body burden from a largely invisible phenomenon to a visible and relatable one.[28] This has also resulted in new relationships between environmental advocates and scientists, as organizations hire scientists or collaborate with them to conduct biomonitoring studies.[29] Advocacy biomonitoring is part of a larger trend of what sociologist Sara Shostak calls "moving environmental regulation inside the human body," which is when the biomedical gaze moves from outside the human body, where collective risks can be considered, to inside the human body, where personal exposure is studied.[30]

One of the most comprehensive and highly publicized advocacy biomonitoring efforts was produced by the EWG. Headquartered in Washington,

DC, the EWG was founded in 1992 by Ken Cook, who is president of the organization. The EWG operates several environmental advocacy programs, but it is best known for its work on toxics and environmental health. In 2003, the EWG released the report *BodyBurden: The Pollution in People*.[31] This eighty-three-page document, available on the organization's website, revealed the biomonitoring results of nine volunteers. It described ubiquitous chemical exposure from the most familiar and mundane commodities and environments: "There are hundreds of chemicals in drinking water, household air, dust, treated tap water and food. They come from household products like detergent, insulation, fabric treatments, cosmetics, paints, upholstery, computers and TVs, and they accumulate in fat, blood and organs, or are passed through the body in breast milk, urine, feces, sweat, semen, hair and nails."[32] The study recorded exposures to 167 synthetic chemicals, including pesticides, PCBs, dioxins, and phthalates. This number was far greater than the 27 compounds measured in the CDC's first national biomonitoring study of 2001 and the 116 measured in the CDC's 2003 analysis.[33] The timing of the *BodyBurden* study coincided with the CDC's 2003 report and showed that the agency's biomonitoring program was missing important exposures in what was supposed to be a nationally representative snapshot of the American body burden.

The day the *BodyBurden* study was released, the EWG ran a full-page advertisement in the *New York Times* featuring a photo of volunteer and Breast Cancer Fund founder Andrea Martin with a caption reading, "Warning—Andrea Martin's blood contains 59 cancer causing industrial chemicals."[34] Journalist Bill Moyers had his blood and urine tested for chemicals by the group, revealing that his blood contained dioxins, PCBs, pesticides, and other compounds. Moyers reported on the EWG study and his biomonitoring results in his PBS program *Trade Secrets*.

The EWG is not the only environmental health group to use advocacy biomonitoring. Organizations such as Commonweal, the Washington Toxics Coalition (now Toxic Free Future), and the Oregon Environmental Council have also used this technology.[35] In table 1, I list twenty-seven advocacy biomonitoring reports produced by seventeen organizations (some as coauthors) between 2003 and 2015.[36] As the table shows, the EWG has produced the most studies. Some of these measured PBDEs in breast milk, chemicals in the umbilical cord blood of newborns, PBDEs in mothers and toddlers, and endocrine-disrupting chemicals in adolescent girls. The EWG even published a report measuring the body burdens of pets.[37]

TABLE 1 U.S. Advocacy Biomonitoring Reports, 2003–2015

Organization	Year	Title
Environmental Working Group	2003	*BodyBurden: Pollution in People*
Environmental Working Group	2003	*Mother's Milk*
Silent Spring Institute	2003	*Household Exposure Study**
Northwest Environment Watch	2004	*Flame Retardants in the Bodies of Pacific Northwest Residents*
Commonweal Biomonitoring Resources Center	2005	*Taking It All In: Documenting Chemical Pollution in Californians through Biomonitoring*
Environmental Working Group	2005	*BodyBurden: The Pollution in Newborns*
Northwest Environment Watch	2005	*PBDEs Greater Than PCBs in 30% of Breast Milk Samples from the Pacific Northwest*
Environmental Working Group	2006	*Across Generations: Mothers and Daughters*
Environmental Working Group	2006	*The Human Toxome Project*
Pesticide Action Network	2006	*Airborne Poisons: Pesticides in Our Air and in Our Bodies*
Silent Spring Institute	2006	*Findings of the Cape Cod Breast Cancer and Environment Study*
Washington Toxics Coalition / Toxic Free Legacy	2006	*Pollution in People: A Study of Toxic Chemicals in Washingtonians*
Alliance for a Clean and Healthy Maine	2007	*Body of Evidence Report: A Study of Pollution in Maine People*
Mossville Environmental Action Now	2007	*Industrial Sources of Dioxin Poisoning in Mossville, Louisiana: A Report Based on the Government's Own Data*
Oregon Environmental Council	2007	*Pollution in People: A Study of Toxic Chemicals in Oregonians*
Commonweal Biomonitoring Resources Center and the Body Burden Work Group (with Alaska Community Action on Toxics)	2007	*Is It in Us? Toxic Trespass, Regulatory Failure, and Opportunities for Action*
Environmental Working Group	2008	*Fire Retardants in Toddlers and Their Mothers: Kids and Contaminants*
Environmental Working Group	2008	*Polluted Pets: High Levels of Toxic Industrial Chemicals Contaminate Cats and Dogs*
Environmental Working Group	2008	*Teen Girls' Body Burden of Hormone-Altering Cosmetics Chemicals: Teens are Vulnerable*
Alliance for a Clean and Healthy Vermont	2009	*Toxic Exposures in the Green Mountain State*
Environmental Working Group	2009	*The Pollution in Minority Newborns*
Environmental Working Group	2009	*Pollution in 5 Extraordinary Women: The Chemical Body Burden of Environmental Justice Leaders*

(continued)

TABLE 1 *(continued)*

Organization	Year	Title
Physicians for Social Responsibility, in collaboration with American Nurses Association and Health Care without Harm	2009	*Hazardous Chemicals in Health Care: A Snapshot of Chemicals in Doctors and Nurses*
Washington Toxics Coalition	2009	*Earliest Exposures*
Learning and Developmental Disabilities Initiative	2010	*Mind, Disrupted: How Toxic Chemicals May Change How We Think and Who We Are*
Environmental Working Group	2014	*No Escape: Tests Find Toxic Fire Retardants in Mothers—and Even More in Toddlers*
Moms across America	2014	*Glyphosate Testing Report: Findings in American Mothers' Breast Milk, Urine and Water*

NOTE: Search criteria included 2015, but no biomonitoring reports were located for this year.

*The Household Exposure Study results were published as scientific papers in academic journals. See, e.g., R. Rudel et al. 2003.

The first of these reports was published in 2003, a time of vast improvement in biomonitoring technology, which allowed for better, more sensitive detection of compounds whose concentrations were too low to be detected by previous technologies.[38] Even though organizations like the EWG have wholeheartedly embraced advocacy biomonitoring, regulators and industry routinely reject studies using the technology, claiming a lack of evidence that exposure leads to disease or health disorders.[39] However, regulators and industry do accept the CDC national biomonitoring reports, which are technical and less personal, as data are aggregated to provide a nationally representative sample. Most importantly, the CDC does not make any statements about the public health impacts of exposure—that is, the agency does not take a position on the potential harm of chemical exposures.

Similar to the CDC's methods, advocacy biomonitoring takes samples of human tissues and measures the presence of multiple compounds, including BPA, phthalates, heavy metals (e.g., lead or cadmium), persistent organic pollutants (e.g., dioxins, PCBs, and DDT), PBDEs, organophosphates (fungicides and pesticides), and volatile organic compounds (e.g., tetrachloroethylene, toluene, xylene, and 1,3-butadiene).[40] Unlike CDC reports, however, advocacy biomonitoring reports outline concerns surrounding low-dose exposures to such chemicals, even when their tests detect levels in human tissues that are too low to be considered acutely toxic by standard EPA and industry definitions. As the Alliance for a Clean and Healthy Maine writes in their *Body of Evidence* report,

> We don't understand very well the combined effects of these chemical exposures on human health, especially on fetuses and children who are more sensitive to toxic effects.... Chemicals that interrupt the intricate processes of developing life can, at high levels, wreak havoc in the form of severe birth defects, or at lower levels cause subtle but important changes in development that surface later in childhood as learning or behavioral problems, or in adulthood in the form of certain cancers or deteriorating brain function.[41]

Here, the focus is not only on low-dose exposures but also on *multiple* chemicals circulating within the body—framing the human body as a chemical "cocktail," to use the words of Steve Lopez, a journalist and volunteer for Commonweal's *Taking It All In* study. Referring to his personal biomonitoring report, Lopez writes, "It turns out I'm a walking cocktail of toxic chemicals. None of this came as a surprise. We've all ingested and inhaled chemicals in our lifetimes, and some of them linger in the body for decades. What's different in my case is that I've got the evidence right here in front of me."[42]

Unlike CDC reports, which feature anonymous data, advocacy biomonitoring reports often list the names of volunteers, provide photos of them, display their personal chemical profiles, and give statements summarizing their reactions to their personal biomonitoring results. The Commonweal and Body Burden Work Group report from 2007, for example, includes a table documenting the number of compounds detected in each participant. Participants who underwent all of the tests had fifteen to seventeen compounds, but specific exposure profiles differed in small ways. Mattie Hunter, for instance, a fifty-three-year-old woman living in Illinois, had "the project's highest levels of diethyl phthalate, above the CDC's 75th percentile," while father and son Bryan and Terry Brown were the only two participants whose bodies showed traces of contained brominated diphenyl ethers 85 and 138. The report speculates that they were exposed to the compounds through accidental poisoning of feed grain in Michigan in the 1970s.[43] By reporting the small differences in the chemical burdens of each volunteer, reports reinforce that body burdens are distinctive—no one person's chemical profile is identical to another's. As sociologist Rebecca Altman observes, "Many of these studies are powerful because they prompt readers to wonder, 'Could this be in me?'"[44] By providing photos, biographies of volunteers, and tables that list each volunteer's results, these studies *personalize* body burdens.[45] Personalization helps make body burdens a relatable phenomenon to *individual* people, but it also drives home the message that chemical pollution is a *shared* experience—it is in all of our bodies. Environmental health movement groups acknowledge that advocacy biomonitoring has successfully raised public awareness of the poor regulation of endocrine disruptors and the ubiquity of environmental chemicals more generally.[46] But advocacy biomonitoring does not draw attention to all bodies in the same way.

THE TOXIC MATERNAL BODY

More than just personalizing chemical body burdens, advocacy biomonitoring genders the problem of chemical body burdens by presenting women's preconception and their pregnant and breastfeeding bodies as vectors of chemical risk. Men carry chemical body burdens, but women's burdens receive far more attention from environmental health movement organizations owing to the fact that women gestate and birth babies and lactate.[47] The environmental health movement's relative focus on the contamination of women's bodies is related to campaigns about threats to children's health. During pregnancy and breastfeeding, women's bodies mobilize fat stores and minerals in bones to support fetal and infant growth. This process makes needed energy and minerals—along with any chemicals that are stored in fat and bones, such as lead and PCBs—available to the fetus or infant. Biomonitoring of umbilical cord blood reveals that chemicals in the mother's blood stream cross the placental wall and enter the fetus.[48] Environmental groups like the EWG, the Natural Resources Defense Fund, and the Pesticide Action Network tell the public and policymakers that babies are born prepolluted. The first tests of umbilical cord blood were conducted in the EWG's *BodyBurden: The Pollution in Newborns* study. The report placed the burden of responsibility for this pollution on society: "As a society we have a responsibility to ensure that babies do not enter this world pre-polluted, with 200 industrial chemicals in their blood."[49] In subsequent reports, however, the EWG emphasized the problem of infant body burdens as a problem related to *maternal* bodies.[50] This zooming in on mothers' bodies and actions mirrors the dominant medical and public health perspective, which downplays structural factors that lead to poor health, such as poverty and stress, and instead prioritizes patient lifestyles.[51]

In the EWG's *Across Generations* study, for example, the authors wrote, "Studies show that a mother confers a portion of her chemical body burden to a child in the womb, and continues to pass down pollution after birth through her breast milk."[52] The document shows a photo of a mother gazing down at her infant, with a timeline below the image showing "daughter's age when she has excreted 99% of her mother's pollution" (1 year for methylmercury and 166 years for lead).[53] This powerful image presents the maternal body as a pathway that transmits environmental chemicals to the next generation. A child is polluted via its mother. The mother's body, not the polluted environment, becomes the focus of the campaign.

Reports publishing the reactions of volunteers to their personal biomonitoring results reinforce this message of maternal responsibility for infant body burdens. In the Washington Toxics Coalition's *Earliest Exposures* study, for example, researchers took blood and urine samples from nine pregnant women.[54] When the organization released the study on its website, it also published video interviews with three of its participants. In one video, volunteer Molly Gray says this about getting her results:

> I did a lot throughout my pregnancy to do my best to avoid toxic chemicals. At least the ones that I know of. I started before pregnancy, I started to clean up my yard, my house, my work, my car—all the environments I was going to be, basically. I took huge caution in what was going to be in the inside of my body. . . . I felt disappointed when I got my results, I was disappointed in the fact that I felt that I had done so much both before pregnancy and during pregnancy so that I wouldn't have those results.[55]

In this excerpt, Gray expresses frustration that her actions were not effective, showing how she internalized the responsibility for her infant's body burden. Yet her response also highlights the limits of consumption—a theme I address later in this chapter.

The reproductive equation, where men's responsibility for fetal health ostensibly ends at conception, is powerful in the environmental health movement literature on body burdens.[56] Men's bodies are rarely discussed; when they are, the reference is usually to occupational exposures or cancer and infertility. When reports mention biological fathers' role in transmitting chemicals, they focus on *occupational* hazards, with some mention of everyday exposures from consumer products or items in the domestic environment. In the Pesticide Action Network's 2004 report on chemical trespass, for example, the authors note that when a child's father works in agriculture, the child is at greater risk of genital birth defects, cleft lip or palate, and other birth defects.[57] If reports mentioned domestic exposures, the concern was about men's infertility rather than about the health of the future child. In the few other instances where male bodies are mentioned in advocacy group reports, they are cast as *receiving* threats from chemicals rather than *transferring* them to future children. This framing of male bodies stands in contrast to what political scientist Cynthia Daniels identified as "reproductive masculinity," a set of beliefs and assumptions that men's bodies are invulnerable to environmental harm and that men bear little responsibility for transferring chemical harm to future generations.[58] EWG references the extreme vulnerability of the male reproductive system and the risk to male bodies from endocrine disruptors. One of its fact sheets published in 2014 entitled "Men's Health: Six Surprising Things That Can Affect Male Fertility" indicated that men's domestic chemical exposures are linked to declines in fertility. This sheet stressed the importance of "avoiding risks that can impair proper development of a man's hormone and reproductive systems" and references research finding that "several types of toxic chemicals that everyone encounters in daily life can alter sperm and semen in ways that may impair fertility."[59] A Healthy Child, Healthy World (HCHW) blog post acknowledges men's virtual absence in environmental health discourse, stating, "It's well known that what a woman eats, drinks, breathes and puts on her body while she's pregnant or nursing can all affect her reproductive system and the health of her baby. But new research reveals that a *man*'s exposure to chemicals play an important role, too."[60] The post details the results of a study showing that men's exposure to toxics may impact the length of time to conception and then offers "easy tips for potential moms *and* dads to avoid the common chemicals identified in the study."[61] Groups advance a notion of reproductive masculinity that *emphasizes,* rather than downplays, the vulnerability of the male reproductive system.[62] Notably, the emphasis remains on male fertility, not on men's role in transferring health risks to their children.[63] Significantly, in contrast to how women's bodies are discussed, men's bodies are not implicated in the future health of children, even though health research now suggests that men's preconception exposure to chemicals, like women's, likely does affect the future health of their children.[64]

Men's exposure to environmental chemicals is significant not only because it can cause threats to fertility but also because health conditions such as schizophrenia and autism may be linked to genetic mutations in sperm.[65] While several of the reports I analyzed shared the shock and disappointment mothers experienced when learning that their bodies contain environmental chemicals that can be passed on to the fetus or breastfeeding infant, only one biomonitoring report mentioned the reactions fathers had to the knowledge that their bodies also transmit chemical risk. This was the Learning and Developmental Disabilities Initiative's *Mind, Disrupted,* which provided the paternal perspective on responsibility for children's body burdens. "As a father of four boys," says Stephen Boese, one of the organization's leaders in New York State, "one of whom lived a short life of overwhelming disability, I am keenly aware that prevention of learning and developmental disabilities is both an individual and a community responsibility."[66] Several pages later, a second father reflected on how his exposures to endocrine disruptors might be responsible for his sons' autism: "As a parent of two boys with autism it's very frustrating because I can't help but wonder, stepping back from my own personal history, about what I've been exposed to. It's amazing to me how much body burden I have and what that means for my children."[67] This reflection of a father on his preconception lifestyle was a rare exception in environmental health movement publications, which focus overwhelmingly on women's reproductive bodies.

The disproportionate attention to women's bodies is explained in part by the movement's incorporation of the developmental origins of health and disease (DOHaD) model to explain future disease states and disorders.[68] According to this model of disease causation, fetal exposure to maternal stress, toxics, and malnutrition, among other stressors, can cause subtle changes in fetal development that result in behavioral disorders or disease that will surface later in the child's life and may even be passed on to future generations.[69] The timing of exposure matters during what is termed "critical windows of vulnerability." Exposure to a compound during a critical window of fetal brain development or reproductive system development can result in changes to cell differentiation, leading to diseases or disorders that may not appear for months or even years after birth.[70] These mutations and alterations can also have transgenerational effects, meaning that a parent's exposure to a toxic substance will effect development of future generations, even when those generations were not directly exposed. In one animal study, for instance, researchers administered small doses of a mixture of plastics made up of BPA, DEHP, and dibutyl phthalate (DBP) to pregnant females (called the F_0 generation) and found an increased incidence of reproductive disorders and obesity in both the children (the F_1 generation) and the great grandchildren (the F_3 generation) of the treated animals (the F_2 generation was not studied in this case).[71] So, even though the grandchildren were never directly exposed to the plastics treatment, the development of their reproductive and endocrine systems was affected by their grandmothers' exposure. DOHaD studies typically examine *maternal* exposure to environmental contaminants. Certainly, fetal development occurs within female bodies, and, in humans as well as in other mammals, eggs (or oocytes) are formed in utero. So if a mother is exposed to an endocrine disruptor during weeks eleven to twenty of her pregnancy and is carrying a female fetus, the fetus's eggs could be impacted by exposure, thereby setting the stage for the intergenerational transfer of disorder or disease.[72] Environmental harm can also be passed down transgenerationally through sperm, but male bodies are comparatively absent in DOHaD studies.[73] The prioritization of mothers' bodies in this model overlaps with social and cultural attention to maternal accountability for children's health that excludes serious consideration of how males are part of the reproductive equation.[74]

Environmental health movement organizations draw on the DOHaD model to place enormous emphasis on how women's lifestyle choices can be at odds with what is best for the fetus—what scholars refer to as the maternal-fetal conflict.[75] The maternal-fetal conflict is especially visible in materials from the HCHW. In its e-book *Easy Steps for a Safer Pregnancy,* the authors tell pregnant women:

> Your baby's first home isn't her nursery or even your house. It's your body. And you're not just your baby's first environment, you're also the source of everything she needs to grow and develop. If you think about it this way, taking care of yourself when you're pregnant is your first official job as a parent. Scary, sure. But it can also be empowering. . . . Avoiding environmental toxins is possible; it's just about getting the right advice.[76]

An accompanying infographic with the caption "When Looking Good Is Bad for Baby: How to Avoid Toxic Personal Care Products in Pregnancy" shows an illustration of a pregnant woman applying bright red lipstick. She is seated at a vanity laden with beauty products, and inside her pregnant belly is the shadow of a fetus.[77] While the intent is to alert women to the danger of unregulated beauty products and the impacts of cosmetic ingredients on fetal health, the overarching message of the infographic equates beauty work with maternal selfishness and lack of concern for fetal health.[78]

The Breast Cancer Fund's study *Disrupted Development: The Dangers of BPA* references the DOHaD model and advises women to change their shopping habits to prevent their future daughters from developing breast cancer. The report mentions that "prenatal BPA exposure can affect the development of mammary glands, the brain and other organ systems, increasing risk for later-life disease."[79] Breast Cancer Fund demands regulatory reform, but adds, "Until we see decisive governmental action to protect women from BPA exposure, reproductive health practitioners should integrate information about the risks and how to avoid the chemical (as well as other toxic exposures that may be harmful to reproduction and fetal development) into their routine patient education and interaction."[80] The report ends by advising mothers to "change your shopping list," putting the responsibility on women's shoulders to make up for the lack of regulatory restrictions on BPA.

Groups like the HCHW and Breast Cancer Fund (renamed Breast Cancer Prevention Partners in 2017) extend the idea of maternal selfishness by casting everyday choices of what to eat and apply to the body as potential threats to fetal health. The movement deploys not only a message of pollution as personal but also a message of pollution as gendered. This framing establishes new, and I would argue unfair, measures for evaluating women's lifestyles. If a pregnant or breastfeeding woman knows that conventional strawberries contain pesticides, is she then selfish to eat them? What if she wants to apply a perfume that the EWG's Skin Deep Cosmetic Database identifies as having phthalates? By providing ample advice for how to minimize exposure to environmental chemicals, environmental health groups have heightened the message of women's personal responsibility for controlling chemical exposures.

"TEN THINGS YOU CAN DO!" MANAGING THE
TOXIC BODY AND THE POLLUTED HOME

In addition to adopting advocacy biomonitoring that directs attention to the maternal body, environmental health groups have turned their attention to dangers of the home. That is to say, the outdoor environment is no longer the sole concern of these organizations. Today's movement points to the contamination of indoor air, which can be many times more polluted than outdoor air. Organizations such as the Silent Spring Institute have tested indoor air and dust and found chemical byproducts from furniture, carpeting, detergents, and adhesives—compounds that also show up in human biomonitoring studies.[81] As the movement became aware of the toxicity of indoor environments and endocrine disrupting compounds in everyday objects used at home, many organizations began to offer precautionary consumption advice by developing safe shopping guides and consumer product databases that allow individuals to find less toxic commodities. Later in the chapter, I theorize why the movement turned its attention to safer shopping, but before exploring that question it is important to first understand the vastness and complexity of precautionary actions recommended by organizations within the movement.

In table 2, I list the range of precautionary actions recommended by twenty-seven environmental health movement organizations that are actively working on body burden issues. These include the Breast Cancer Fund, the EWG, the Silent Spring Institute, and the Campaign for Safe Cosmetics, among others. Much of the advice overlapped across the guides, and most organizations provided five to ten tips per guide. Taken together, environmental health groups recommend nearly sixty precautionary actions. The most common advice is to avoid plastic water bottles and containers, avoid products with synthetic fragrances, buy organic fruits and vegetables, find furnishings that do not contain PBDEs, choose cookware that does not have Teflon-based coatings, and make homemade cleaning products in lieu of buying conventional products. Notably, when groups recommend *avoiding* a product or food, they typically recommend *finding* an eco-friendly alternative. Many organizations produced multiple guides that addressed different aspects of daily life—for example, one for selecting produce, another for choosing safer plastics, another for selecting safer foods, and yet another dedicated to cosmetics. Consequently, an individual searching for information about safe shopping will find that the list of recommended precautionary actions is long.

The EWG is the most prolific producer of precautionary advice, having released over seventy consumer guides (not including biomonitoring studies and other reports on environmental health topics) since 1995. Every year, it publishes the *Dirty Dozen Guide* and the *Clean Fifteen* (which rank fruits and vegetables according to the pesticide residues they retain after washing or peeling). It also produces the highly popular Skin Deep Cosmetic Database, which, as of May 2017, has analyses of approximately sixty-six thousand products, including cosmetics, shampoos, lotions, and baby personal care products, and flags ingredients that are carcinogens, suspected carcinogens, reproductive toxins, and endocrine disruptors.[82] In 2014, the organization released another safe shopping database, this one dedicated to food. Called Food

TABLE 2 Precautionary Consumer Actions Recommended by Environmental Health Advocacy Organizations

Action	Concern
In the Home	
Find a chemical-free carpet	VOCs (volatile organic compounds), perfluorinated compounds
Find a chemical-free crib mattress	Flame retardants
Find a couch without brominated flame retardants	Flame retardants
Use plants to filter air	Off-gassing of furniture
Use eco-friendly cleaning products or make your own	EDCs (endocrine disrupting compounds)
Do not use air fresheners	EDCs
Use low-VOC paint	VOCs in indoor air
Use an air filter	Fine particles in air
Take your shoes off at the front door	Heavy metals from soil
Do not use furniture made of composite or particle board	VOCs
Damp mop regularly to remove flame retardant laden dust	Flame retardants
Avoid commercial dry cleaners	VOCs
Avoid conventional pesticides in home and yard; use natural or homemade pesticides	Pesticides
Avoid chemical fertilizers in yard and garden; use eco-friendly alternatives	Fertilizers
Avoid vinyl in flooring, blinds, and mattress covers; use eco-friendly alternatives	EDCs
Avoid phthalates in children's toys; use eco-friendly alternatives	EDCs
Buy eco-friendly children's jewelry and painted toys	Heavy metals
Test home for radon	Radon
Turn on a fan in kitchen to air out harmful particulates from cooking	Fine particles in air
Open windows to bring in outside air	VOCs in indoor air
Avoid nonstick cookware; use eco-friendly alternatives	Perfluorinated chemicals

(continued)

TABLE 2 *(continued)*

Action	Concern
In the Home	
Use an eco-friendly detergent or make own detergent for dishes and laundry	EDCs
Use lead-free ceramics	Heavy metals
Find flame-retardant-free children's sleepwear	Flame retardants
Allow new furniture to off-gas before bringing it into the home	VOCs
Buy clothes made from natural fibers that have not undergone chemical treatments (e.g., stain proofing, wrinkle proofing)	Perfluorinated chemicals
Find less toxic electronic devices	Heavy metals, EDCs
Find eco-friendly art supplies	Heavy metals, VOCs, PVC (polyvinyl chloride)
Food	
Buy certified-organic foods	Pesticides
If buying conventional, avoid the Dirty Dozen	Pesticides
Avoid synthetic additives (e.g., artificial thickeners, colorings, sweeteners)	Chemical additives
Avoid canned food; eat fresh or frozen food	BPA
Avoid rice grown in areas known to have high levels of arsenic in soil	Arsenic
Do not microwave food in plastic containers	EDCs
Cook from scratch to avoid processed foods	Chemical additives
Look at country of origin labels to avoid foods grown in countries with poor chemical regulations	Pesticides
Filter water with a good quality carbon filter	Heavy metals, pesticides, byproducts of chlorination, other compounds
Eat a diet low in animal fats or trim fat from meats	Pesticides, EDCs

Avoid food packaging with plastic or nonstick compounds	EDCs
Avoid farmed fish; buy wild-caught, low-mercury fish whenever possible	Heavy metals
Avoid polystyrene food containers (#6 plastic)	EDCs
Avoid PVC in food packaging or water bottles (#3 plastic)	EDCs
Avoid BPA in food and water storage containers (#7 plastic)	EDCs
Choose powdered baby formula over liquid formula	BPA
Avoid meats with antibiotics or dairy with rBGH; buy meats from producers that do not use these additives or select certified-organic meats	EDCs, antibiotics

Cosmetics and Personal Care

Make your own cosmetics using natural ingredients	EDCs, carcinogens
Avoid antibacterial soaps; use eco-friendly alternatives	Triclosan
Avoid lipsticks containing heavy metals; use eco-friendly alternatives	Heavy metals
Avoid conventional lice shampoos; use eco-friendly alternatives	Pesticides
Avoid DEET-based insect repellents; use eco-friendly alternatives	Carcinogens, EDCs
Avoid conventional hair dyes; use eco-friendly alternatives	Carcinogens, EDCs
Avoid synthetic fragrances; use eco-friendly alternatives	EDCs
Avoid hair relaxers; opt for natural hairstyles, wigs, or weaves	EDCs
Avoid chemical hair detanglers; use eco-friendly alternatives	EDCs
Avoid nail polish and nail polish removers	EDCs, VOCs
Avoid conventional sunscreen; use eco-friendly alternatives	Carcinogens, nanoparticles, EDCs
Avoid products containing cocamide DEA, sodium lauryl sulfate, phthalates, quaternium-15, formaldehyde, and 1,4-dioxane; find eco-friendly alternatives that do not contain these compounds	Carcinogens, EDCs
Avoid conventional face paints	Heavy metals, EDCs

Scores, it identifies potentially harmful chemicals in over eighty thousand food products. The EWG also produces a database for safe sunscreens. Several women I interviewed for this book were aware of these databases and had used them, and nearly all of them had heard of the EWG's *Dirty Dozen* list. Some had looked up this list on their own, but most had heard about it through other organizations or from blogs, Facebook posts, or friends.

Simple Steps?

The range of actions listed in table 2 brings to mind Andrew Szasz's concept of the inverted quarantine—the idea that individuals can create their own private commodity bubble to quarantine themselves from the polluted external environment.[83] These actions are presented by movement organizations using a cultural script of "things you can do" that reminds individuals of their personal responsibility to tackle collective problems, while also providing reassurance that there are tangible solutions to the problem of widespread toxic pollution.[84] These reports, guides, and websites all reinforce the message that safe consumption can be both *simple* and *effective*. In their brochure on finding safe food for Thanksgiving, the Breast Cancer Fund speaks of "simple and inexpensive replacements" to canned foods that have BPA linings.[85] This advice presumes that the reader has the time and the means to cook from scratch or find preserved vegetables that come in glass jars or tetra-pak cartons instead of in cans. The guide advises readers to avoid canned pumpkin purée, among other canned foods, reassuring them that making pie from scratch is rewarding work: "Sugar pie pumpkins are readily available at many grocery stores. Making a pie from scratch takes a little more work, but is worth the effort. And nothing beats the smell of roasting pumpkin in the oven."[86] In the Coalition for a Safe and Healthy Connecticut's brochure, *Top Ten Tips to Reduce Toxins in Your Home,* the authors describe making home-made cleaning products as an "easy and inexpensive" alternative to buying conventional products.[87] In *Out of Harm's Way,* by the Greater Boston Chapter of Physicians for Social Responsibility, the organization writes about "simple steps" that can be taken, such as avoiding pesticides in food, lead in paint, and mercury in fish.[88] Organizations emphasize the proper timing of these actions. They must be enacted before pregnancy, if possible, and most definitely during pregnancy and breastfeeding.

This language of simplicity and ease belies the complexity of precautionary consumption and the uncertainty that individuals feel when they adopt these actions for the first time. In one report, the EWG writes, "When possible, it is best to avoid #7 plastics, especially for children's food. Plastics with the recycling labels #1, #2 and #4 on the bottom are safer choices and do not contain BPA. Find baby bottles in glass versions, or those made from the safer plastics including polyamine, polypropylene and polyethylene."[89] According to this excerpt, findings safer plastics is straightforward (just look on the bottom of a bottle for the triangular symbol with a number next to it). In practice, say, while shopping at the grocery store, one must first remember to look at the number on the bottom of a plastic bottle and then try to recall if that number indicates a "good" plastic or a "bad" plastic. To provide any kind of reliable protection from exposure, these steps must presumably be implemented *all the time*. If a shopper forgets, or is too busy or tired, they inevitably come into contact with the dangerous conventional item they were warned to avoid.

While each step might seem simple on the surface, the time required to carry out these actions is significant, particularly if individuals choose to implement more than one tip or piece of advice. I explore this issue in greater depth in chapters 5 and 6. Scanning an ingredient list for hidden nanoparticles, synthetic additives, or a chicken's antibiotic-free status involves extra labor when shopping. Because there are dozens of environmental chemicals that organizations warn against, shoppers must somehow remember all of them. Organizations try to make this easier for consumers by offering smartphone apps that allow shoppers to scan a product barcode to identify harmful additives or by providing online pocket guides that list chemicals to avoid.

A Job for Women

Due to the kind of labor these recommendations require and where that labor takes place, in addition to the gendered language and images used in these documents, this advice is directed at women. The idea that safe shopping is a woman's responsibility is reinforced across many of the materials I examined. Consumer guides frequently use photos and illustrations of women, often pregnant or holding babies or children. These women are typically shown in domestic settings or with children, and in many of the photos, the subjects are light-skinned or white. Photos of men are rare, and when they do appear, they are shown with women or in occupational settings (such as hospitals or construction sites). These photos belie the gender-neutral language used in these materials, which refers to the adults in a child's life as "parents" or "caregivers" and uses the plural pronoun "we." Moreover, by showing primarily white subjects, these materials reinforce a racialized depiction of precautionary consumption, casting it as a white practice and minimizing how chemical risks and associated protective actions are equally relevant to black and brown bodies.

Such attention to the domestic environment is reminiscent of the urban environmental movement of the late nineteenth and early twentieth centuries.[90] Part of the progressive movement and led by white, upper-middle-class, educated women such as Ellen Swallow Richards (the first woman to graduate from MIT), the urban environmental movement fought to improve sanitation and domestic life by educating low-income, immigrant, and middle-class women on the science of the "right living conditions."[91] Educating these women was considered crucial for protecting families at a time when there was little to no regulation of food (indeed, it might be tainted with arsenic or lead) and there was minimal public infrastructure to ensure clean water and prevent the spread of communicable disease.[92] As I discussed in chapter 2, this domestic activism was integral to pressuring government to pass the Pure Food and Drug Act of 1906, the first time a logic resembling the precautionary principle was used to regulate the food system. There are many parallels between the early urban environmental movement and today's environmental health movement. Both demand that women educate themselves to compensate for a lack of structural environmental health protections. Both invoke white subjects as the target audience and presume an audience of middle-class individuals who have the means to improve their living conditions by making their homes and food safer. Both also emphasize consumer citizenship, particularly when women use their power as consumers to push for structural change.[93]

PRECAUTIONARY CONSUMPTION
AS CONSUMER CITIZENSHIP

By promoting precautionary consumption, environmental health movement groups may be engaging in a larger project of effecting change through the market. Corporations, as I showed in chapter 2, have a great deal of power in a regulatory system built on the proof-of-harm model. Thus, by bringing corporations on board to lead with "greener" practices—promising a loyal consumer following—groups may have some hope of addressing the ubiquity of toxic substances in the consumer landscape. Indeed, as social scientists Bhavna Shamasunder and Rachel Morello-Frosch discovered in their interviews with environmental health movement representatives, some groups see consumer pressure as the most productive avenue for change—albeit change that happens company by company. In the words of one environmental health movement scientist they interviewed, "I think that there's certainly been an indirect ripple effect as chemicals like bisphenol A and perchlorate pop up in almost everybody in the whole population, and then NGOs [nongovernmental organizations] start freaking out about the high prevalence in everybody's bodies, and then the public pressure ultimately on industry makes them rethink their product composition."[94]

Groups use a language of consumer empowerment in their materials on safer shopping to frame individual acts of consumption as part of *collective* social action. Consumers, this language suggests, are empowered by safe shopping guides; they can easily protect themselves—and their families—from chemicals while *also* changing the world. As I show in chapters 5 and 6, because of how labor is divided within households, the responsibility to act as an empowered consumer falls to mothers.

This is a message of consumer citizenship, a form of political action that occurs through shopping and boycotts.[95] Consumer citizenship represents a kind of "individualized collective action" where individual consumption choices aggregate and scale up to send signals to the market that then motivate further investment in sustainable and more socially just production.[96] There is a win-win logic at the heart of consumer citizenship, as changes to lifestyle and shopping benefit the planet as well as the individual shopper or eater.[97] Beginning in the 1980s, eco, or "green," shopping became trendy, and environmental advocacy groups supported calls for greener consumption.[98] The first mass-market green shopping guide was *The Green Consumer Guide: From Shampoo to Champagne; High Street Shopping for a Better Environment,* published in Britain in the late 1980s.[99] It quickly became a bestseller. The authors consulted with environmental groups before writing the book and were surprised to discover that nearly 90 percent of the organizations they contacted believed that consumer action could lead to environmental improvement. They tell readers, "The real message of the guide is that the Green Consumer is here and is already having a tremendous impact. . . . So don't worry that your decision to buy or not to buy scarcely registers on the scale. Market researchers, and the companies they serve, sit up and take notice when thousands of people begin to behave in the same way."[100]

This appeal to individual consumers can be found in some of the staunchest critiques of industrial pollution. *Our Stolen Future* urges readers to use precautionary consumption. In the chapter "Defending Ourselves," Theo Colborn and her coauthors entreat readers not to feel overwhelmed by the dangers of endocrine disruptors and slip into a state of denial or hopelessness about the problem.[101] They advise taking action immediately by, for example, avoiding animal fats, choosing certified-organic foods, and never microwaving food in plastic. The authors do, nevertheless, remind readers that these individual actions are merely stopgaps: "While individuals can do a great deal to protect themselves, these efforts must be matched by broad government action to eliminate synthetic substances that disrupt hormones."[102]

This pairing of individual self-protection with appeals for regulatory change is at the heart of the environmental health movement's support for precautionary consumption. Most of the organizations addressed in this chapter combine these two messages in their advocacy campaigns. In a recent video celebrating the twentieth anniversary of the EWG, the organization's president, Ken Cook, explains why the organization has invested so much in producing safe shopping guides:

> A lot of people have realized, watching what happens particularly in Washington [DC], that it's very difficult to get things done. And parents would ask, "Well, that's all well and good to try and reform the toxic chemical laws, but what am I supposed to do, wait five or ten or fifteen years? I've got an infant. You mean to tell me that when he's fifteen, the chemicals that are in him now will be tested for safety by the government? I don't want to wait. How do I avoid those?"
>
> So with all that tremendous need out there we have to do two things. One, we have to keep the pressure on Congress and keep the pressure on the administration to fix our broken legal system to have strong regulations that protect public health. In the meantime, we have to tell consumers, "While the government is taking its good time to act, we're going to be here to give you the best advice we can so you can protect your family and your health."[103]

In this video, Cook suggests that the public wants immediate solutions to the problem of environmental chemicals in food and everyday products. As he mentions, changing government regulation is a slow, arduous process, whereas consumer responses can happen almost immediately. This is the appeal of precautionary consumption: it can be implemented quickly, as long as individuals know what to do, can afford to do it, and have the time to implement all of the steps.

Cook's comments also reveal how groups continue to lobby for better environmental and chemical laws. Although their websites are packed with precautionary consumption advice, these organizations also make it easy for visitors to write to members of Congress and demand better chemical safety laws. Groups like Safer Chemicals, Healthy Families inform website visitors that safer shopping is merely one step in the process of making the world safer for children. Visitors are encouraged to write to Congress to demand better chemical regulation. The Natural Resources Defense Fund provides this caveat to its advice on preparing the body for breastfeeding:

> Many of the contaminants in breast milk cannot be removed by short-term lifestyle changes. For example, a short-term switch to a low-fat, organic diet will likely not affect levels of DDT, dioxins and other persistent chemicals in a woman's breast milk. These chemicals must be addressed by stopping pollution at the source. Some of the contaminants, however, can and should be avoided by women—mercury contaminated fish and solvents in household products, for example.[104]

The upside of precautionary consumption is that it gives customers some hope when facing a seemingly intractable problem. The downside is that it represents a product-by-product, chemical-by-chemical, and individual-by-individual approach to a much larger problem. I return to this problem in the last chapter of the book. To be sure, not all organizations emphasize consumer action. Breast Cancer Action, an organization based in San Francisco, is dubious that precautionary consumption provides real protection from breast cancer, stating, "No matter how much organic we eat, how quick we are to rid our kitchens of plastic, how much effort we put into safe cosmetics, we can't just opt out of the toxins that come to us through our daily environment."[105] The organization does not provide safe shopping advice.

CONCLUSION

Spurred on by concern about endocrine disruptors, environmental health movement organizations lobby for structural reform based on the strong precautionary principle. Facing considerable hostility and opposition from industry and government, groups have turned their attention to advocacy biomonitoring and educating the public about the dangers of endocrine disruptors in the home. Groups present chemical body burdens as a threat to maternal bodies by emphasizing the ways in which women's preconception, pregnant, and breastfeeding bodies transmit chemicals to fetuses and infants. When men's bodies are mentioned, it is to warn about threats to male fertility from endocrine disruptors. By producing countless safe shopping guides that implicate women's domestic labor, these groups reinforce an image of precautionary consumption as mother's work while simultaneously marking the authority of mothers as experts on safer shopping. By directing attention to mothers' bodies and domestic labor, groups influence how some mothers shop—especially mothers with access to resources, like time and money, that allow them to modify their lifestyle. Environmental health organizations have successfully pressured manufacturers and retailers to manufacture and carry safer products. While increasing the number of green and nontoxic commodities in the marketplace is a promising strategy, it is not clear that it will benefit everyone equally. Consumers without time to read about precautionary consumption or study product labels at the store, or who lack the money to afford more expensive "green" or organic items will not benefit from a two-tiered retail landscape where green and nontoxic products are sold alongside conventional commodities. The entire retail landscape must reflect the precautionary principle so that safer products are not a *choice* but rather the only option. I return to this point later in the book.

Even though precautionary consumption fits into the model of consumer citizenship, environmental health movement groups recognize the limitations of this strategy, seeing it as a stopgap measure that provides temporary protection while the wheels of regulatory reform slowly turn. Groups continue to push for structural reform that would provide more universal protection from environmental chemicals. It is possible that industry will respond to the pressure from consumers and begin removing all harmful chemicals from production. But consumer citizenship can work only if it leads to large-scale change to the retail landscape and if industry invests in developing replacements for existing chemicals that are truly safer for human health and the environment.

In the next chapter, I investigate how messages of consumer empowerment and safe shopping have spread into the marketplace as part of an expanding retail landscape predicated on customers' distrust of conventional commodities and the imperative of precautionary consumption.

FOUR

———————

Be a Super Shopper!

PRECAUTIONARY CONSUMPTION AT THE GROCERY STORE

The highest standards weren't available, so we created them.

WHOLE FOODS MARKET, *The Whole Deal*

Wouldn't it be more fun to shop for groceries if you didn't have
to worry about what food additives to avoid? Good news, we're
looking out for you.

WHOLE FOODS MARKET, "Quality Standards"

On a cold day in January 2012, I stood in the yogurt aisle of my local supermarket, taking stock of the endless varieties in front of me: Greek, strained
Icelandic, sugar-free, low-fat Oreo flavored, goat's milk, and agave sweetened.
One Stonyfield Organic tub stood out from the others. Its foil lid was deco-
rated with a photo of a white woman dressed in a superhero outfit, one arm
holding a bag of groceries and the other confidently positioned on her hip.
The text box beside her read, "Our superheroes can see right through food
labels. When you know your food, you can protect your family . . . and the
whole planet."[1] This superhero was, presumably, able to swiftly navigate all
the features in this convoluted landscape of potentially dangerous consumer
goods, including the long, multisyllabic ingredient labels found on most tubs
of modern-day yogurt. The superhero who can look *into* food encapsulates
the gendered labor and underlying logic of precautionary consumption. The
shopper—typically a woman—summons her power as an informed consumer to find safe foods for her family. Labels proclaiming "all natural"
ingredient lists and organic certification seals give her the x-ray vision to see
inside the product and confirm that it is indeed safe and up to middle-class
standards of quality. These labels are integral to the shorthand methods (or
heuristics) that shoppers like superhero mom need to navigate the dangerous
consumer landscape and "know" their food.

As the regulatory system fails to protect consumers, the market for green products swells. Certified-organic foods are now widely available in most supermarkets in the country. One report estimates that three out of four grocery stores in America carry certified-organic products.[2] Foods and personal care products are more likely than ever to carry a label declaring they are free of the chemical du jour that has slipped through the wide cracks of the regulatory system.

The supermarket occupies a lowly status in the hierarchy of retail spaces. It is rarely depicted as a glamorous site, and grocery shopping is portrayed as the epitome of the mundane. It is no coincidence that this task is gendered labor. The Private Labels Manufacturing Association reports that although women's labor force participation is increasing and women are doing slightly less cooking and meal preparation, women continue to be the primary household shoppers, whether this involves going to the store, placing an online grocery order, or making the grocery list.[3] The United States Bureau of Labor Statistics reports that married women do more grocery shopping than married men, regardless of employment status.[4] Supermarkets are well aware of this fact and have evolved to both shape and respond to the needs of women shoppers.[5] Over the past decade, grocery stores have responded to anxieties about chemicals in food and consumer products by carrying more organic foods, non-GMO foods, and nontoxic personal care products. Most mainstream supermarkets in the United States, including Walmart, Kroger, Costco, Publix, Wegmans, ShopRite, and Safeway, now carry these items, in addition to "health" foods and eco-friendly commodities. In 2012, Kroger introduced a line of Simple Truth products, touting them as "free from 101 artificial preservatives and ingredients that some customers have said they do not want in their foods."[6] In general, precautionary consumer items mark themselves as a bit more special than the conventional products sitting a few inches away. The availability of these products within major supermarkets attests to the mainstreaming of precautionary consumption.

Nowhere is the rise of precautionary consumption more visible than within the walls of Whole Foods Market stores. Founded in 1980 in Austin, Texas, Whole Foods Market is now the tenth largest supermarket chain in the United States and the largest to specialize in certified-organic foods and so-called health foods.[7] Inside any Whole Foods Market location, there are hundreds of foods, personal care products, and other consumer items that promise to be "better" or "safer" than their conventional counterparts. It is the country's only certified-organic grocer, and it brands itself as "America's healthiest grocery store."[8] In 2016, Whole Foods Market operated 456 stores in the United States, Canada, and Britain and reported $15.7 billion in sales.[9] In the United States, where most of its stores are located, Whole Foods Market operates in forty-two states, including Alabama, California, Florida, Georgia, Wisconsin, and Texas.[10] In 2017, activist investors bought shares in the company and shortly thereafter sold it to Amazon in a deal valued at $13.7 billion.[11] Under Amazon's ownership, Whole Foods Market is predicted to dominate the grocery sector as both an online and a brick-and-mortar retailer.

In the previous chapters, I have shown how regulatory failure in tandem with environmental health movement campaigns have contributed to the rise of precautionary consumption. In this chapter, I draw from my research over a two-year period at nine Whole Foods Market locations in New York City to examine how the company and the hundreds of brands it sells have kicked precautionary consumption into high gear.[12] While Whole Foods Market is certainly not the only market actor encouraging precautionary consumption, the company has been vital in marking the grocery store as a primary site where a new, much more encompassing form of precautionary consumption is possible. More than this, Whole Foods Market has helped to normalize precautionary consumption as a "better and safer" kind of grocery shopping. By creating a major retail space for natural and organic products, it has helped this segment of the food and consumer product market expand.[13]

INSIDE A PRECAUTIONARY CONSUMPTION PARADISE

Whole Foods Market reinforces precautionary consumption as a consumer imperative, and its decor and signage mark other retail spaces as comparatively dangerous. It bans 120 ingredients from its food products and 75 compounds from its personal care products. No other major grocery store, including Trader Joe's, vets their products to this extent. The interiors of Whole Foods Market stores are saturated with the language of precautionary consumption. These messages bombard the shopper before they even walk in the door. In one of my visits to an Upper West Side location of the store in New York City in early 2015, the windows had several colorful banners proclaiming, "0 synthetic nitrates or nitrites allowed," and "400 ingredients not allowed in our Premium Body Care." Walking through the main entrance, I saw a large sign hanging from the ceiling greeting shoppers: "Welcome to America's Healthiest Grocery Store." Turning to descend the escalator to access the main section of the store, I caught sight of another sign boasting, "The table brings us together, our ingredients set us apart." Reaching the produce section, I gazed at the neatly ordered displays of prepared foods and the bins overflowing with both certified-organic and conventional fruits and vegetables. Scattered among these displays were more signs attesting to the company's mission and high standards. One read, "Responsibly Farmed. Our farmed fish and shrimp are third-party verified to ensure that our strict standards are met. Ask your fishmonger about our rating system." Two feet away from this sign hung another, announcing, "Supporting Organic Farmers."

Taken together, these signs tell consumers that they have entered a "safe" place, where food has been verified as healthy and has a low environmental impact. They assure shoppers that they can browse freely and easily without having to read the labels, as the company has already vetted the products for sale. "Trust us to do the research so you can shop with peace of mind," urges one of Whole Foods Market's webpages.[14] Precaution is established here, the store says; one can be safe here, not sorry.

Whole Foods Market's emphasis on health and quality ingredients represents a shift from its earlier marketing efforts, which promoted ethical shopping.[15] The store still advertises its commitment to environmental sustainability and labor justice, but its shelves speak to the company's priority of offering abundant product choices and top-quality items. Shoppers who love Whole Foods Market talk about the aesthetic experience of the store and the offerings of gourmet food; they are less likely to see it as place where they can uphold environmental or ethical principles. Whole Foods Market is, in the view of some, a shopping "destination" and "vacation."[16]

Values Matter

In 2014, the year I started making regular site visits to Whole Foods Market stores in New York City, the company began promoting a flashy advertising campaign called Values Matter, complete with television commercials. In-store advertisements featured glowing, healthy-looking models and inspiring text. One read "Eat like an idealist" and was accompanied by a photograph showing a pregnant woman with a young girl cuddling her belly. Another declaring "Grow up strong and harmless" showed a white, preadolescent girl standing on a rock, arms outstretched to show her strength. At Whole Foods Market, according to an in-store flyer, "values are inseparable from value." In the so-called anthem for the campaign, the company emphasized the role of transparency as part of its brand: "We're hungrier for better than we ever realized. We want to know where things come from. We want to know what happens to it along the way."[17] One in-store advertisement showed a young Black woman smiling while standing in a field of grain and holding a chicken. Superimposed on this image was the text, "Know what kind of life your dinner lived."

The Values Matter campaign married the company's existing message of ethical shopping with a newer message that set the company apart from other corporate grocery stores: ultratransparency. As part of delivering ultratransparency, Whole Foods Market prominently advertised nine different quality standards. These rating systems evaluated products in the store. Some specified unacceptable ingredients in food, personal care products, cleaning products, and dietary supplements, while others outlined animal welfare, labor, and environmental standards.

In 2017 (prior to being acquired by Amazon), the store merged some of the systems and added one for eggs, leaving a total of six quality standards. In the store, some of these rating systems are displayed next to the items for sale. In the cleaning products aisle, for example, each product has a color-coded rating score. The score ranges from red (products that are deemed unacceptable and not carried by the store) to green (products containing ingredients that are considered safe and environmentally friendly). On its website, the company asserts that this system replaces formal regulations, stating, "Even for 'natural cleaning products,' there are no regulations for listing ingredients on packaging—except at Whole Foods Market®. We developed the Eco-Scale rating system that, among other things, requires that every ingredient be listed."[18] The premium body care standards at Whole Foods Market are also displayed prominently in the store.

The quality standards are published on the company's website, accompanied by photos of farm fields, Whole Foods Market employees, farmers, and fresh vegetables. These photos evoke the image of food coming directly from farms. No intermediaries—the processors, distributors, and industrial spaces that are part of getting food into stores—are shown in these photos. These photos and signs are part of an ethos of local food and a farm-to-store experience that purports to let the shopper "see" where their food came from. These images reinforce the quality standards the company so prominently advertises. The women I interviewed valued the farm-to-table philosophy, and this is consistent with other research suggesting that more and more consumers prefer to "eat local" or grow their own food and, ideally, talk face-to-face with farmers about how their food is grown.[19] Of course, not all Whole Foods

Market products are local. Its processed foods are necessarily the products of a long and complex commodity chain involving corporate farms, large food-processing companies, and the various "middlemen" who broker their journey to the store. In the winter, much of the fruit for sale at New York City stores comes from outside New York State or even outside the United States. Whole Foods Market—like other supermarkets—buys from wholesale distributors, the ultimate middlemen.[20]

The transparency at Whole Foods Market is exceptional compared to other grocery stores in New York City. Other major supermarkets in the city, such as Fairway Markets and C-Town Supermarkets, as well as national chains like Trader Joe's (considered Whole Foods Market's main competitor) do not advertise a set of quality standards. Most independent health food stores in New York City do not display a set of quality standards or rating systems.[21] However, some boutique, independently owned butcher shops, like Harlem Shambles in central Harlem and Honest Chops in the East Village, openly advertise quality standards of purity and transparency to shoppers—both in-store and online. Honest Chops, for example, tells customers that it "promises to be transparent. No question is off-limits!"[22]

While transparency is a trend across the food industry, it is the centerpiece of Whole Foods Market's brand. In *Conscious Capitalism: Liberating the Heroic Spirit of Business,* cowritten by Whole Foods Market's founder John Mackey and Rajendra Sisodia, the authors state, "Transparency is not an end in itself; it is important because it builds trust in the organization. When we keep something hidden, the motivation is almost always a lack of trust."[23] Many of the women I interviewed for this book (whom I will discuss in more detail in chapters 5 and 6) shopped at Whole Foods Market because they trusted the company to carry fresh foods of decent quality and because the store represented the best alternative to the conventional supermarkets in their neighborhood. They found their local stores to be overpriced, dirty, and full of expired or low-quality goods. Kannitha, a married, Asian American, middle-class mother of two children, tried to avoid her local conventional stores as much as possible. "The supermarkets they have here, . . . the produce is just terrible [and] the quality," she explained. "The cleanliness is just really terrible. I never really go there for produce. I go there for boxed things like milk, juice, pasta sauce." Many of the women I interviewed mentioned store cleanliness and the poor quality food at conventional supermarkets. Arissa, a married, Asian American, middle-class mother of two, told me that she had seen fresh chicken unloaded from a delivery truck outside her local grocery store, where it was left to sit out in the hot sun. Indeed, the stores these women identified have been charged with numerous violations by the city's health department, including those regarding dirt, pests, and expired food.[24]

Commodity chain transparency is vital to Whole Foods Market's brand, and it is also essential to practicing precautionary consumption. Transparency, whether it is clear labeling of all ingredients in a product or a quality standard that prohibits certain ingredients, allows consumers to make their own precautionary judgments and thus exercise perceived control over what they put into their body. Several of the women I interviewed for this book trusted Whole Foods Market to screen products—that is, to sell safer and healthier versions of the commodities they could get elsewhere. They paid attention to the company's quality standards. Jennifer, a white, middle-class mother of two, suffered for months from chronic sinus congestion and frequent headaches. After doing some online research, Jennifer wondered if she was sensitive to the synthetic preservatives and fragrances in the conventional products she had been using, so she began shopping at Whole Foods Market for soaps, shampoos, lotions, and cosmetics. After switching, her conditions eased. "I pretty much only buy at Whole Foods now," she explained, "just because I have a general notion that it's good for beauty products." Indeed, Whole Foods Market maintains a list of four hundred unacceptable ingredients in its personal care products. Allison, a married, Asian American, upper-middle-class mother of two, shops at Whole Foods Market because she trusts the store's rating system for meat:

> It is really important to me to know that it is organically treated and that there are no pesticides and no chemicals. The eggs are from cage-free, pasture-raised chickens, and the beef as well. I really only get beef from Whole Foods. . . . Like, all the beef and the pork and the chicken, they have all these standards: one, two, three, four, five. Five is the highest, and so I get the five or the four maybe.

Importantly, several women looked at Whole Foods in a more critical light, seeing it as quite the opposite of an ethical market actor, and refusing to incorporate it into their precautionary consumption routines. In contrast to Allison, Fiona, a white, middle-class mother of a toddler, refused to shop at Whole Foods Market because she did not trust the company's claims about quality and health:

> You see this all over Whole Foods: . . . meats that are referred to as "natural." I'm like, "Okay, what does that mean?" Whole Foods has, I think, the most

pernicious marketing of their meats. You see all this chicken that's "natural" and "air chilled." . . . I feel like I'm being lulled into thinking that I'm doing something good for the Earth by shopping at Whole Foods. They are selling me that myth more than anything.

Kathleen, a white, middle-class artist and mother of a young child, shopped at local health food stores and farmers' markets. She trusted the smaller stores and farmers' markets, explaining, "They've been in the neighborhood for a really long time, and they're committed to a certain lifestyle, and also they're committed to bulk. I trust the stores. I value their mission." She avoided Whole Foods Market, citing CEO John Mackey's opposition to the Affordable Care Act, and contrasted her local store's treatment of employees with Whole Foods Market's employee practices: "They [Whole Foods Market] check their [employees'] bags and their person for stolen items, every day, publicly. That is just so fucked up, I'm sorry. That is just really shaming, and that just doesn't give them any dignity."

All of the women in this study spoke positively about the independently owned health food stores in the city. Few, however, actually shopped at these stores because they were not in convenient locations and their prices, on average, were higher than Whole Foods Market's, making them too expensive. In upper- and middle-class neighborhoods in New York City, Whole Foods Market is an affordable shopping space. For lower-income shoppers with few choices in their neighborhood, traveling to a Whole Foods Market can offer some discounts (see chapter 6). But when Whole Foods Market moves into a low-income or gentrifying neighborhood, it can make life more difficult for its neighbors. Harlem residents reported seeing a "Whole Foods effect" of rising residential and commercial rents soon after the company announced a new store in the neighborhood.[25]

Whole Foods Market is only one element of the consumer culture of precautionary consumption. Also key are the things for sale within the store, which use savvy branding and labeling to convey similar narratives of purity, health, and wholesomeness.

THE PRODUCT PACKAGE

Whole Foods Market, along with the packaging encasing most of the food it sells, is part of a supermarket narrative that tells consumers many stories: the story of how a company started, the story of how animals are treated before they are slaughtered, the story describing the lives of the workers who produce the food.[26] To borrow a phrase from journalist Michael Pollan, Whole Foods Market is the land of "storied food." As Pollan observes in his book *The Omnivore's Dilemma,* "It's the evocative prose as much as anything else that makes this food really special, elevating an egg or chicken breast or bag of arugula from the realm of ordinary protein and carbohydrates into a much headier experience, one with more complex aesthetic, emotional and even political connotations."[27] Nearly a decade after the publication of Pollan's book, the shelves of Whole Foods Market are still laden with storied food. Take, for example, the text on a package of Jovial Organic Einkorn Crispy Cocoa cookies that I found at the store in 2015: "The eggs are from hens that are pasture-raised and truly free to roam on a small countryside farm. Extracted from prehistoric salt deposits, this salt is a product of centuries of natural evaporation of seawater. Socially and environmentally responsible palm fruit oil helps reduce deforestation and preserves biodiversity."

Products at Whole Foods Market (and increasingly at conventional grocery stores) are plastered with text and symbols signifying purity and naturalness—from the standard organic certification seal to claims such as "phthalate-free," "certified by the Non-GMO Project," "from grass-fed cows," and "nothing artificial." In addition to all this text, the packages include the standard markings found on all food packaging, including nutritional information, ingredients, a list of allergens, and kosher and halal certifications. Products marketed to mothers or labeled as children's products carry messages about the need to protect vulnerable children from synthetic chemicals, sugar, and salt.

As part of my research on precautionary consumption, I cataloged the claims and labels on products for sale at Whole Foods Market (see the appendix for an outline of the methodology). Many of the products I reviewed were not sold exclusively at Whole Foods Market and could also be found at independently owned health food stores, conventional grocery stores, and online health food vendors. But Whole Foods Market was unique in that it specialized in precautionary consumer products and carried a far greater variety of these products than did any other store. Especially prevalent in Whole Foods Market stores are products that carry a "clean label."[28] Clean labels claim that a product is free of certain ingredients, and these products represent an area of significant market growth.[29] Table 4 displays the many other precautionary claims that can be found on the labels of foods and consumer

TABLE 3 "Nothing's in Here": What Products Using a Clean Label Promise Not to Contain

Personal care products	Food	Cleaning products	Other consumer products
Ammonia	Added sugars	Added synthetic ingredients	Biologically toxic chemicals
Animal ingredients	Antibiotics	Bisphenol A	Bisphenol A
Artificial flavors	Artificial colors	Chlorine	Chlorine
Artificial foaming agents	Artificial flavors	Dyes	Endocrine disruptors
Artificial/synthetic colors	Aspartame	Fragrances	Flame retardant chemicals
Artificial/synthetic fragrances	Bisphenol A	Gluten	Heavy metals
	Corn syrup	Harmful chemicals	Latex
Camphor	Gelatin	Harmful heavy metals or chemicals	Lead
Chemicals	Genetically modified organisms/ingredients	Perfluorooctanoic acid	Melamine
Chlorine		Petrochemicals	Nitrosamines
DEET	High fructose corn syrup	Petroleum	PBDEs
Detergents	Hormones (synthetic)	Phosphates	Perfluorinated compounds
Dibutyl phthalate	Pesticides	Polytetrafluoroethylene	Phthalates
Dye	Preservatives	Polyvinyl choride	Plastic
Fluoride	Recombinant bovine growth hormone	Sodium laureth sulfate	Polyvinyl chloride
Formaldehyde	Sucralose	Toxic chemicals and flame retardants	Volatile organic compounds
Formaldehyde derivatives	Synthetic colors	Triclosan	
Fragrance or scent masking agents	Toxic persistent pesticides		
Heavy metals	Toxic pesticides		
Icky chemicals			
Mineral oils			
Nano (nanoparticles)			
Parabens			
Paraffin			
Polyethylene glycol			
Petrochemicals			
Petrolatum			
Phenoxyethanol			
Phthalates			
Preservatives			
Resorcinol			
Silicones			
Sodium laureth sulfate			
Toluene			
Toxin			
Triclosan			

SOURCE: Data were collected between 2014 and 2016 from an analysis of product labels of commodities sold at Whole Foods Markets in New York City. Note that a "clean label" states that a product does not contain a particular compound or substance.

products for sale at Whole Foods Market. Food packages most often made multiple claims, such as a package of cookies that claims to be both "small batch" and "GMO-free."

According to historian Tracey Deutsch, shopping did not always involve this much reading.[30] When the conventional grocery store rose to prominence in the 1950s, market research suggested that shoppers (i.e., women) preferred simple packaging with as little text as possible. Yet over the following several decades, food packages became adorned with ever more information. Nutrition labels that indicate the calorie, fat, and sodium contents of products were first introduced by the FDA in 1973 and then revised in 1990, when the agency's secretary complained that current provisions were too lax: "The grocery store has become a Tower of Babel and consumers need to be linguists, scientists and mind readers to understand the many labels they see."[31] In contrast to the shoppers of the 1950s, consumers today want *more* information about their food and look to food packaging to obtain it.[32] Such information is communicated through voluntary labeling—that is, labels that are not required by law (see chapter 2).[33] Consumers look for the USDA Organic certification seal when searching for organic options, but they also look for stickers suggesting products are "natural," produced locally, or free of GMOs.[34]

Karen, a married, white mother of two children, spoke of how she looks for these labels and how they are important when she is deciding what food to buy for her children:

> Usually, [with] the big commercial brands, it's not organic. It has high-fructose corn syrup, it has food coloring and everything. . . . I am watching for an organic label if I can—and if it's within reason, price-wise, and something that the kids will eat and will like. If two brands are similar and [the kids] will eat both, I would get the organic one, just because I don't want food additives or chemicals.

Consumers like Karen turn to certified-organic food or to food with clean labels as a reaction to the increasing complexity, invisibility, and secrecy that characterizes the industrial food system. As popular documentary films like *Supersize Me* (2004), *Food Inc.* (2008), and *Fed Up* (2014) illustrate, agribusiness and major food processors have considerable power over food production and processing and have a vested interest in controlling the public's access to information about where their food comes from, how it is processed, and what effects it has on their health. As consumers demand greater transparency in the industrial food system, companies have responded by adopting clean labeling practices to advertise what is *absent* from their products while keeping ingredient lists short and simple.

These clean-label claims reflect an increasing number of exposés of unpopular (and invisible) ingredients used in food production. When the USDA, for example, allowed the controversial recombinant bovine growth hormone (rBGH) to be used in milk production, organic producers and some small milk producers began adding an "rBGH-free" label to their products.[35] High-fructose corn syrup (HFCS) was in the spotlight from 2006 to 2012 owing to books and films that attributed its use to the rise in type 2 diabetes and obesity in the United States. Accordingly, "HFCS-free" labels began to appear on food products like bread, soda, cookies, and applesauce. Producers replaced HFCS with cane sugar, which caused the price of sugar to rise. Some producers, feeling the price pressure and detecting consumer indifference to HFCS over time, have added the ingredient back to their products and quietly removed the HFCS-free label from the package.[36] This HFCS bait-and-switch is testament to the unreliability of voluntary changes to production recipes as a solution to building a healthy food system. It also demonstrates how careful consumers must be if they want to detect these small changes to their foods.

Precautionary consumption involves not only reading a product package but also decoding its assurance of safety, wholesomeness, and purity. And there is a lot of decoding to do. To provide an illustration of the volume of reading that has become part of precautionary consumption, I list in tables 3 and 4 many of the precautionary and clean labels claims that were prominent on foods and other consumer products sold at Whole Foods Market from 2014 to 2016. These labels were voluntary; they were chosen by producers to enhance the look and appeal of their products. They also help consumers navigate a potentially hazardous consumer landscape. Trusting that these labels are transparent and truthful is a matter of faith.[37] The women I interviewed looked for labels such as "antibiotic-free," "cage-free," and, of course, "certified organic" to help them quickly make a product choice. Several women could provide me with a rapid-fire list of unacceptable and acceptable ingredients, but as much as they seemed to have mastered the lexicon of chemical avoidance, they admitted that learning to read a label was a lot of work. It required mastering a new language of descriptors for production processes (e.g., "cage-free" and "tended by hand") and synthetic chemicals (e.g., "perfluorinated compounds"), as well as their acronyms (e.g., PFCs).

TABLE 4 General Claims Made on Commodities Marketed as Healthy, Nontoxic, or Organic

Personal care products	Food	Cleaning products
100% natural	100% pure	All natural ingredients
100% vegetarian ingredients	Cage-free	Certified organic
95% plant based	Certified humane	Environmentally friendly
Certified organic	Certified organic	Free and clear
Certified organic facility	Certified vegan	Made from cornstarch
Full disclosure of ingredients according to PCP Standards	Fair trade	Made from naturally derived ingredients
	Free-range	Natural
	From family farmers	Non-GMO Project verified
Hypo-allergenic	Grass-fed	Plant-based
Made on an organic farm in the USA	Handmade	
	Humanely raised	
Made with organic ingredients	Made from single source	
	Milk from grassfed cows	
Natural	Never hybridized	
Natural cleaning agent	Non-GMO Project certified	
Naturally derived	Nonleaching	
Nontoxic	None of those weird, vexatious sweeteners	
NOP certified organic	Nothing added and nothing taken out	
Not tested on animals		
Pure flower and plant extracts	Pasture-raised	
	Real ingredients	
Pure	Real pure	
Sustainable	Responsibly grown	
Vegan friendly	Small batch	
	Subject to European regulations	
	Tended by hand	
	U.S.-grown soybeans	
	Vegan	
	Vegetarian	
	Vegetarian feed	
	We use real milk	
	Worry free	

SOURCE: These claims were visible on the front or back of product packages. These data were collected between 2014 and 2016 from an analysis of commodities sold at Whole Foods Market stores in New York City.

The work of reading a label frustrated Marcy, a married, white, middle-class mother of twin girls, who had this to say about food labels:

> I think learning to read a label is a huge thing. . . . You find things that can be hidden in a term as benign-sounding [as] "natural flavors." You will see that on a label on anything. . . . Without a doubt, there are chemicals within that, and it is legal for them to list it that way. And citric acid, which sounds lovely, like orangey and lemony or something, but it comes from corn. If it's not

organic, it's GMO without a doubt. Learning what some of the ingredients are and what some of the possible risks are from those ingredients, like the carrageenan which is in everything. The amount of chemicals in everything, in terms of cosmetic products or cleaning products—again, the labels are crazy. They can say "all natural" or even "organic," and then you read the label, and there may be some percentage of ingredients that are organic, but the rest is just the same garbage that could be anything else.

Food packages with precautionary messages establish a reason for concern while also promising an answer. A package indicating a product is "worry free" or "without toxic pesticides" suggests that other commodities might be worrisome or contain toxic pesticides but reassures consumers that this one is "safe." In some cases, a package provides a long list of ingredients that it promises are *not* in the product, and this list can sometimes be longer than the actual ingredient list. Siggi's Icelandic-Style Skyr yogurt has eight clean label and general health claims (including "all natural" and "no sucralose"), which is double the number of listed ingredients. KIND nut bars implement their tag line—"Ingredients you can see and pronounce"—quite literally, wrapping their bars in a package with a clear plastic window that allows the consumer to see the contents.[38]

The same way a brand makes a pair of shoes more than footwear (e.g., sneakers become Nikes or Reeboks), these precautionary claims give food a desirable status by rendering a commodity more meaningful and by promising something beyond the pragmatic utility or purpose of the item. The seal for USDA Organic or the Non-GMO Project brands a food as *superior* to conventional foods as a result of the producer's adherence to a set of standards. While consumers recognize advertising as an exaggeration meant to influence their purchases, the claims on precautionary labels hold special importance, particularly when it comes to foods for infants and children. As mothers like Marcy and Allison explained, precautionary consumer labels matter a great deal to them; they look for them while shopping, and they take the precautionary assurances seriously. Even though Marcy is skeptical that labels give her the full picture of what went into a product and how it was produced, she still looks for them.

I found that packages for items marketed for children or infants used the strongest language of quality, purity, and safety. A package of Earth's Best Organic baby cereal, for example, claims: "All babies begin life 100% pure ... Feed them accordingly." Kabrita, a brand of infant formula, announces this on its package: "Kabrita is sourced from humanely raised goats in the

Netherlands. European regulations limit the use of antibiotics and growth hormones; so our goat milk is not exposed to potentially harmful levels of pesticides, growth hormones, or antibiotics. Kabrita ingredients are non-GMO." The package references E.U. regulations as a reassurance that the product is safer than competing brands of formula, which are subject to looser U.S. regulations. ThinkBaby, a company that makes stainless steel dishes and cups for infants and toddlers, includes this text on the box of its Complete Baby Feeding Set: "Research has linked many chemicals in use to cancer and hormone disruption. Hormone disruptors may lead to a large number of developmental problems in children. ThinkBaby™ operates with the singular purpose of protecting children during the most fragile developmental stages through the use of safe materials." Here, the package raises a concern and references a scientific paradigm (exposure to endocrine disruptors at a young age can lead to a number of developmental problems) and offers a solution (ThinkBaby has made a product with safe materials).

Baby items frequently paired anxiety-inducing language about other products with a promise that the item making the claim could be trusted. Sometimes, a package would identify the owner of the company as a mother, thus reinforcing that shopping for children is women's work and that good mothers choose these safe products. The founder of Late July, an organic brand whose snacks can be found at health food stores and large grocery stores across the country, informs buyers, "As a mother, I'm constantly in the position where I need to give my son a snack on the go, but I'm not willing to sacrifice the quality of the ingredients for convenience. These bite size crackers were developed with him in mind. Our family hopes you enjoy them." The motto of California Baby, a company that makes personal care products for children, is "Developed by a mother, California Baby® has your child's best interest at heart." In my review, references to mothers were more common than references to fathers, although a few companies, like Ella's Kitchen, refer to the owner as a concerned father who cares about his children's health.

STOKING ANXIETIES WHILE PROMISING TO FIX THEM

The marketing of precautionary consumer items stokes anxieties about synthetic chemicals while simultaneously offering a way to safety. A claim that a product is free of "icky chemicals," to quote a bottle of Babo Botanicals diaper cream, makes that product appear safe and pure, but it also suggests that brands that do not make this claim are suspect. Moreover, products sold at Whole Foods Market are situated in an environment that is already heavily branded as precautionary, such that shopping at Whole Foods Market stores involves interpreting and navigating a constellation of signs and symbols all meant to convince consumers that shopping is safe. The quality standards, labels, claims, and narratives about a product's simplicity or naturalness paint a picture of an item that has been vetted by trustworthy authorities: Whole Foods Market and the manufacturer of the product. For example, when a tube of Tom's of Maine "non-nano" baby sunscreen is sold at a store that has already signaled that "values matter," the legitimacy of both claims is increased.

Significantly, the packages and store environment afford a highly mediated view *inside* a product, thus allowing individuals to enact their desired level of precaution. In other words, the more consumers can see (e.g., what ingredients are added, where the product was made, who made it, and the quality-assurance standards of the company selling it), the more information they have to evaluate whether a product is safe. Of course, this is not true transparency but rather a stylized presentation of what a product contains and how it was produced.

Political theorist Chad Lavin surmises that contemporary food discourses are saturated with fear and anxiety because of broader concerns about the limits of personal responsibility and the powerlessness of political structures to address increasingly scientific, technological, and global problems. His synopsis overlaps with Ulrich Beck's assessment of the risk society.[39] Both Lavin and Beck point to a modernity where individuals, rather than institutions responsible for the well-being of the collective, manage risks stemming from a highly complex, coupled, and global system. When problems arise, such as food pathogens in meat, high pesticide residues on strawberries, or toxic chemicals in a children's toy, no discernable institution or organization is responsible for addressing the problem. This diffuse and ambiguous organization of responsibility for risk is what Beck calls "organized irresponsibility."[40] Individuals search for safety, and often the market is the first to respond by producing options that can be purchased, such as local meat from a family farm, certified-organic strawberries, or toys made by an ecologically conscious company. Yet, as this chapter reveals, the very market that promises to help consumers escape risk also amplifies discourses of anxiety, thus bringing more consumers into the fold of precautionary consumption.[41]

Accompanying the promise of transparency is the message of consumer empowerment and control. Messages of empowerment are, of course, present across all types of advertising, not just that found on precautionary consumer goods. In the case of Whole Foods Market and nontoxic commodities, however, empowerment works together with indicators of transparency to suggest not only that shoppers can become healthier though their purchases but also that they can take control over their exposure to chemicals. Inside a Whole Foods Market store, signs and product labels celebrate consumers' power to, in the words of Stonyfield Organic, "see right through food labels," and they congratulate shoppers for choosing to make purchases at the store, as Whole Foods Market does at its shop entrances. Shoppers feel like the supermom on the yogurt tub; shopping is a necessary chore, but, if done "correctly," it can be an empowering mechanism for self-protection. The flipside of consumer empowerment is, of course, consumer accountability and threat of failing to harness consumer power. When chemicals enter bodies (as they inevitably do), or worse, when a person is diagnosed with an illness linked to chemicals in food or consumer products, they are urged to become *more* knowledgeable consumers.

The marketing of precautionary consumption draws on the neoliberal ideology of individual responsibility for risk that celebrates the freedom of choice and promotes a message of consumer empowerment through shopping. Food studies scholar and geographer Julie Guthman looks at the expansion of food labels with considerable skepticism. She asks whether these labels put power in consumers' hands or take it away by giving consumers an even greater burden of self-protection. She sees them not just as an outcome of neoliberalism but also as a mechanism that reproduces it.[42] In other words, precautionary consumer labels are both a response to a regulatory system that allowed harmful chemicals to enter the market and cues to individuals on how to protect themselves and their children from the effects of this system. This neoliberal approach that prioritizes the power of the market over government regulation aligns with Whole Foods Market's cofounder John Mackey's philosophy toward government and capitalism. Mackey was a vocal critic of the Affordable Care Act that was signed into law by President Obama in 2010. Mackey argued that individuals, not the government, should promote better health, starting with advocating for improved access to supermarkets carrying healthy food—access that Whole Foods Market hopes to provide.[43] Whole Foods Market offers its employees incentives to change their eating habits, including paying expenses for over-weight, diabetic, or otherwise unhealthy employees to attend one of their week-long Total Health Immersions workshops, which involve one week of exercise, diet control, and "intensive education about healthy eating and life-style."[44] As CEO of Whole Foods Market, Mackey has positioned himself as a kind of Grocer-in-Chief who will shape diets and shopping habits to create a nation of healthy subjects, with Whole Foods Market as its main supermarket.

But for a person to truly take control of their health and diet, they need to know as much as possible about what they are putting onto their skin and into their body, such that transparency of ingredients becomes absolutely vital to the project of "healthy living." Transparency is a limited and easily manipulated claim. Consumers have to trust that companies are disclosing everything and telling the truth. Whole Foods Market has come under scru-tiny for price gouging, unsanitary conditions in its stores, and overstating its commitment to buying local foods, as mentioned earlier in this chapter. While the company offers a rating system for meat, a significant proportion of the meat that I cataloged during my site visits to its New York City stores met the company's lowest standard, Step 1.[45]

Although many of the women I interviewed looked for organic certifica-tion seals and clean label claims, they also suspected that these labels made exaggerated or untruthful claims. They have good reason to be skeptical. In 2007, the environmental health movement group Silent Spring Institute tested forty-three products that were labeled as green alternatives. They found that many of them contained some toxic ingredients, such as synthetic fragrances and phthalates, and that "eco-friendly" sunscreens marketed for children contained suspected carcinogens.[46] In 2017, the *Washington Post* discovered that conventional soybeans and corn from China were being shipped through Turkey to the United States, where they were falsely labeled as USDA organic and delivered to U.S. organic dairy farms.[47] Even "true" USDA certified-organic products are permitted to contain some synthetic ingredients and can be grown with certain synthetic pesticides, which con-tradicts one of the central goals of the organic movement, which is to produce food without any synthetic pesticides and few, if any, synthetic additives.[48] Food processing and agribusiness industries lobby the USDA to allow more and more of these substances as they develop new processed or convenience organic foods that they want to bring to market.[49]

On the one hand, the increased consumer demand for more environmentally friendly and "healthy" product choices appears to be positive news, particularly if it responds to consumer concerns about toxics in food and household products. On the other hand, while the range of these products expands, the number of new conventional food and consumer products also increases, meaning that consumers have *more* product choice overall.

While having more choice is celebrated as one of the benefits of industrial capitalism, it comes with costs that are not always easy to quantify.[50] Even "regular" grocery shopping, with no thought to whether something is organic or nontoxic, is a complicated endeavor. Interviews with women reveal the work it takes to navigate a supermarket and find the desired items, accommodate each family member's individual tastes, stay within a budget, contend with other shoppers, manage the moods and whims of the child (or children) they may be carting around with them, and avoid expired food, messy aisles, or poor lighting.[51] Renowned food politics and nutrition scholar Marion Nestle knows all too well the difficulties individuals encounter when grocery shopping. She found herself continually bombarded with the same question: "Why is it so hard to know what foods are good for me?"[52] This question, and the widespread consumer confusion she encountered in her research, inspired her to write *What to Eat*. The sheer length of the book—six hundred pages—attests to the complexity of grocery shopping. *What to Eat* guides shoppers through the nearly 320,000 food and beverage products available for sale across the United States. Her book is divided into chapters according to sections of a typical grocery store—for example, one chapter is devoted to produce and another is focused on "the processed section."

Precautionary consumption adds to the already highly complex task of deciding what to eat. It introduces a new layer of complexity to shopping. More labels and more choices are not always the signal of a better marketplace. Greater choice and more precautionary claims on commodities do little to help consumers, especially those without much time or income at their disposal. Reading a label might be second nature to some shoppers, but it involves learning a new vocabulary. Studies suggest that green consumption requires more time, energy, and money than more typical or conventional forms of consumption.[53] Consumers find labels confusing, particularly when they have to navigate multiple messages, such as deconstructing an ingredient label while also decoding a nutrition facts table.[54] When shoppers are pressed for time, are experiencing stressful living conditions, have low incomes, or do not speak or read English, reading a label to identify synthetic additives, let alone prepping a home-cooked meal, is unimaginable, as I discuss in chapter 6.[55] Precautionary consumption involves knowing what is important to notice and what is not—and what certain claims really mean. "Phthalate-free" might sound nice, but what does the average consumer know about phthalates and why they should be avoided? If something is labeled "non-GMO," is it also certified organic? These are questions the women I interviewed ask themselves when they read labels. I turn to their experiences in the next chapter.

FIVE

The High Stakes of Shopping

PRECAUTIONARY CONSUMPTION AS MOTHERS' WORK

"There is a long history of society blaming mothers for the ill health of their children," wrote Sarah Richardson and her colleagues in a widely discussed social commentary published in *Nature* in 2014.[1] This history is central to explaining the rise in precautionary consumption. The current generation of mothers is subject to an especially intense medical surveillance that considers them "vectors for fetal risk"—a characterization not extended to men.[2] As I have written about elsewhere, many women in their reproductive years are aware that environmental contaminants can cross the placenta and are present in breast milk, and they begin thinking of their bodies as their baby's first environment.[3] These women see themselves as gatekeepers of their children's exposures to toxic chemicals. While pregnant, they view chemicals in much the same way as other substances that are prohibited during pregnancy. Many go about avoiding bisphenol A and conventional food in the same way that they do alcohol.[4] After the birth of a child, precautionary consumption continues to be important; many mothers reflect on the contaminants contained in their breast milk. Some buy nontoxic products for their baby, like organic crib mattresses, shampoos, creams, and sunscreens. Once the baby is ready, they offer organic foods. They do this because, as mothers, they are held individually responsible for producing healthy, "normal" children. Health professionals remind mothers that their job is not only to "produce a healthy newborn but to produce a human being biologically predisposed to be healthy from birth to old age."[5]

Motherhood therefore involves two major responsibilities: managing one's own body as the child's first environment, and taking care of household consumption and foodwork (which includes food planning, meal preparation, and grocery shopping) after the child is born. Precautionary consumption bridges these responsibilities. In previous chapters, I explained the rise of precautionary consumption as a combination of factors, including routine regulatory failure, the expansion of major environmental health campaigns, and the growing market for "clean" products and organic foods. In this chapter, I examine the lived experience of precautionary consumption by drawing on interviews I conducted with thirty New York City mothers to learn how much precautionary consumption is part of their foodwork and shopping routines. I chose to interview women, and mothers more specifically, about precautionary consumption because mothers are most likely to participate in precautionary consumption, particularly during and after pregnancy.[6] In what follows, I describe the many ways precautionary consumption is practiced and the reasons the mothers in my sample practice it. I show how these women became aware of cultural ideals of femininity and good motherhood when they entered their reproductive years and how this translated into a deep sense of accountability for the future of their children. Precautionary consumption offered these women a way to respond to these cultural ideals, and they wove precautionary consumption into existing caregiving and foodwork routines.

Before I investigate this interplay of gender, embodiment, and consumption, I show what precautionary consumption routines actually look like in "real" life—that is, outside the pages of an EWG shopping guide or on the product packages and store signs in Whole Foods Market.

PRACTICING PRECAUTION

All of the women I interviewed bought some organic food products each week, which is not surprising given that the Organic Trade Association estimates that 81 percent of U.S. parents buy certified-organic food "at least sometimes."[7] In 2015, when I was conducting interviews, organics was set to bring in $45 billion in the United States, and access to organics was rapidly expanding throughout the grocery sector.[8] Most women also bought some nontoxic cleaning products and personal care products, especially lotions, sunscreens, and baby shampoos. Yet, across the thirty women I interviewed, no precautionary consumption routine was alike. Drawing from the descriptions these women gave of the various things they do to try to avoid synthetic chemicals in food, the home, and the environment more broadly, I have identified three types of precautionary routines: basic, moderate, and comprehensive.[9] Eight of the women I spoke with had a basic routine, eleven had a moderate routine, and eleven had a comprehensive routine.

A basic precautionary consumption routine involved occasional purchases of certified-organic products. This kind of routine described Gina, a married, white, upper-middle-class homemaker and mother of two children. Gina left a stressful professional job after the birth of her first child and was now a full-time homemaker. She bought organic milk for her children and occasionally purchased organic fruits and vegetables, but only when they were in season or on sale. She tried to avoid synthetic and artificial preservatives in processed foods, like cereal or crackers. She rarely bought nontoxic personal care products. Women with basic routines spoke of the cost, hassle, and time precautionary consumption required. Carol, a single, white, middle-class, stay-at-home mother of a toddler, had a basic routine because she did not enjoy grocery shopping, and despite living in an affluent neighborhood with a Trader Joe's and Whole Foods Market a few blocks away, Carol had no interest in making a "a special [grocery] trip to buy special eggs." Instead, she drove to Costco once a week with the father of her child, and bought all of her groceries in one trip. She bought organic food only when it was convenient and affordable.

A moderate routine is intended to control chemical exposure across a range of food and consumer products, but there is a clear limit where the time, hassle, or expense get to be too much and precautionary consumption is put on hold, at least temporarily. This moderate approach was taken by Abby, a married, white, upper-middle-class mother of two children. Abby, a part-time healthcare worker, shopped at an independently owned organic grocery store in an upscale Brooklyn neighborhood and bought organic fruits and vegetables if they were listed on the EWG's *Dirty Dozen* list of produce containing high pesticide residues. She recently threw out her plastic containers and replaced with them with glass after learning that compounds in plastic can leach into food: "I'm always looking at that—if something is BPA free—and [asking] what are the ingredients of food, stuff like that." Abby did all of the grocery shopping and cooking for her household, as her husband worked long hours as a financial advisor. Convenience and practicality determined her limit with precautionary consumption. If she knew a cleaning product contained a toxic ingredient but was effective at polishing the tub or disinfecting the sink, she continued to use it. She would not, however, make a similar exception for products for her children, such as their shampoo, as she reasoned that their bodies deserved a higher standard of protection. If Abby was tired and short on time, she would pick up a conventional, processed food for dinner rather than push herself to cook something organic from scratch. Even so, Abby tried to buy as much organic fruit as possible because of concerns about her children's exposure to pesticides. In other words, she was driven by a sense of responsibility to protect her children's health, but she recognized the limits to what she could accomplish as a working mother with limited time and energy.

In contrast to a basic or moderate approach, a comprehensive precautionary consumption routine is designed to avoid as much exposure to environmental chemicals as possible. Such a routine looks very much like the routines recommended by organizations within the environmental health movement, as discussed in chapter 3. In this chapter, I go into detail about what these routines involve because of how the women I interviewed connected the accomplishment of precautionary consumption to normative femininity and motherhood. Women with comprehensive routines estimated that anywhere from 70 to 90 percent of their weekly groceries were certified organic. They read ingredient labels, compared ingredient lists across brands, and consulted EWG shopping guides. They made or bought natural or nontoxic cleaning supplies, and shopped at their local farmers' market. They purchased natural cosmetics and, if they could afford it, eco-friendly furniture (such as crib mattresses) for their home.[10] They read books, magazine articles, and blog posts on the topic of chemicals in food and household commodities. In contrast to women with basic or moderate routines, they did not stop at "good enough" precautionary consumption. Rather, they felt guilty or anxious that they were not doing more. Marcy, for example, was fully invested in precautionary consumption. A married, white, middle-class mother of preschool-aged twins, she bought all organic foods for her children (with few exceptions) and, despite working full time, made her own toothpaste and cleaning supplies. Like other women with comprehensive routines, Marcy was not satisfied with her dedication to precautionary consumption: "Oh my God, I feel like I'm failing at something almost every day. That's the other thing about trying to do any healthy thing, whether it's food or anything else. . . . The more you know, the more there is to know."

Fiona, a married, white, middle-class writer and mother of a toddler, had a comprehensive routine that was similar to Marcy's, and she also contended with strong feelings of guilt. When I interviewed her at a café near her office, she told me about her son's diet, emphasizing the absence of premade or processed foods: "The most processed thing that [my son] eats are those Annie's [Cheddar] Bunnies, but other than that, he's never had a pouch [of baby food]. He's never had baby food from the jar. He's only had food that I've made for him or that his daycare makes for him." Like other mothers aiming to raise an "organic child," Fiona told me about how her son eats wholesome, home-cooked foods.[11] The small choices that involve weighing one risk against another came up a lot in my interviews with mothers. Fiona underscored the mental labor that goes into making seemingly simple choices: "I just think there's so much gray area around this sort of stuff. Is it better to give your child [conventional] grapes than no grapes?"

The day before, Fiona was grocery shopping and wanted to buy asparagus for her son—"It's like candy to him. I'm like, 'This is great. He loves asparagus.'"—but when she found asparagus grown in Mexico, she hesitated. Although the vegetable is on the EWG's *Clean Fifteen* list, she did not know whether imported asparagus qualified for the "clean" rating. Standing in the produce aisle of her local grocery store, she wondered, "Do I buy this? Do I not? We know that Mexico still sprays DDT. Is this conventionally grown asparagus actually safe?" She bought it but also grabbed a bag of organic sugar snap peas, reasoning that they might somehow cancel out any risk posed by the imported asparagus.

The comprehensive approach to precautionary consumption is in line with the ideologies of "intensive mothering" and "total motherhood."[12] These ideologies prize a mother's total commitment to her children and suggest that mothers must always try harder, be more organized, and be better informed about the best practices of child rearing. The careful attention to detail that this intensive form of precautionary consumption entails—considering pesticide residues and a product's country of origin, for example, while also wanting to reward a child for his love of vegetables—brings to mind the "calculative rationality" that is central to the discourse of risk and the responsible subject, and responsible mothering in particular.[13] According to today's standards of "good motherhood," moreover, it is not enough to have a healthy child who loves vegetables; that child must also consume organic food and have few pesticides and other synthetic chemicals in their body.

To be clear, these concerns are more than just expressions of upper-middle-class anxiety. As chapters 2 and 3 demonstrate, precautionary consumption is a response to ubiquitous environmental pollution and a poorly regulated food system and retail landscape. Safe shopping guides and biomonitoring reports published by environmental health movement groups, and the marketplace for nontoxic commodities and organic foods, circulate a discourse of maternal responsibility for protecting children's purity and future health.

What is surprising, as I explore in this chapter, is how this responsibility is normalized by the women in my sample as just another part of motherhood. Precautionary consumption coheres with existing social and medical discourses of gender, motherhood, and personal responsibility.

DISCIPLINING THE FEMININE BODY, PRIMING THE MATERNAL BODY

On the surface, precautionary consumption appears to be a more complicated form of shopping involving the added twist of reading ingredient labels a bit more carefully or taking the extra time to weigh the high price of organic produce against the potential future health costs of a child's exposure to pesticides on conventional produce. Yet precautionary consumption is more than just shopping. It is a practice through which femininity and motherhood are produced and reproduced, and the way mothers talk about precautionary consumption is a window into their negotiations with the normative expectations of middle-class motherhood at a time when individuals are expected to take personal responsibility for collective risks—like environmental chemicals in food and consumer products.

As a sociologist, I take the perspective that femininity is both embodied and produced in interactions, and that this embodiment and "doing" of gender is always in reference to a cultural definition of normative femininity.[14] The contemporary American cultural definition of normative femininity holds that the ideal woman is thin and light-skinned[15] and knows how to cook and care for others. She is careful about what she eats but not too obsessive.[16] By keeping a close watch on what she incorporates into her body, she stands a chance of being considered attractive and youthful and of producing healthy, "normal" children.[17] This ideal woman is a self-regulating subject who monitors her own weight and the size of the women around her.[18] She keeps her body under constant control—especially during pregnancy.[19] The dominant discourses about good health and nutrition are technologies of power in the Foucauldian sense.[20] Women internalize what seem like common sense scientific messages, such as "eat a balanced diet," "cook from scratch," and "avoid chemicals," and these messages have a profound impact on women's relationship to food. Put another way, caring about food and controlling diet is a biopolitical project, as it is a form of power where individuals govern their own bodies from the inside out.[21] In the case of chemical body burdens, this biopolitical project includes preventing chemical trespass into the feminine body as part of keeping it "pure" for its future function during pregnancy or breastfeeding. As I found in my interviews, the skills and knowledge involved in this project begin well before motherhood. They are honed through women's drive for thinness and weight control.[22]

Although upper- and middle-class women have been exposed to the thin ideal since childhood, they do not really gain full control over their food and what goes into their bodies until they begin shopping for their own groceries and cooking their own meals. Among the women I spoke with, most of whom had at least some college education, this period started after graduation from college, when they moved into their own home, either alone or with a romantic partner. Around this time, they began thinking more seriously about how to manage their weight, improve their diet, and cook appealing meals for their boyfriends or husbands.[23] This transition required them to learn to read food labels to determine sugar and fat content and to identify potentially harmful chemicals, like preservatives, food colorings, and other synthetic compounds. Underlying their concerns was a desire for thinness, disease prevention, *and* healthy future children, but these concerns were voiced using the language of health and nutrition.[24] Through dieting, women learned a set of skills that were vital to precautionary consumption.

This trajectory, starting with dieting and leading to practicing precautionary consumption, was especially evident in my interview with Allison, a married, middle-class, Asian American stay-at-home mother of two children. Allison gave an account of how her approach to precautionary consumption had changed over time that mapped onto key moments in her reproductive life course. She began dieting after college and then used precautionary consumption several years later as part of preparing her body for pregnancy. While in college, Allison ate mostly packaged ramen and food from the school cafeteria. "The packaged ramen is really bad for you. It has all these chemicals in there," she tells me as we sit at her kitchen table on a day when her son was home sick from school. "All we got [growing up] was home-cooked Chinese meals every day, twenty-four seven, 365 days a year. . . . When I got to college, I saw all these different ways of cooking and eating. I said, 'Oh, this is great!' I gained so much weight. I ate everything. I would try every single dessert because I never got any of that [growing up]." When she met her husband, he joked that she ate "horribly" and promised to help her improve her diet:

He really taught me how to shop for good foods, how to eat more vegetables, and eat salads. I never liked salad. I never ate that stuff before, so he was a big influence. Then his sister was even more like [an] authority on this stuff. She is crazy actually. She is totally obsessed. She grinds everything. She is making her own enzymes to make the yogurt and kefir. She makes everything from scratch.

After getting married, Allison wanted to get her body "healthy enough to be able to have a healthy baby." She gave up meat and began exercising, eating more fruits and vegetables, and avoiding processed foods, and she maintained these habits during pregnancy. She switched to organic foods when she was breastfeeding because of concerns about pesticides in her breast milk. While pregnant, she looked to her husband's sister as a role model, as she always bought organic food, filtered her water, and used only nontoxic personal care products. She saw her sister-in-law as the embodiment of a wife and mother whose clean, healthy, and fertile body produced a healthy daughter, who is "solid as a rock and never gets sick. You can look at her and know she is solid." By referring to her niece's body in this way, Allison connects her sister-in-law's rigid precautionary consumption regime to the production of healthy children. To achieve this same robust health for her own children, Allison feeds them only certified-organic food.

Allison's trajectory—from dieting for "health" to practicing precautionary consumption for the sake of her children—shows how the clean, "chemical-free" maternal body, like the slender body, is the contemporary embodiment of normative femininity. Informed interest in precautionary consumption is not so different from the informed interest in "healthy eating" that is integral to women's performance of thinness.[25] Moreover, after marriage or partnering and the arrival of children, the pressure on women to practice precautionary consumption increases, as it is integral to the performance of good mothering.

This performance can begin early, as I saw with Bianca, a twenty-five-year-old, middle-class, single, Black-Hispanic woman who had recently graduated from college and was working as a financial planner. She and her boyfriend of several years were thinking of moving in together in the near future, and she was hoping to have a baby soon. Bianca told me that when she was in college, she had lived with a group of health-conscious "vegans who had all these special machines that they would use for cooking or making juices or freeze-drying foods or packaging foods." Her friends, she explained, not only modeled good eating but also monitored her weight: "If I'm gaining too much weight, [a friend will] politely say, 'Oh, you're kind of'—this happened a few months ago, where I was getting kind of big. She politely said some things to me, like, 'Maybe you should try eating more fruits and vegetables.'" This suggestion, however politely it was delivered, is an indirect reprimand for failing to maintain the thin ideal and serves a reminder to Bianca that her weight is under constant surveillance.[26] Bianca was not offended by her friend's suggestion; rather, she was grateful that her friend gave her such "practical" advice. In fact, Bianca felt that exerting control over her body through food now extended into planning for a future pregnancy: "I want to do my research and make sure I keep a diet that is healthy for the pregnancy. Also, [I'm] staying away from the chemicals and stuff because of sensitivities. And I'm already worrying about a natural diet for children, once they're born." Bianca had started eating more organic foods and had recently switched to phthalate- and sulfate-free cosmetics. When I asked her why she felt it was important to avoid chemicals *before* she became pregnant, she shrugged and paused for a moment. Then she smiled, telling me, as though it was obvious, "It's very important—having a good start for the baby. I want my baby to be healthy."

Bianca's reaction—that a healthy baby is an obvious reason for planning ahead—speaks to how normative femininity and motherhood are guided by a set of commonly understood rules that, presumably, define how all women (even those who are not mothers) should prepare their bodies for pregnancy. These rules are embedded in social, cultural, and medical discourses of what Miranda Waggoner calls "anticipatory motherhood."[27] The CDC, for example, actively encourages all young women to prepare their bodies for pregnancy as early as possible, in case they have a unplanned pregnancy, and especially if they are planning to become pregnant at some point in their reproductive lives.[28] Several other women I spoke with talked about preparing their bodies for pregnancy and said their interest in doing so was sparked by a desire to have the cleanest and healthiest body possible to increase the odds of having a successful pregnancy and a "perfect" child. When I interviewed Monique, a married, white, upper-middle-class professional, she was five months pregnant with her first child. We met on a cold winter evening after she had worked a long day at her job in the fashion industry. Monique first became aware of the issue of chemical body burdens when she was in her midtwenties and started grocery shopping on her own. At this point, concerns about chemicals did not influence how she shopped; she was more concerned about calories and convenience. But when she was in her midthirties, she was faced with in vitro fertilization as her only option for conceiving and began taking an interest in organic food and nontoxic products after reading the book *Inconceivable,* by Julia Indichova.[29] Monique was inspired by the book's advice, and chose not to pursue in vitro fertilization. Instead, she gave up coffee, stopped eating takeout food, and began cooking from scratch using organic foods she bought at Whole Foods Market and an independent health food store in her Brooklyn neighborhood. A few months later, she told me with a smile, she became pregnant. Monique considered infertility to be the result of poor personal choices—such as making the decision to eat takeout food, drink coffee, and consume conventional fruits and vegetables. Her husband made some changes to his diet as well, but far fewer than Monique did. Precautionary consumption was, in other words, a gendered responsibility tied to maintaining a fertile body. Monique's experience speaks to the reproductive equation: in the world of medicine, the health of women's bodies matters from preconception through pregnancy, while the health of men's bodies stops being important after conception.[30]

Consequently, the trajectory of being responsible for future children's health is a long one, and it starts early for women. This trajectory is socially defined, as women encounter messages encouraging them to take control of their bodies. Initially, these messages tell women to maintain a thin body; later, they become about developing a pure maternal body. After women give birth, they are urged to cultivate an organic child, deepening their sense of responsibility for their child's future.

The pure, vulnerable child is a potent cultural symbol, and a *contaminated* child is one who has lost his or her innocence too early.[31] Mothers connect the threat to their children's purity to their own contaminated bodies and consumer choices, as I saw with Cerena, who had one of the strictest precautionary consumption routines of anyone I encountered in this study. Cerena was a married, upper-middle-class, African American mother of two young children. She attributed her interest in precautionary consumption to two things. This first was her Southern identity. She spent her summers in the South, eating food grown on her family's farm. She ate pecans fresh off the tree and picked pears and persimmons that grew in her grandmother's garden. These were the freshest foods possible, in her view, and this way of eating was central to her identity and was how she wanted to raise her children.

"I still have that very strong connection to [the South]," she told me, "and that way of communing with nature in that sense, I guess." But the second experience that ultimately put her on the path to practicing precautionary consumption was watching the film *Erin Brockovich,* years before she was even thinking of having children. One scene deeply disturbed her:

> They had that one scene where, you know, the kids were bathing in the water. I was like, "So bathing in tainted water, that's absorbing into your skin?" And you think babies are really buoyant because they're chubby and they're fat, and that's what makes them so cute and lovable. And they have all these fat cells, and [the pollution is] being absorbed into their fat cells and resting there until it re-emerges later in life. I was just like, "Oh my God." I freaked out, and that's when I started doing research.

Cerena reasoned that if toxic chemicals leaching into the groundwater had harmed the residents of Hinkley, California (the case that made the activist Erin Brockovich famous and on which the film is based), chemicals used in agricultural production, cleaning products, and cosmetics might be harmful to her health, and she began preparing her body for pregnancy, even though she was years away from trying to conceive. She started to buy more organic foods and nontoxic personal care products and eliminated processed and conventionally grown foods from her diet. When she was pregnant, she upped the ante: "I was doing research, the [EWG's] *Dirty Dozen,* all sorts of stuff." Her husband was skeptical that these measures were necessary, but Cerena recalls telling him, "You don't know how things build up in your fat cells and have an adverse effect, not necessarily now, but later down the road, on you, on the baby." The fat cells Cerena was referring to were her own cells, not her husband's, reflecting her understanding of the reproductive equation. After her daughter was born and began breastfeeding, Cerena became "even more fanatical," explaining that she was thinking, "Whatever I'm processing is becoming milk, and I'm feeding it to her." If her body was pure, she could pass on to her children the legacy of purity and good health that she considers central to her Southern upbringing. Cerena made all of her children's meals from scratch and bought only organic, fresh, and whole foods for them. Cerena's actions were consistent with the discourse of individual responsibility for risk, and her experience with precautionary consumption shows how individual responsibility for risk adds to the burden of unpaid domestic labor. Cerena's husband was not part of this picture, which was not unusual among the women I interviewed.

Although all of the partnered mothers I interviewed were in heterosexual relationships, men were notably absent from their accounts of precautionary consumption. Their partner's roles in grocery shopping, avoiding chemicals, and monitoring children's health did not come up in the interviews until I asked about them. Women presented the men in their lives as supportive bystanders. Marcy said of her husband, "I already kind of had that mindset, and he didn't, although I think he is more than happy to come along for that ride." Referring to her husband, Fiona spoke of the "demoralizing fact that the other person is not as into it as you are." She explained: "He goes along with it, and I think he benefits from it, and he's on board with it, but he's not initiating it." Karen, a white, middle-class speech therapist with two young children, said of her husband, "He definitely does not care as much about organic choices as I do. When I started out, he said, 'It's just too expensive. I don't want to buy quality stuff.'" Monique resented that her husband did not participate in precautionary consumption: "I think that I'm leading it, and he's accepting of it and likes it, but I say things and he'll sort of ignore me, but then he'd look at it online and say, 'Oh, did you know this?' And I was like, 'Yeah, I told you that *three* times!'" Just as I found in my other research on precautionary consumption, these women portrayed men as secondary actors who showed some interest in the practice but did not take charge of it. Women actively protect precautionary consumption—a practice that is connected to their sense of identity as good, caring mothers—from what they characterize as men's interference. Indeed, mothers' consumer choices are seen as a marker of their investment in their children, while this same pressure is not placed on fathers.[32]

Women were careful to perform precautionary consumption on their own without asking for help from male partners because drawing too much attention to the practice sometimes generated criticism about its cost or convenience. Some women encountered judgmental looks from their partners, like a roll of the eyes to suggest they are "crazy" about chemicals. Kannitha, a married, middle-class, Asian American mother of two young children, felt judged by her husband whenever she asked to leave the apartment windows open to refresh the indoor air: "He doesn't really think about [chemicals] that much. It's not on the top of his mind for him in any shape or form. Sometimes he thinks I'm crazy when I say, 'Oh, we need to leave the windows open when we're leaving the house.'" In this case, being "crazy" is defined as showing concern about chemicals at a level that interrupts what the partners of these women consider a normal routine. Indeed, social commentary on parenting tends to pathologize the anxious mother and to suggest that her fears and controlling behavior are excessive and should be kept in check.[33] Consequently, precautionary consumption is like other performances of femininity, such as beauty and bodywork, in that a woman's investment of time and effort in these areas should appear invisible and effortless.[34] Women who invest too much or too visibly in precautionary consumption risk being labeled "chemophobic" hysterics.[35]

There were exceptions to this kind of muted accomplishment of precautionary consumption. Cerena was one of the few women I interviewed who reported that she argued openly with her husband about precautionary consumption. Cerena had rules about what food could be brought into the home, and if her husband bought something that she considered unacceptable (such as conventional cranberry juice with added sugar), she sent him back to the store to return it. "When I tell him to take it back he doesn't like it though. I'm sure he probably hides it in the trunk of his car and takes it to work with him," she laughed. When she suggested they replace their couch with one free of brominated flame retardants, her husband contended that their current couch was perfectly fine:

> I just had this big mini discussion or argument with my husband. I was thinking, we need a [new] couch. He was like, "No." I was like, "There are flame retardants on everything. They come out in breast milk, now all these studies are coming out, yada, yada, yada. . . . Every time [our daughter] hops up on a pillow, you don't know what kind of things are flying up into the air and being inhaled, and blah, blah, blah." He was like, "We are not getting rid of the couch."

Cerena did not push the issue. She hopes they can buy a new couch some day, but in the meantime, she has covered the old couch with a thick cloth that she reasoned might prevent flame retardant dust from spreading throughout the house.

Although she acknowledged that the work was tiring, she appeared happy to be the gatekeeper of environmental contamination in the home. In fact, like other women I interviewed, Cerena did not resent the work she invested in precautionary consumption, and she protected this work from the interference of her husband and other family members. This sequestration of precautionary consumption from other household tasks allowed Cerena to have full control over it.[36] In many middle-class households, mothers are seen as the gatekeepers of health, and fathers are seen as subtly undermining mothers' priorities for maintaining family health by prioritizing convenience and efficiency in the interest of getting the basic care work done.[37] Still, doing all of the work associated with precautionary consumption comes with a steep price: exhaustion. Cerena worked late into the night preparing home-made lunches and prepping for the following evening's dinner. In the middle of the night, while nursing her daughter, she read blog entries and magazine articles on her phone. When I asked her how she found the time to do all of the domestic work, research environmental health, and maintain a full-time job, she joked, "Do I sleep? No." As Anita Garey discovered, cutting back on sleep is a strategy working mothers use to create time to maintain an ideal household—one that more resembles the home of a full-time homemaker.[38] Rather than letting things go, women like Cerena give up sleep. Cerena's precautionary consumption routine adds to an existing load of paid and unpaid labor, which already consumes all of her time.[39]

A few of the women I spoke with said that their partners had taken the initial interest in precautionary consumption, but this happened *before* the arrival of children. After becoming fathers, men become helpful bystanders. As mentioned earlier, Allison learned about healthy eating from her husband, but she was the one who managed precautionary consumption for the family. Gina also told me that she learned about the practice from her husband, who had learned about it from his brother. Despite her husband's concerns about chemicals, Gina was the one who maintained a precautionary consumption routine, although this routine was basic, as she found it exhausting to juggle all of the domestic responsibilities and precautionary consumption. Referring to her husband, she explained, "He really feels strongly about eating healthy and reading about chemicals. He will not let the kids have cereal that is pre-served with BHT [butylated hydroxytoluene]. For the kids, I will only buy brands that have natural preservatives because he's really serious about that." Gina had never heard of BHT before her husband mentioned it, but she took his lead and began avoiding the ingredient as much as possible.

Yet Gina resisted adopting a comprehensive precautionary consumption routine. One day, she recalled, her husband had been talking to his brother about the dangers of conventional sunscreen. He suggested that the family switch to all-natural sunscreen. Gina looked up the best eco-friendly brands using the EWG online sunscreen database. She then found these brands at her local Whole Foods Market and compared prices to find the most affordable one. After considering the cost, she realized she could afford the eco brands for her children but not for herself or her husband. She bought natural sunscreen for the children for a brief period and then gave up. "Now all our family will use the same sunscreen," she said, explaining that the decision was the result of "convenience, economy, [and] I'm not carrying around a gazillion sunscreens for everyone." When I asked Gina why she switched back to conventional sunscreen, she replied with a sigh, "I don't care to spend that much mental energy worrying about all this stuff; there's enough other stuff to think about." Gina was upfront about the mental energy that precautionary consumption requires. While her husband raised the issue of chemicals in sunscreen, it was Gina who did the work of looking up the brands, going to the store to compare prices, buying the "right" kind, and then hauling them around to her kids' outdoor activities. Looking at Gina's situation, it is clear that precautionary consumption is not mother's work because of some essential characteristic of women tending to worry more. Rather, precautionary consumption becomes women's work by virtue of the social expectations of who will take charge of protecting children and who will do the shopping. As I show next, this gendered arrangement is connected to social attributions of responsibility for children's health.

THE HIGH STAKES OF FEEDING A CHILD

While all parents want their children to be as healthy as possible, raising a child with few exposures to environmental chemicals is a much more involved process than conventional child-rearing, requiring minute calculations about what is safe, what is best, what is the least toxic. While there are differences in how the women I spoke with practiced precautionary consumption, one theme stands out across all of the interviews: feeding a child at this cultural moment is a high-stakes job. Women hoped to inoculate their children from future health problems by prolonging a kind of embodied purity that they believed would eventually erode as the children grew up. Underlying this belief was the idea that children start life as pure and that chemical exposure happens as a result of maternal bodies and consumer choices. Marcy, for instance, referred to this as starting children "from scratch":

> It's about wanting them to be as healthy as possible. . . . They are only kids for such a tiny amount of time, but I'm starting people from scratch. . . . The

knowledge comes in the face of something you just always assumed was fine. You're sitting there with a tiny little body in a bathtub or with the food in her mouth, or whatever, and you go "Oh, these choices are all going to have long-term effects." Or not. Maybe they won't, but you can't possibly not want to err on the side of caution on all of those things.

Naomi, a married, white, middle-class public health consultant with a school-aged boy, used a language of purity when talking about when her son was first born: "Just realizing you have this baby who was just born. He was pretty pure, if you want to look at it that way, and I want to try and keep it that way, if possible." She surmised that this was the case for a lot of parents in her social circle: "I think having children really is a tipping point for a lot of people. They will start buying organic milk for their children, or they will buy organic vegetables." Mothers like Naomi feel it is their job to keep their children "pure" for as long as possible because the stakes of feeding children are so very high. Kannitha felt the same way, and she came up with a plan to manage precautionary consumption on a middle-class budget that was fairly common among the women I interviewed. She bought organic foods only for her children, and she and her husband ate conventional food. She justified this plan using the language of precautionary consumption: "It feels just almost like precaution. In their lifetime, I'm sure they're going to get some bad stuff, . . . and I'd rather have them get a good start before that happens."

Most of the mothers I interviewed saw the beginning of life as a moment of total purity; they described their babies as largely untouched by industrial pollution and talked about the future of their newborns as still in the making. They felt that contamination had less to do with a polluted external environment that contaminated all bodies (their own and their children's) and more to do with their individual, personal choices—the food they chose to put in their babies' mouths, as Marcy put it. Both Marcy and Kannitha used the language of precaution in their interviews. Because the impact of the consumer landscape on children's health is impossible to predict, these women considered precaution to be the best solution to such high-stakes uncertainty.

Beyond feeding a child "pure" food, the project of starting a child "from scratch" involves trying to predict and control other kinds of risks that are also beyond a parent's personal control. Fiona, for example, was concerned about epigenetic mutations from chemical exposures. Epigenetic mutations are changes in gene activity that do not alter genetic makeup but can have an effect on embodied traits and biological processes, including the emergence of disease.[40] The DOHaD model, discussed in chapter 3, envisions epigenetic mutations as the primary mechanism that sets future disease states in motion.[41] As Fiona explained to me, "If I can control certain risks, I'm going to control them for [my son's] well-being. I'm thinking about his brain development. I'm thinking about his whole body development. I'm thinking about, if I give him this, is he going to be more likely to get cancer, a childhood cancer, or cancer when he's eighty? I don't want that for him. I want him to be as healthy as possible." Turning to the issue of chemicals, she added, "We don't know what the impact of these chemicals will be for him ten years from now."

Fiona's comments point to how managing risks to children involves envisioning all threats to a child's future and feeling wholly responsible for mitigating them. Biomonitoring research, however, tells us that infant bodies contain traces of hundreds of chemicals that are absorbed in utero, so a pure infant body is a false or elusive ideal.[42] The science surrounding the causes of disease like cancer and autism draws on epigenetic explanations for the cause of disease and increasingly points a finger at women's bodies as a child's first environment—an environment that could be rendered "safer" if women applied better health practices earlier in their reproductive life course.[43] Put another way, epigenetic science, in tandem with the DOHaD model, has merely amplified women's feeling of personal responsibility to manage all risks to current and future children, and as mothers like Fiona attest, this responsibility has been incorporated into the everyday calculus and worry surrounding their childrearing.[44]

Importantly, the interviews I conducted illuminate how environmental health movement messages of strengthening regulation are overshadowed by the far more potent discourse of individual, maternal responsibility. The message from advocacy organizations about safe shopping and the message of empowered consumption in the marketplace is that women can actually control their exposure to chemical risk. Compared to the message of regulatory reform, the appeal to do more precautionary consumption has far greater cultural currency in this neoliberal moment.

ILLNESS AS AN ORGANIC AWAKENING

In a neoliberal society, good health, like good mothering, is an individual imperative, and illness is commonly attributed to a person's failure to adopt good health habits. These habits—what Michel Foucault would consider "technologies of the self"—are circulated through health promotion messages that encourage individuals to modify their lifestyles (e.g., by cooking homemade meals) and consumption habits (e.g., by eating more fruits and vegetables and choosing foods low in sugar and fat).[45] Alan Petersen and Deborah Lupton refer to this as the "new public health" that collapses the "distinction between the production of health and the consumption of health."[46] In the new public health era, smart consumption is equated with good health. Precautionary consumption fits well within this model, as it promises exactly this: better health through safer consumption. Accordingly, the women I interviewed viewed precautionary consumption as critical to preventing health problems. For a few, precautionary consumption was also a response to a previous or existing illness, such as cancer, fibroids, or severe allergies. And while health problems initiated this practice, the transition to motherhood intensified it, as mothers hoped to prevent their children from developing the same illnesses or disorders.

Lilly, a married, middle-class, white artist with a school-aged son, was one of the mothers I interviewed who had encountered multiple health problems leading up to her adoption of a highly comprehensive precautionary consumption routine. We met in her apartment one morning while her son was at school. She was busy prepping an organic lamb dinner so it would be ready to put in oven after she picked up her son from school. Lilly worked part-time, and her husband worked long hours at a middle-income job. She did all of the domestic work, including the cooking.

Lilly traced her precautionary consumption routine back to two health crises. The first involved a miscarriage. "I was [in my late thirties] when I got married, and I got pregnant on our honeymoon, but then I had a miscarriage," she explained. "I was completely paranoid because I just didn't want to ever go through that again. Although people said it was common and everything, I was intent on doing whatever I could do." Indeed, about 20 percent of pregnancies end in miscarriage, even among healthy women.[47] Consistent with the logic of the new public health, however, Lilly attributed her miscarriage to personal faults: bad eating and lifestyle habits. She soon picked up *The Organic Pregnancy,* a book coauthored by Alexandra Zissu, who writes for the Moms Clean Air Force website—an environmental health movement organization that produces precautionary consumption advice.[48] She found the book to be full of helpful advice:

> I was . . . concerned about the pregnancy and just want[ed] to make sure everything went well. It was totally shocking for me [to read] things like "Don't

go to the swimming pool, there's all this chlorine. Get an organic mattress." But I was motivated. . . . That book really changed my life, I think. I was like, "Oh my god!" Here, in our culture, you go to college, you meet somebody, you have an engagement party, you have a wedding, you get all made-up [with cosmetics]. Then you go have a baby, and everything is like, "Screech!" All of sudden, you find out about all this stuff, and all the crap that you've been ingesting. . . . It was like a big wake-up call.

Lilly heeded this wake-up call and embraced precautionary consumption. She changed her diet and discarded all of her Chanel makeup ($700 worth of products, she estimated). Lilly's changes signaled her readiness to embrace a cleaner, more precautionary lifestyle as part of preparing for motherhood. Motherhood became a consumer project where concern for the self was replaced by concern for the future child. As Barbara Kingsolver writes in the introduction to *The Organic Pregnancy,* "When someone has taken up residence in your belly, you're forced to slow down and think beyond yourself. First, of your own baby."[49] Several months after adopting these shopping and lifestyle changes, Lilly became pregnant again and gave birth to a healthy son. She attributed her successful pregnancy to these changes.

Two years later, Lilly experienced her second health crisis: breast cancer. This time, it was Lilly's doctor who pointed a finger at Lilly's dietary and lifestyle habits: "My doctor said three words that really changed my life. I always say it *wasn't* 'You have cancer.' It was 'Don't eat pesticides.'" Lilly began listing for me all of the things she had done "wrong" leading up to her diagnosis, including giving up the organic lifestyle she had adopted during pregnancy and eating food for pleasure: "I took a wine tasting class, I had big steaks, I drank wine. I would have a bit of chocolate and [a] croissant every day. I really was trying to lean into food as a source of pleasure and support. It was the perfect storm for cancer." Croissants and chocolate are not toxic, nor are they linked to cancer, but Lilly presented her lifestyle as overly indulgent, such that cancer became the logical consequence for failing to properly discipline her cravings for pleasurable food. Her self-blame aligns with the new public health model's vision of accountability for disease. Precautionary consumption becomes just another strategy of health promotion under this model. Lilly's experience with illness, combined with her sense of responsibility as a mother, made her acutely aware of potential environmental exposures: "I know about the molecules that you breathe in, but I was surprised when I heard that it might be unhealthy to sleep on a mattress with flame retardants or to have your kid in pajamas with flame retardants. It didn't occur to me initially that having something on the person's skin or in their living room could be a problem."

After her diagnosis, Lilly, her son, and her husband drastically changed their lifestyle, but Lilly did all of the actual work of precautionary consumption. She tried to avoid as many chemicals as she possibly could. She and her family drank purified water stored in an expensive glass and a ceramic water cooler to avoid chemical residues from plastic water jugs. She prepared all of her family's meals using certified-organic produce and organic, grass-fed meat. She and her husband slept on an organic mattress, as did her son. She used all nontoxic cleaning products. She made multiple shopping trips every day to find just the right kind of chicken or fish. Many of her actions were in line with advice offered by breast cancer advocacy groups like Silent Spring Institute and Breast Cancer Prevention Partners.[50]

For Lilly, this allocation of time, energy, and money into shopping, feeding, and caring for herself, her husband, and her child was an investment in future health. She acknowledged the extent to which this practice drained her financial resources but found ways to make it work, such as taking a part-time job, dipping into her savings account, and finding a rent-stabilized apartment: "The most terrifying thing about cancer was I knew I'd be okay, but I just didn't know how I was going to implement the lifestyle change on our budget." Lilly mentions the terror of failing at precautionary consumption because she sees it as vital to preventing breast cancer from recurring. She had enough class-based resources that she could accomplish her ideal precautionary consumption routine, but doing so required considerable expense. I delve more deeply into the class privilege of precautionary consumption in the next chapter.

Christine, a low-income, middle-class, married, white mother of two young children, also started practicing precautionary consumption after experiencing health problems, and when her symptoms improved, she adopted this lifestyle for her whole family. From early childhood through college, Christine had been plagued with severe allergies. Recalling her first visit to an allergist, she told me, "I was only using 40 percent of my lung capacity, my breathing was so restricted by my allergies. . . . I started doing allergy shots when I was five years old. I went to kindergarten with a kit full of ice packs for my headaches, allergy shots for my allergies, and over-the-counter medicines for all of my symptoms, and glasses."

After moving to New York City, she and her husband became interested in food and borrowed documentaries about the food system from the local library. They switched their diet to organic food and avoided synthetic chemicals in cosmetics and cleaning products. Christine's allergy symptoms faded away soon after making these changes, and that increased her desire to raise her children with minimal exposure to synthetic chemicals:

> My kids haven't had any ear infections. They haven't had a lot of the common sicknesses that kids go through. They haven't had that. My younger son, he's three, he's never had an ear infection, . . . and that's been really motivating to keep doing it. Just to see them not get sick when their friends are sick. . . . I still get colds, but when I was growing up, and until I started eating healthy, I had a sinus infection or upper respiratory infection almost always. . . . Seeing my kids not have to go through that is really exciting.

Precautionary consumption offers Lilly and Christine an escape from their illnesses and a sense of security that they will not return. Their own experiences with illness made them even more dedicated to precautionary consumption when they became mothers and were not responsible just for preventing their own illnesses from returning but also for safeguarding their children's health.

CONCLUSION

Precautionary consumption seemed normal to many of the mothers I spoke with because of its overlap with the thin ideal, contemporary mothering ideologies, and the neoliberal logic of personal responsibility for health. For many young women today, the healthy body is not only thin, youthful, and fertile but also "clean"—and attaining this ideal requires a concerted project of careful consumption of food and personal care products. Striving for this body started in earnest when women first began doing their own cooking and food shopping—a time when they learned to read nutrition and ingredient labels. Men's responsibility in the reproductive equation and responsibility for family health was nearly always defined as temporary and secondary to women's concerted project of precautionary consumption.

While onerous, precautionary consumption provided women with a sense of control over a largely intangible threat to their children's health. As a self-directed project, it reinforced a powerful feeling of accomplishment. For many women, the addition of yet another responsibility was offset by a feeling of control acquired through greater "freedom of choice."[51] Through the expansion of choice over the possibilities for managing exposure to chemical risk, the mothers I spoke with felt some control over their children's future health.[52] Precautionary consumption involves navigating multiple and overlapping contexts that hold mothers accountable for their own health and their children's chemical body burdens and praise the agentic, proactive consumer.

Most of the women profiled in this chapter were able to experience precautionary consumption as a worthwhile practice that "good" mothers do because they had sufficient household income to afford organic foods and nontoxic products and enough time to learn about chemical avoidance and research best practices, organize shopping trips to economize on eco-friendly purchases, and read ingredient labels carefully. Many also had easy access to commercial spaces that sell certified-organic food and nontoxic products. For upper-middle- and middle-class shoppers, precautionary consumption is less a function of informed choice (something that is widely celebrated by companies like Whole Foods Market and the brands it sells) and more about class privilege.

But how do mothers who do not have these resources manage precautionary consumption? I turn to this question in the next chapter by focusing on the classed and racial privileges that make precautionary consumption easier and delving into the experiences of low-income and working-class mothers who struggle, for various reasons, to implement precautionary consumption.

Precautionary Consumption
as a Class Act

Marc&mark teaches nannies of affluent parents how to prepare healthful, organic meals that don't come frozen or under plastic wrap. "Some of these nannies already do the cooking in the family, but they're throwing chicken fingers in the oven, or worse, the microwave—they're doing the bare minimum," Mr. Leandro said. In today's foodie culture, in which some fifth graders would rather feast on hand-delivered lunches of locally procured salmon over turkey on rye, the company is playing to moneyed, obsessive parents striving to tutor their children's palate much the way they would their math skills.

CAROLINE TELL, *New York Times*

Stories like this one—of rich parents who spare no expense in giving their children the best of everything, including local, organic food—contribute to a kind of stereotype of precautionary consumption that I frequently encounter in talking to academic audiences about this practice. To be sure, to engage in precautionary consumption, an individual needs enough money to afford more expensive food and personal care products, access to stores that sell these products, and the time and know-how to sift through an overwhelming amount of information designating "safe" and "unsafe" ingredients. However, precautionary consumption is not solely a project of upper-class mothers. Several women I interviewed had low incomes but still managed to practice fairly comprehensive routines, and their experiences reveal the nuances and complexity of precautionary consumption.

Mothers' approaches to precautionary consumption look very different depending on how much money they have, their access to organic foods and nontoxic goods, how much time they have to read ingredient labels and weigh the costs and benefits of organic food relative to conventional food, and whether their lives can accommodate the mental effort associated with the complex decisions involved in learning and practicing precautionary consumption. Even when the cost of precautionary consumption is manageable, it is an additional domestic responsibility that consumes a mother's time and energy, particularly as the learning curve for this practice is steep. There are ways of reducing this effort, but they typically involve money. Two upper-middle-class mothers that we met in the previous chapter, Abby and Cerena, saved some time and effort by doing most of their shopping at stores that specialized in organic foods. Shopping at these stores meant that they had considerably higher grocery bills than most of the other women I interviewed. Abby and Cerena spent more money to save time and effort, yet they still remained entirely responsible for family foodwork. Middle-class mothers, who were also responsible for all cooking and shopping for their households, did not have the luxury of shopping at specialty food stores. They shopped at multiple grocery stores to find bargains and take advantage of sales. They were able to save money by doing their shopping at two to three supermarkets—such as Costco, a local grocery store, and Whole Foods Market—but making these extra trips took time and effort. Fiona, for example, went to a farmers' market to buy organic meat for her son but bought conventional meat for herself and her husband at a local grocery store. Middle-class women such as Fiona had moderate constraints on choice—constraints that were inconvenient but not stressful or arduous. Working-class and low-income women, in contrast, faced much more limited and, sometimes, stressful choices. They could not afford certain products (such as organic mattresses) and could not adopt certain expensive practices (like replacing plastic storage containers with glass or stainless steel containers). Even so, they managed to piece together moderate and sometimes comprehensive precautionary consumption routines. While the previous chapter discussed how women were introduced to precautionary consumption and the reasons they gave for engaging in it, this chapter narrows in on the class dimensions of precautionary consumption. This exploration reveals the invisible but significant resources that some mothers use to accomplish this practice.

I focus on mothers who contended with low-wage or precarious work, disruptions to family stability, or single parenthood, all of which made precautionary consumption difficult. To be clear, none of the women I interviewed were very low-income or poor (see table A3). All had small incomes from their own paid labor, the paid labor of a spouse or partner, or child support. Some lived in subsidized housing or had spouses who earned government benefits. The mothers I spoke to chose to practice precautionary consumption because they were concerned about their children's health. Caring about consumption in this particular way allows women to lay claim to the status of the good, caring mother—a status that is so often denied working-class, low-income, and single mothers.[1] This chapter demonstrates the tremendous pressures all mothers, regardless of social class, feel to protect their children from chemical exposures.

IT'S EXPENSIVE TO EAT PURE

It stands to reason that it is nearly impossible for those living in poverty to practice precautionary consumption.[2] Market survey research suggests that for women with household incomes less than $25,000 a year, purchasing organic products drops to the bottom of priority list. But when household income is above that amount, buying organic is a moderately important priority, regardless of whether it is $50,000 a year or above $100,000 a year.[3] The price premium for organic food products has dropped over time, but it still ranges from 7 to 82 percent, depending on the item.[4] Many conventional supermarkets, like Aldi, Kroger, Shop Rite, and Safeway, now sell organic foods and have their own lower-cost, generic organic brands. But even with a modest price premium, organic food is not a choice for families who cannot meet basic living expenses. Moreover, food assistance programs like Women, Infants, and Children (WIC) do not allow for the purchase of many organic foods, including organic baby food,[5] and access to grocery stores that sell fresh food, let alone certified-organic food, is limited in some parts of the United States, particularly in rural areas, low-income neighborhoods, and minority neighborhoods.[6] In New York City, where I conducted much of the research for this book, access to fresh food has improved because of programs designed to draw in supermarkets and fresh produce vendors. In 2008, for example, the city began issuing licenses to street vendors through what is called the Green Cart program, which brought more fruits and vegetables to the city's street corners.[7] A year later, the city offered financial incentives for supermarkets to open in poor neighborhoods.[8] Whole Foods Market has expanded in New York City, with twelve stores as of July 2017, and while this has undoubtedly improved access to organic food for some residents, the new stores have opened in affluent or rapidly gentrifying neighborhoods. In the low-income neighborhoods of South Bronx and east Brooklyn, grocery stores, and stores selling organic food in particular, remain hard to find.[9]

Even though access and affordability are barriers to precautionary consumption, the picture I paint in this chapter pushes back against the assumption that low-income women never buy organic foods and upper-middle-class women drop wads of cash at Whole Foods Market and their local farmers' markets. Several women in my sample defied this depiction. Precautionary consumption can be affordable—to a point.

Sarah, for instance, an Asian American, working-class, single mother of a teenage daughter, bought some organic foods and cooked most of her meals from scratch. Her ex-husband worked in the food business, and he introduced her to organic foods. Buying organic became a priority for Sarah after a childhood friend died from pesticide exposure. Sarah grew up in a farming community but had not reflected on the dangers associated with farmworkers' pesticide exposures until her friend's death. Deeply saddened by the event, she considered how, as a consumer, she contributed to farmworkers' daily exposure to pesticides. This led her to rework her small budget to buy more organic food. Even though she worked in retail, she managed to do this because she lived in an affordable apartment in Queens and received some child support from her husband. Her coworkers, in contrast, did not have these same privileges, and while they were eager to buy more organic food, their wages were too low to do so. Sarah told me that she had one coworker who bought organic food if she had enough money for that week: "[But when] she's in a pinch, just like every parent, I guess, she will succumb to McDonald's. But [organic is] not on the top of her list if your kid is complaining and you just want to get something in their stomach."

Leanne, a married, working-class Latina mother of a toddler, grew up in a low-income family in the Bronx. Many of her family members bought conventional, processed foods because they were affordable. Leanne worked three days a week while she finished her college degree, so she did not have extra money to spare on organic food: "I really want to purchase organic stuff for my family, but at times I can't afford it." Leanne told me that she had recently gone to the store to buy an organic broiler chicken, but when she found that an organic chicken was eighteen dollars while a conventional chicken was seven dollars, less than half the price, she settled for the conventional chicken. She had a list of foods she prefers to buy organic, but she would only buy them if they were on sale or the same price as the conventional variety. Leanne had access to a well-stocked discount grocery store a few miles from her home. She had a car and could drive to the store to stock up on groceries for the week. The foods she bought were affordable and fresh but rarely organic. A short distance away from this store is a large, suburban Whole Foods Market. Leanne told me that although she loves Whole Foods Market, it is out of reach for her:

> My ideal place would, honestly, be to shop at Whole Foods. I went to Whole Foods maybe once or twice last year to pick up something small, like their oatmeal and stuff like that, but just walking down the aisles [I see that] they have so many options and so many different things that you don't really see in just a regular supermarket. They have a whole lot of sections of organic food, grass-fed meat, and so forth. Their prices are honestly a little bit ridiculous if you just are on a set income—and I'm only working three days. If I was working full-time and I could afford that, I would honestly just shop there.

If she had more money, Leanne would do *all* of her shopping at Whole Foods Market. A diet of all organic food is a luxury for Leanne and she considers Whole Foods Market to be an ideal shopping space because it offers a large choice of organic commodities and sells specialty foods that are difficult to find in other supermarkets.

Not all women I interviewed had access to a large discount grocery store. Many did not have a car and lived in Manhattan, Brooklyn, or Queens, where Whole Foods Market offered more organic foods at lower prices compared to the smaller supermarkets in these neighborhoods. These women did not buy all of their groceries at Whole Foods Market; instead, they learned how to navigate the store to locate the low-cost items.

One of these women was Ellen, a Black, married, working-class mother of two daughters. Her husband was between jobs when we talked, and the family struggled to make ends meet on Ellen's small income from her job as a clerical worker. Even so, Ellen relied on buying fresh produce at Whole Foods Market. We sat down during her lunch break at a busy café near her workplace, and she told me her story of coming to the United States from the Caribbean, turning to processed food for convenience, and then changing her diet after suffering from endometriosis. Her endometriosis was so severe that her husband began investigating homemade remedies. He decided that they should eat more fresh vegetables and greens, like kale, and use more turmeric and apple cider vinegar in recipes to reduce inflammation and cleanse the body. As the one responsible for all of the food shopping and cooking, Ellen implemented this change and was pleased when the symptoms of her endometriosis subsided. Even though this new diet incorporated more fresh and organic foods and was aimed at improving her overall well-being, it meant that she had to give up her favorite Caribbean foods, such as fried conch (a type of seafood), and change the menu of typical weeknight dinners to incorporate more vegetables and fewer carbohydrates. Laughing, she recalled hosting her husband's friend, also from the Caribbean, who teased Ellen when she served potatoes, a green salad, and a small serving of meat: "I served it and he's going, 'Where's the food?' . . . When he's finished, he's like, 'That's the appetizer?' I said, 'No, I promise you, that's not considered an appetizer!' For the man, especially. They must have lots of rice, a big piece of meat, potato salad, macaroni—three starches, three carbohydrates, and meat. So he said, 'Where's the food?'"

Not only was this way of eating disconnected from Ellen's traditional foodways, it also strained her budget, especially because she was feeding a family of four and shopping in her low-income neighborhood in Brooklyn, where fresh vegetables were expensive. To save money, she decided to start shopping at the Whole Foods Market close to her office. She planned her shopping trips strategically, buying items on sale at Whole Foods Market and everything else at her local supermarket. Every week, Ellen checked the Whole Foods Market flyer and planned her shopping around what was on sale. Ellen enjoyed the store and spoke of the good taste of organic food, and she wished she could buy more of it. Yet she had to limit what she bought: "I'm trying not to go over budget. That's why I don't buy a lot of organic." She laughed, "It's expensive to eat pure."

As much as Ellen liked Whole Foods Market, she distanced herself from "other" Whole Foods Market shoppers, who, she claimed, go to the store because of its status as an elite shopping space: "Shopping there is about status. It makes people feel good to shop there. These are the ones who fill their carts with everything, even their toilet paper!" I interpret Ellen's comments as her way of marking herself as a budget-savvy Whole Foods Market shopper, but they are also a commentary on the social class divisions within this retail space. Whereas Ellen had to watch every penny she spent at Whole Foods Market, the shoppers around her seemed to have no trouble filling their carts with expensive organic and gourmet items. Her decision to shop there, Ellen reasoned, is not only savvy but also responsible; otherwise, she would be paying for medication and doctors to treat her endometriosis. The cost of shopping at Whole Foods Market, she says, is "definitely higher. But when you compare it to the cost of getting sick and medication, it's low in comparison. . . . But before, the things that we bought were much cheaper." As I showed in chapter 4, Whole Foods Market actively cultivates this sense of personal responsibility for health, casting itself as the solution to the country's health problems.

For another woman I interviewed, eating "pure" had been a pleasure that she had enjoyed as part of a middle-class life, but it ended when hard times hit. Chitra, a South Asian, low-income, single mother of a preschooler, experienced a major slide down the class ladder that required her to make a significant change in her food shopping and diet. When we met for our interview she had an afternoon free—a rare occasion for a single mother working multiple part-time jobs and attending school part-time. Born in India, Chitra grew up in the Middle East and settled in New York City in her early twenties. Before becoming a mother, she had a professional job with a generous salary, but it was stressful and required long hours and international travel. After meeting her partner, she became pregnant and left her job, thinking that she would switch careers after spending some time at home with the baby. But a few weeks after her son's birth, Chitra's life changed. Hurricane Sandy hit New York City, and her home in Queens was destroyed. She separated from her partner, and she and her baby lived in temporary shelters and short-term apartments for four years before she was able to find a rent-stabilized apartment in Manhattan.

Precautionary consumption was a privilege that Chitra had enjoyed in her "previous" life—when she had a professional job, a good income, and a nice home. At that time, Chitra ate a raw, organic food diet. She cooked her own meals and paid attention to everything she put in her body. She told me that her body had been fit, strong, and healthy. After becoming a mother and then losing her home, relationship, and job prospects, she could no longer afford organic food, and she relied on WIC benefits to feed her son. As much as she wanted to buy organic food, she could not, owing to her low income and restrictions put in place by WIC: "You can't use [WIC] vouchers in Whole Foods and TJ's [Trader Joe's]. . . . Unfortunately, with WIC, you cannot get organic milk; I don't know why. They've made fruits and vegetables organic. And yogurt, you can get organic with WIC. But somehow, you can't buy all kinds of dairy. Cheese and milk is not organic. Their explanation is: 'Well, there's not enough evidence that it really makes a difference.'"

It was not only the expense of organic food that bothered Chitra but also the fact that her son had stopped eating the only healthy foods she *could* afford: "It's frustrating because I used to give him everything, fruits and vegetables, he used to eat everything, and then all of a sudden he wants sugar all of the time." The middle-class mothers I interviewed similarly complained about their children's refusal to eat vegetables, but this challenge was personally painful for Chitra. As the women profiled in chapter 5 demonstrate, having a child who loves vegetables is the hallmark of good, middle-class motherhood. But low-income mothers struggle to afford fresh vegetables and risk wasting these vegetables if their children are reluctant to eat them.[10] Chitra attributed her son's refusal to eat fresh fruits and vegetables to changes in her own eating habits as a result of her stressful life. In contrast to the raw food diet she had maintained in her previous life, she now craved comfort foods like pasta, bagels, pastries, and dairy products—foods that she had rarely eaten when she was an employed professional. "There tends to be— honestly, it's very bad—an element of sugar in all my food," she explained, "because I'm using sugar as my saving grace, my energy." Chitra observed how these foods made her feel lethargic soon after eating them but offered a fast, easy escape from the stress of juggling multiple jobs, having little money, and single parenting. Changing these eating patterns seemed insurmountable to Chitra: "I'd be better off without the breads, without the gluten, . . . and [without] the sugar. . . . I know there's other options, but they're damn expensive, and I can't afford them." Chitra felt she had so little time to prepare healthful meals, and when she was not working, she was exhausted and emotionally drained: "In fact, it's crazy I don't know how to cook even one meal a day. I wish I could do that, but I just cannot do it. . . . Yeah it's hard. And then you feel guilty. I mean moms have a lot of guilt. This is just one of them to add to the big bucket."

A raw food, organic diet, though totally inaccessible for Chitra, still remained central to her identity. But because she could no longer afford this diet, she saw herself as a hypocrite:

> A lot of people, ironically, find me healthy and health oriented, which is really weird. Probably because I know so much. Even though I feel like I'm a hypocrite inside, I'm still able to talk about it, and I know I'm on the way to recovering, to turning things around and doing things like joining the gym and doing the gardening. Those are all intertwined and they motivate me. These are my motivators. I'm basically laying the brick and mortar for a comeback.

Chitra's shift in class status from middle-class to low-income required her to give up precautionary consumption. Her reference to a "comeback" is a comment on her slide down the class ladder and her desire to move back up. Her sense of loss and her feelings of guilt reflect the fragility of class status during neoliberal times, when a person's sense of self-worth is tied to paid work and the loss of class status is understood as personal failure rather than the consequence of structural conditions. Chitra viewed her life circumstances as the outcome of bad choices, not as the consequence of having few social and structural supports to assist her recovery from a natural disaster, a separation, and unemployment.

Chitra's interview not only illuminates the feelings of failure mothers experience when they do not live up to middle-class ideals of mothering, but also reveals how precautionary consumption requires much more than income. Investing in special diets, reading labels, and forgoing foods that are deemed "bad" because of their high sugar content—these actions require a great deal of *work*. When life is stressful, particularly due to temporary housing, a low income, and the lack of a supportive partner to help raise a child, there is no extra time or energy to put effort into precautionary consumption. Chitra experienced stress from her difficult life conditions, and public health research suggests that when individuals are stressed from a combination of overwork, lack of sleep, family responsibilities, poverty, household conflict, or neighborhood violence, they experience cognitive overload that influences their food choices.[11] They are more likely to turn to energy-dense, easy-to-eat foods that provide them with a sense of immediate pleasure. These choices reflect structural conditions that inflict stress on individuals, not necessarily a lack of choice of good supermarkets or a poor understanding of how to eat "well."

INVESTING TIME

Contrast Chitra's experience with those of Christine and Dahlia, two white, lower-income mothers who managed to accomplish comprehensive precautionary consumption. Although money was tight, they were able to take advantage of flexible time to accomplish this routine. These women invested time and energy into becoming the best experts of their own children—a job that mothers take on in response to intense social pressure to produce healthy, pure, and perfect children.[12]

Christine, introduced in chapter 5, described having severe respiratory problems and chronic allergies before she started practicing precautionary consumption. She grew up in a middle-class family in the Midwest, but she had lived on a low income since moving away from home. She worked part-time in education, and her husband did not work due to a permanent disability. He recently became eligible for disability benefits, and until his benefits came through, the family depended on Supplemental Nutrition Assistance Program (SNAP, or food stamps) to buy groceries. Despite her family's meager income, Christine practiced a comprehensive form of precautionary consumption. She bought almost all organic foods and cooked most of the family's meals from scratch. She bought nontoxic personal care and cleaning products and made some of these products herself.

When I asked Christine how she managed her routine on a low income while also caring for young children and working part-time, she told me that she was able to invest *time* in practicing precautionary consumption, including learning the basics of this practice and doing price comparisons while shopping:

> I would say something that was really important, besides the learning curve and the slow transition to swapping brands and then eliminating that product completely, was the time it took reading labels. . . . It's exhausting. I can still easily spend an hour and a half at the store buying five things. Having a smaller budget and having every product impacting our budget, I have to take into consideration the unit price. Per pound, or per pint, or per pill, how much is the unit price? I have to compare the integrity of the product. I have to read the labels, look up what other people are saying. I have the Amazon price compare app. You can scan it [a product], and it pulls it up on Amazon and tells you how much it is on Amazon.

The investment of time to calculate unit prices requires a kind of mental space to be thoughtful about consumption choices; it involves reading price tags and ingredient labels and weighing the benefits of buying a more expensive organic item against the risks of buying a cheaper but more toxic item. What I have learned from interviewing mothers for this and other studies is that an initial investment of time, where a shopper has the mental space to learn to "read" the retail landscape, is essential to building an efficient shopping routine that saves them time down the road.[13] Several of the women profiled in chapter 5 spoke of how the learning curve for precautionary consumption was steep, requiring a lot of time and effort. But once they learned what brands were "good" and affordable, their routines became comparatively easy. Of course, this is the logic of neoliberal risk management: consumers must educate themselves to make the best decisions and reduce their exposure to risk. But good choices depend on underlying social, economic, and political contexts. Individuals who are already worse off cannot simply avoid chemical exposures or pull themselves out of economic distress or poverty by becoming better consumers and "making better choices."[14] My sample does not capture women living in poverty, but it does include women with lower incomes. Their cultural capital, benefits from social programs, and support of another adult in the home, gave them flexible time and cognitive energy to think about precautionary consumption, which they could leverage to work around the financial constraints in their lives.

Christine exemplified the lower-income, middle-class shopper with these extra resources. Even with a low household income and a husband unable to work because of a long-term disability, her middle-class upbringing provided her with cultural capital in the form of consumer confidence and the skill to simultaneously economize and sort through a lot of information about toxicity and quality of products. Her husband's disability benefits freed Christine from the constraints of a SNAP food budget. Still, their income was not much for a family of four, so she shopped at four different stores, each offering a unique discount on a certain category of organic food. She shopped at Costco for fruits, vegetables, and frozen products; a local big box store and Trader Joe's for nonperishable items; and at Whole Foods Market for everything else. If she could find a better price for a food product on Amazon, she would order it on her phone. Christine knew the price-per-unit weight or volume of the products she bought and was able to stretch her small budget to accommodate a comprehensive precautionary consumption routine. She used whatever free and flexible time she had to shop for the lowest-cost organic products and to sort through labels, logos, and ingredient lists to determine the "truthfulness" of precautionary claims.

Christine had this time because of her flexible, part-time work schedule and her supportive husband who was at home and could care for the children while she shopped, meaning that she could shop alone. Without the pressure of addressing children's physical and emotional needs during grocery shopping, she could expend extra energy comparing prices and reading ingredient lists. Shopping alone is a major advantage in the realm of consumption. Combining domestic work like shopping and cleaning with childcare makes this work more stressful, difficult, and time consuming.[15]

Christine also learned about precautionary consumption *before* having children, meaning that she became "literate" in the intricacies of precautionary consumption before she had to juggle additional responsibilities. The stress of a "learning curve," as she put it, came at a moment when she had free time but not necessarily more money. When she gave birth to her first child,

Christine had already done background research on what to buy, making precautionary consumption for her new infant automatic and relatively easy.

Dahlia, a married, white, low-income mother of three children, also had flexible time to accomplish a comprehensive precautionary consumption routine on a low income. Her husband was a college student, and their family relied on SNAP benefits to pay for groceries. They lived in a one-bedroom apartment in an affordable neighborhood in New York City, which meant her husband had to take a long subway ride to get to school. Dahlia did not work outside the home, but she homeschooled her three children and did all of the cooking and planning for grocery shopping. Her husband did most of the actual shopping, stopping at the supermarket on his way home from school.

Dahlia told me of how she had earned a college degree before becoming a mother and had learned about organic food production in college, where she also became interested in healthy eating. After having a child, Dahlia registered for free cooking classes at her local food pantry and learned about baking, canning, and fermentation. She used those skills to stretch her limited SNAP benefits: "It's really challenging when you get a sporadic amount every month and you're trying not to eat processed food. It's amazing how much less processed food costs than whole foods." Like other women in this study, Dahlia justified spending the family's food assistance dollars on organic food by referring to how her investment was protecting her children's future health:

> You really have to make priorities when you have a limited income. Buying healthy food is really important to me and for my children. I feel like that's one of the best things I can do for them—besides making them not be jerks. I'm helping their bodies to be as strong as possible.... [My husband and I] had discussions about it when we were first trying to figure out the finances of it. Like, 'Organic is so much more expensive. Is this the right choice?' Thinking about what we would rather spend our money on: good, healthy food, or down the road spend it on healthcare stuff. We both really see the connection between taking care of our bodies and our health. If you're going to put junk in your car, you're going to have engine troubles.

Dahlia increased her consumption of organic foods once she became pregnant, as she worried that chemicals in her food would affect the development of the fetus. She internalized the responsibility for health and saw it as an individual choice—one that could be made by paying attention to her budget and ranking her priorities.

Her husband did the actual grocery shopping, but like the mothers profiled in the previous chapter, Dahlia made the shopping list and specified
exactly what brands he should buy and where he should buy them. Her lists
were planned strategically to save money. She knew where to find the most
affordable organic food in the city. Some foods were more affordable at
Whole Foods Market; others were cheaper at Trader Joe's. She would occasionally buy products at the local farmers' market when she knew the prices
and quality would be good. Good quality organic food was not readily available in her neighborhood, so all of her groceries came from stores that were
close to her husband's college, which was in a higher-income neighborhood
with more choice in supermarkets.

As a married, white, college-educated mother, Dahlia could safely occupy
the role of homemaker in a low-income family that collected SNAP benefits.
She described herself as a willing stay-at-home mother who had chosen motherhood as a "job." Part of this job was to invest in precautionary consumption
by making meals from scratch, finding the best price on organic foods, and
educating her children about healthy eating:

> I consider it my job description to be a mom. Knowing that what I do takes a
> lot of resources and mental energy and time. . . . It takes a lot of brainpower to
> think about. I feel like I also have this body of knowledge related to little
> things that I committed to over time because I've had a specific interest in
> this, and so it's stuck more, . . . and I'm passionate about it, and it's something
> I really think is important.

Having the choice to stay home with one's children is itself a privilege, especially for a low-income family. Dahlia was aware of this privilege, remarking
that her family's low-income status was temporary. Eventually, her husband
would finish school and get paid work.

The intensive aspects of childcare, such as precautionary consumption, are
not always viewed by mothers as onerous.[16] Mothers like Dahlia consider
their investment of time and effort as part of a deliberate project of raising
children, a stance that draws heavily on the ideology of intensive mothering.[17] Intensive mothering demands that mothers invest themselves completely in the lives of their children as part of raising them to be emotionally
secure and healthy adults, but this can come at the expense of mothers' own
leisure time and well-being.[18] Rather than complain about the work of precautionary consumption, Dahlia told me that she enjoyed the time she spends
figuring out what to buy and where to buy it:

It's tricky, but I enjoy it. Do you know what I mean? It's like a puzzle, and it's something that I enjoy doing, figuring out. When I write a list for my husband, I do it by section of the grocery because for . . . that kind of thing, it's like filling out a form. It fits my personality really well, and it's one way for me to feel like I am contributing. It satisfies me, and it also makes me feel like I'm contributing to my family's well-being.

For Dahlia and Christine, extra time was a resource that allowed them to cook healthy, homemade food and craft complex but affordable shopping routines. They swapped paid work for intensive mothering, which included the practice of precautionary consumption. Coming from middle-class backgrounds, these women could take risks lower-income women could not. This is a privilege not available to most other low-income families, where mothers must work to feed their families and have little extra time to cook or compare the prices of organic items. These mothers turn to processed foods, and when they cannot get to an affordable supermarket, they must rely on a local shop, which may offer undesirable but convenient foods.[19]

LOOKING TO THE UPPER CLASS

Of all of the interviews I conducted, one of the most illuminating for revealing the intersection of race, class, and gender in precautionary consumption was the interview I did with Hannah, a Black, working-class, single mother of an adult son and a five-year-old daughter. We met for our interview near the end of the school day at a café a block away from her daughter's school. Hannah had a well-paid part-time job at a restaurant and lived in a rent-controlled apartment in Manhattan. When she first became a mother, twenty years ago, Hannah had not thought about organic food or worried much about chemicals. She was newly married, young, and overwhelmed at the time, and it had not been on her mind. When her son turned five, she enrolled him in daycare and began working as a nanny in a wealthy neighborhood in Brooklyn. Once immersed in this white, upper-class environment, she began to observe how organic food was part of a larger array of practices meant to provide children with the very best. She recalled this time very clearly:

I met these British nannies, and they taught me so much. They went to these expensive nanny schools in England. They were so intelligent and so smart, and I just learned so much from them. . . . This was a mainly white [neighborhood], and they only feed their kids the best. The parents are wealthy. They live in a whole brownstone, and they're feeding their kids the best. They're going to the butcher and getting the best meats. They're buying organic foods. . . . Even if it isn't organic, it might be natural, and they're not sending their kids to McDonald's. They're not feeding their kids this stuff. Along with their diet, they're educating them.

In the case of food, the "best" is local and certified organic. The "worst" food, Hannah suggested, is fast food. Realizing that she had much to learn about parenting, Hannah started reading about organic food and healthy lifestyles. At the time, she had separated from her husband and had little money and no access to a computer. So on her days off she took her son to a Barnes & Noble bookstore in her neighborhood. While he played and read children's books, she browsed books about organic lifestyles and natural child-rearing. These books emphasized that providing children with organic food was just as important as cultivating other aspects of children's growth and development, such as encouraging reading in very young children. She tried applying what she learned to her five-year-old son but eventually gave up because she believed that you had to "get all of this stuff into your kids by the age of two." Hannah's belief that she had somehow missed the opportunity to give her son the "right" upbringing reflects the unforgiving discourse of early childhood development that specifies windows of opportunity that must be seized. According to this discourse, if these windows are missed, a child will be at risk for everything from depression and disease to low educational attainment and learning disabilities.[20]

A decade later, Hannah became pregnant with her daughter, and she immediately began to implement all that she had learned about organic food and lifestyles. Her dedication to precautionary consumption increased "tenfold," in her words. She drew on the same language of childhood innocence that I observed among other mothers I interviewed. "I just wanted her to be as pure as possible, her body to be as pure as possible," she told me. "I didn't want her to have junk in her body, because what is in the inside shows on the outside." Hannah fed her daughter mainly certified-organic food and very few processed foods. She made all of her daughter's meals from scratch and always packed a homemade lunch for her to take to school. Although her son (who was twenty years old at the time of our interview) still lived at home, Hannah explained that, because he was fully independent, he shopped for his own food and made his own meals, which largely involved heating up processed foods like frozen pizzas and burritos.

Hannah's affordable housing and the high hourly wage she earned from her job at an upper-class restaurant allowed her to work part-time and use her remaining time to care for her children. This care involved shopping for the best deals on organic foods. Like Dahlia, she went to Costco for the cheaper organic items available there and to Whole Foods Market for items that were not available at Costco. She also saved money by making meals from scratch—something she could do in the afternoons and evenings when she was not working. She told me that her food budget consumed most of her income, but she presented this as a deliberate choice: "I spend way too much money on all this stuff, and I really can't afford it, but my priorities are food. Everything else falls by the wayside. I don't need any more clothes. I don't need any more shoes. I just need healthy food for my child." Hannah drew attention to how Whole Foods Market has a reputation of being an expensive grocery store but framed the store in a positive way—as a place that allowed her to implement her standards of healthy eating: "I mean, everyone calls it 'Whole Paycheck' because it's really expensive, but I feel like if I get the organic healthy foods that I want, it shouldn't matter the price." She could balance her budget but was aware that not all people could:

> I know a lot of people cannot afford to eat this way [or] shop this way.... I don't do drugs. I've never done drugs in my life. I don't smoke. I don't drink. I drink socially if I go out. I rarely go out. I don't spend money on bad vices. I would say this is my vice: getting healthy, organic foods. I would rather spend my money on that than on going out, than on cigarettes, than on shopping for clothing.

Hannah's comment about alcohol, drugs, and "vices" could be viewed as a statement about the scrutiny she endures as a Black, working-class, single mother. Her account is consistent with what sociologist Patricia Hill Collins calls "controlling images," or deeply held stereotypes, of Black single mothers, which are damaging and negative. Hannah alludes to the image that Collins refers to as "the welfare queen"—a materialistic, irresponsible, and self-absorbed mother who cares more about her own vices than her children's well-being.[21]

In contrast to white mothers, who are labeled as caring and knowledgeable for buying organic food for their children, Black mothers, and especially Black single mothers, can expect additional scrutiny when they spend money on expensive foods. Sociologist Joslyn Brenton, who has studied foodwork among a diverse group of Southern women, writes that organic food, health food, and retail spaces like Whole Foods Market are typically read as white spaces.[22] That is not to say that women of color reject these spaces; rather, the cultural marking of stores like Whole Foods Market as white spaces is integral to contextualizing how women of color position themselves as organic food consumers.

For Hannah, precautionary consumption aligned with concerted cultivation—the intensive investment of time and energy into extracurricular and enrichment activities for children.[23] She told me that she enrolled her daughter in the "best" extracurricular activities, including tennis and Chinese language classes: "What's important is educating my daughter. She's a girl. She's going to get paid 75 cents for every dollar a man makes, so she needs to be double as smart as the average person, as the average man. You know what I mean? It's all about education." Hannah was emphatic that her strategy of prioritizing organic food had paid off, describing her daughter's excellent health and growth and her success at school. The white upper-middle and middle-class mothers in my study did not highlight fears of discrimination for their children, nor did they list their children's accomplishments so openly. In fact, they were more likely to cite their own failures as mothers, as we saw in chapter 5 with women like Marcy, who felt that she was failing at motherhood every day. Because normative motherhood is coded as white, heterosexual, and middle class, mothers that fit this category feel considerably secure to speak freely about their perceived failures without being labeled "bad." In fact, for these mothers, disparaging one's own parenting may be a way of avoiding the label of the "too perfect mother."

Hannah practiced precautionary consumption because she had flexible time, consumer literacy to implement a complex routine, and moderate financial security. Precautionary consumption was a very deliberate choice that she made after being immersed in a white, upper-class habitus that represented to her the very best way to raise children and the path to class mobility. The stakes of raising her daughter are high because, as Hannah put it, her daughter competes on an unequal playing field.

CONCLUSION

An ethos of neoliberalism undergirds the landscape of precautionary consumption, requiring not only money to make good risk avoiding choices but also time to sort out the best choices, as well as sufficient mental energy to ponder precautionary consumption and then enact it. The women I profile in this chapter show how the imperative for precautionary consumption is based on upper-middle- and middle-class assumptions of flexible choice, time, and creative budgeting. Women living on the margins of normative motherhood because of their class status or race are not shut out of precautionary consumption. But they are required to work harder to actualize it than upper-middle-class and middle-class women. Precautionary consumption is a resource-intensive practice; it demands material resources as well as time and cognitive effort. One of these resources can be swapped for another or combined to make precautionary consumption easier. For instance, when money is tight, mothers like Dahlia and Christine draw on their flexible time and unpaid labor to stretch their dollars further by shopping at multiple stores to find bargains on organic foods and nontoxic goods, cooking meals from scratch, or making homemade cleaners or cosmetics. When time is tight but money is not, women like Abby and Cerena shop at health food stores or Whole Foods Market to simplify the work of precautionary consumption. Importantly, precautionary consumption requires, at a minimum, a great deal of consumer literacy. Women must be comfortable reading and understanding food labels and must also have the opportunity to learn about environmental health issues and the hazards of the industrial food system, typically through online research or social media or by word of mouth via networks of other mothers.

Individuals who lack money, time, and consumer literacy are therefore in a disadvantaged position to practice precautionary consumption. Avoiding toxic exposures is less about a lack of individual willingness to avoid toxics and more about larger, structural factors outside an individual's direct control. Women without stable employment, the help of another parent or caregiver, child support, or educational attainment that would make navigating the grocery store somewhat easier cannot be expected to also incorporate a regime of precautionary consumption to protect their children from chemicals. Precarious employment, a lack of social and public support for low-income families, and unequal access to quality public education will work against any individual's effort to avoid toxics in the retail landscape. Precautionary consumption cannot escape larger social inequalities, and it should not be the primary mechanism for avoiding chemical exposure—a point I address in the final chapter.

SEVEN

Moving toward Environmental Justice

We as a society should be able to take protective action when scientific evidence indicates a chemical is of concern, and not wait for unequivocal proof that a chemical is causing harm to our children.

Project Tendr Consensus Statement

This statement, issued by a coalition of forty-seven environmental health scientists, environmental health advocates, and doctors, was published in 2016 in the academic journal *Environmental Health Perspectives* as a national call to action to address ubiquitous environmental chemical pollution. Referred to as the Project Tendr (Targeting Environmental Neuro-Developmental Risks) Consensus Statement, it is a strong declaration of the increasing urgency of widespread chemical pollution. For decades, scientists have known that environmental chemicals are harming human health and the environment, but even while evidence to this effect has strengthened over time, action that would provide collective, population-level protection has failed to materialize.

Instead, precautionary consumption has grown as a key response to mitigating exposure to tens of thousands of untested, potentially harmful chemicals used in our food and consumer products. The popularity of precautionary consumption is the result of several major social, economic, political, and scientific developments that began more than a century ago, starting with the expansion of unregulated food, pharmaceutical, and consumer product industries. These sectors put little thought into the safety of their products, and at times they deliberately misled consumers. The federal government has never succeeded in putting into place a strong regulatory system to oversee these industries, and over time this system has become increasingly fractured and ineffective at protecting public health. This responsibility has been handed to women, and mothers especially, who are tasked with righting the wrongs of a long legacy of shoddy regulatory oversight of the chemicals used to grow food, make processed foods, and manufacture consumer goods.

While there is a formal system in place to review chemical hazards, this system uses a proof-of-harm model of safety assessment, which requires evidence of harm before restricting the production of new chemical compounds. As actually practiced, the proof-of-harm model gives short shrift to public health and prioritizes technological innovation and profit. Harmful compounds end up in the environment and retail landscape, and in many instances, even when evidence of harm surfaces, corporations have been able to suppress or delay regulatory action. As scientific evidence of the harm posed by chemical exposure in early life grows and solidifies, mothers' preconception, pregnant and breastfeeding bodies and their labor as caregivers are marked as vectors of chemical risk. Because mothers bear the brunt of protecting future generations from exposure to environmental chemicals, they have little choice but to turn to precautionary consumption for help. Mothers are aware that this practice is an imperfect strategy for protection, but the stakes are high. They know that exposure to environmental chemicals early in life can lead to poor health outcomes in their children, and some view failing to read labels to avoid endocrine disruptors as a failure of responsible motherhood.

A more effective and equitable strategy for protecting all bodies from pollution is to institutionalize the precautionary principle within the regulatory system that governs chemical manufacturing. Under such a system, if a manufacturer cannot prove that a compound is safe, they would not be allowed to bring it to market. This type of system already exists in the European Union, and while it is not immune to industry influence, it has nevertheless prevented some harmful compounds from entering the environment and marketplace.

Since the 1970s, the environmental health movement in the United States has lobbied for the institutionalization of the precautionary principle in American environmental and health policy. Alarmed by wildlife studies revealing reproductive problems caused by low-dose exposures to endocrine disruptors, groups demanded the implementation of a strong precautionary principle in federal environmental policy that would stem the production and release of such compounds before the problems observed in wildlife began appearing in human populations. Government and industry ignored their demand, arguing that the precautionary principle was both antiscientific and antibusiness.

With little success at building an environmental policy framework predicated on the precautionary principle, the environmental health movement set its sight on personalizing the effects of pollution by carrying out advocacy biomonitoring, flagging conventional commodities as dangerous, and teaching individual shoppers (mainly mothers) about the dangers of untested chemicals in their food, cosmetics, and consumer goods. In other words, although the precautionary principle could not be institutionalized in federal law, groups realized that it could be individualized and enacted in day-to-day life, especially at the supermarket. This individualization of the precautionary principle is gendered because it demands women's labor and implicates the domains for which women are accountable, namely caring for the maternal body to ensure the healthiest possible pregnancy, and feeding and caring for infants and children.

Responding to the wave of enthusiasm for green consumerism, the market expanded by offering more organic foods and nontoxic consumer products, and it did so with the implicit support of the environmental health movement, which endeavored to educate consumers on the hazards of the retail landscape. Whole Foods Market, the country's largest health food grocery chain, capitalized on growing consumer awareness of toxics. The company has cornered the market for organic food and nontoxic consumer goods, and the conventional grocery sector has followed Whole Foods Market's lead. Grocery shopping now involves navigating layers of precautionary messaging—in stores and especially on product packages. Under Amazon's ownership, Whole Foods Market seems well positioned to profit from widespread environmental pollution and lax regulation of consumer products, and will most certainly expand the distribution of organic and green products into areas lacking easy access to Whole Foods Market stores.

Mothers are especially likely to turn to the marketplace for organic and green commodities to manage an impossible task: preventing chemicals from entering their bodies and their children's bodies. Middle-class mothers in particular worry that the consequences of chemical trespass will be high, and they take charge of this work in order to do it "right." Mothers practice precautionary consumption in different ways, depending on whether they have extra money to spend on costlier items, the flexible time to shop carefully to find the best prices on organic foods and other items, and the consumer literacy to quickly decode the overwhelming array of labels plastered on product packages and keep track of the large number of chemicals they are told to avoid. Mothers who do not have these resources adopt what few actions they can, but for working-class and low-income mothers, precautionary consumption demands too much time, energy, and money.

Stepping back, we might wonder if precautionary consumption could provide a degree of protection, at least temporarily. Is it also possible that the cumulative effect of multiple consumer actions will scale up, resulting in systemic change? Can consumers influence the principles of chemical innovation and manufacturing? Should mothers be the ones who are responsible for promoting this change?

The mothers I interviewed for this book answered these questions and offered their own interpretation of who should be responsible for the problem of environmental chemicals in food, homes, and bodies. In what follows, I look at their responses and then move on to consider whether precautionary consumption is the most feasible option for protection.

WHO IS RESPONSIBLE?

Precautionary consumption requires individuals to agree to two things: first, they must take responsibility for their exposure to a universal risk, and second, they must be willing and able to pay for private options that allow them to manage this risk. This appears normal in a neoliberal era where individuals are urged to take care of their own exposure to risk and become informed consumers who take advantage of ample consumer choice. As we saw in chapters 5 and 6, it is mothers who are most likely to agree to precautionary consumption owing to immense social and cultural pressure to prevent the intrusion of chemicals into fetal and infant bodies. Of course, biomonitoring research has established that babies are born with traces of synthetic chemicals in their bodies, meaning that the body burden begins forming before birth. Consequently, the "pure" child is unachievable yet remains a potent cultural construction. Underlying the cultural construction of the pure child is the assumption that the *mother's* body is the infant's first environment. But does pollution start with the mother's body and end with her domestic labor? Is widespread chemical trespass within her (or any other individual's) personal control? The mother, like the child and child's father, is located in an environment already contaminated with substances that easily pass through the corporeal boundaries of the skin, lungs, and placental wall.

The women I interviewed believed they were responsible for protecting their children from chemical exposures, but they also believed that the government should be more proactive at protecting public health. Yet they had little faith that the government would actually take the necessary steps. As Helen, a divorced, white, low-income mother of two children, put it, "Realistically, the government would be the only group that would be far-reaching enough to be able to provide the oversight or make inspections or whatever it would need to have this happen." Arissa, a married, Asian American, middle-class mother of two children, felt "hopeless" when she thought about how to address the problem of chemicals in food and consumer products: "I don't know where to begin to break down this horrible monstrosity of a problem. I don't know." Justina, a married, white, Italian, middle-class mother of a toddler, compared the cultures of consumption in the United States and the European Union. In her view, the U.S. government's reluctance to regulate chemicals is linked to the culture of "business first" in the United States: "I think that [regulators] are doing nothing. They need to control, but it's hard to control. . . . The U.S. economy is so huge in consumption, so they cannot change that. Everyone wants lower prices and all of that. So it's hard to change policy because of that."

Jodi, a single, white, middle-class mother of a toddler, had little faith that government agencies like the FDA and the USDA would place limits on corporations. In her view, the government protected industry to protect its own revenues: "The FDA and the USDA, they don't regulate [the food system] as they should because they have their priorities about making their own money. . . . I think they need to really step up their game." Her remark refers to how the FDA and USDA are closely tied to the industries they regulate. The FDA's congressional funding, for instance, comes from House and Senate Agricultural committees, which are influenced by the agricultural lobby.[1] The FDA's budget, furthermore, is partially funded by user fees from pharmaceutical companies.[2] The USDA receives its funding from the Farm Bill, which is heavily influenced by the agricultural lobby.[3]

Christine, a married, white, lower-income, middle-class mother of two children, who had once relied on food stamps, saw the government's interference in the food system and retail landscape as a major reason for widespread chemical contamination and the poor quality of the food system. Her remarks referred to a legacy of government support for agribusiness and the food processing industry at the expense of public health:

The government has always played a role in this. Either they change their role or they stop playing a role in it. They've made things accessible in the wrong way. Let's make things accessible for people. For instance, for WIC, there's approved products. . . . You can even buy a box of chips on WIC, but you can't buy organic eggs. . . . I think that they have the ability to play a role in [improving the food system], but they've just done such a bad job.

As the government fails to act, Christine saw consumer education as the only option: "If I was going to spend my time lobbying, it would be in schools, in neighborhoods, and communities. . . . [I would ask,] 'If you want to make the switch to eating organically or eating healthy, what is one thing you want to value right now? Is it meat? Is it grains? Is it snacks? Let's just start with that one thing and then make one switch in that one thing.'"

Monique, a married, white, upper-middle-class woman pregnant with her first child, saw the potential in small, independently owned, mom-and-pop, green companies. Leanne, a married, Latina, working-class mother of one child, likewise believed that eco-friendly companies were listening more closely to people's concerns and moving more quickly than government policy could: "I'm seeing more of a shift. Instead of Kraft Mac and Cheese, you'll see the organic Annie's Mac & Cheese or the Horizon Organic Mac and Cheese. That's why I think that they're listening to us." While these green companies appear to be responding to the public's call for safer and healthier commodities, some companies misrepresent their products. In 2016, for example, the Honest Company was implicated in multiple lawsuits for the misrepresentation of its infant formula as organic, the questionable effectiveness of its "natural" sunscreen, and the presence of sodium laureth sulfate—a compound the company promised it did not use in any of its products—in its laundry detergent.[4] Even if green companies are truly "honest" and appear to be more accountable to public health than conventional companies, their accountability is constrained by their bottom line. In theory, this is not true of a democratic institution, like the government, that is charged with protecting the public good.

Mothers were most optimistic about the potential for consumer education to assist shoppers in discerning what is safe and what is not, effectively arguing for the expansion of precautionary consumption. As Marcy put it, "I think it is an individual's responsibility to find out as much as they can, make the best choices they can make, that make the best sense to them personally [and] to their family." According to the mothers I interviewed, the uneducated shopper was most at risk of chemical exposure, and this person might be a fellow mother, a friend in their social network, a neighbor, or family member. The idea that more consumer education can help reduce public exposure to chemicals is consistent with the logic of the new public health and neoliberal governmentality. As Cerena, a married, African American, upper-middle-class mother of two children, told me, "The people who make the purchasing decisions in your household are the ones who are going to address it [the problem of chemicals in the environment and in our food system], and they're the ones that are going to change it." Cerena's perspective coincides with the safe shopping advice that surrounds her and is rooted in the responsibility she feels as a mother.

CONSUMER CITIZENSHIP

Only a few of the women I spoke with characterized the way they shopped as a form of politics—a kind of "voting with dollars" or "conscious capitalism."[5] When I asked them if shopping could be a form of politics, I received puzzled looks and silence. Three mothers—Christine, Kathleen (a white, married, middle-class mother of one child), and Jennifer (a married, white, middle-class mother of two children)—used the phrase "voting with my dollars" and talked about being "political shoppers." As Christine put it, "There's been a lot of times my husband and I have told people we vote with our money. Every time we go to the grocery store, every time we go shopping, we're voting for something." I expected to hear more respondents use the language of consumer citizenship that I detected in other spaces, like Whole Foods Market, and in environmental health movement shopping guides and websites.

A typical response to my question about shopping as politics came from Dahlia, a white, low-income mother of three children: "I guess the personal as political? I don't know if I agree with that . . . because I feel like politics in general—it's just this whole ball of wax. It's big, and it's so much. . . . It's a loaded word, I feel." My explicit reference to *politics* might have had a chilling effect on my attempt to converse about social change. Drawing from Nina Eliasoph's work on "avoiding politics," I interpret the puzzled responses of my interviewees as a reflection of the culture of political avoidance. As Eliasoph observed, when individuals feel powerless to change large structural problems, they avoid using explicit references to politics.[6] Their comments appear self-interested because they focus on where they have power: in their personal lives. The mothers I interviewed for this book framed precautionary consumption as part of their responsibility to protect their family from chemicals while also highlighting the sheer immensity of the problem of chemical body burdens (a big "ball of wax," to borrow Dahlia's phrase). Given how prominently the ideology of intensive mothering figures in middle-class women's lives, situating precautionary consumption within the existing responsibilities of motherhood was likely a much more comfortable way to talk about this practice. Moreover, for the mothers in this study, precautionary consumption was, first and foremost, a strategy of self-protection and not a form of political action. Precautionary consumption was about *circumventing*—as opposed to transforming—a broken regulatory system and a toxic retail landscape.

Precautionary consumption may not, in other words, be the newest expression of consumer citizenship. Unlike other forms of ethical or green consumption, such as buying energy efficient appliances and fair trade coffee or shopping at local farmers' markets, precautionary consumption does not seem to be motivated by an underlying belief that shopping can change the world.[7]

COULD PRECAUTIONARY CONSUMPTION WORK?

Given the slow pace of regulatory reform, industry's influence over policy and regulation (see chapter 2), and the current political climate in Washington, DC, that strongly opposes environmental regulation, might precautionary consumption be the best and most realistic option for avoiding chemical exposures? After all, in a matter of days, a family can switch to a diet of certified-organic food and thereby decrease at least some of their exposure to pesticides, whereas it could take decades for the government to successfully ban the manufacture and use of all organophosphate pesticides. Moreover, retailers appear poised to take the lead in protecting consumers from some exposures. For example, Whole Foods Market, Target, Walmart, CVS, Costco, and other companies have pledged not to carry products with certain ingredients or demanded that all products sold in their stores fully disclose their ingredients.[8] Some of these companies, like Walmart and Target, have enormous reach across the country, offering comparatively affordable "clean" products that are sold nationwide, not just in major urban centers like New York City. As the federal government appears increasingly less likely to enforce strong chemical regulation, environmental and consumer advocacy groups have set their sights on retailers, and we can expect more stores to make pledges similar to those mentioned above, effectively increasing the opportunities for precautionary consumption.

Unfortunately, even with the support of major retailers, the benefits of precautionary consumption are unclear. There is some evidence, for instance, that a truly concerted effort to consume *only* certified-organic food corresponds to lower pesticide residues in human bodies, even for people living in rural areas where pesticides are applied to agricultural fields.[9] Likewise, some studies find that individuals who eliminate personal care products containing phthalates, parabens, and phenols have fewer of these compounds in their bodies.[10] Crucially, these experiments involved having research subjects adhere to strict diets or personal care routines as part of a controlled study, and researchers measured declines in exposure to a small number of compounds, whereas most individuals encounter dozens of compounds in a single day. To achieve a similar decline in a chemical body burden, outside the context of a controlled experiment, individuals would need to enact comprehensive and sustained lifestyle changes. Early advocacy biomonitoring reports acknowledged limits to precautionary consumption. In the Commonweal *Is It in Us?* report, for example, the writers observed, "Some of our most careful shoppers, those who prefer organic or natural products, have some of the highest individual results of the industrial chemicals which they were tested [for]."[11] As noted in chapter 5, even the women with the most extensive routines sometimes consumed conventional produce or conventionally raised meats or used conventional personal care products. In chapter 6, we saw how difficult it can be to maintain a comprehensive routine without flexible time and a steady household income. Intervention studies suggest that individual-level education and counseling does not always lead to lower chemical body burdens. In one study, for example, researchers provided subjects with a diet low in environmental contaminants and counseled them on healthy eating. Even when provided with a diet of fresh, organic foods, subjects' phthalate levels did not change, leading researchers to conclude that there are many sources of phthalates and that simple dietary changes are not enough to reduce exposure. Rather, they argued for solutions that would prevent phthalates from entering the food supply in the first place. This means introducing strong regulation that prohibits these substances from being used in food processing materials and in food packaging.[12]

There are other reasons to be wary of swapping a basket of polluted goods for a basket of "greener" ones. Once a critical mass of consumers is concerned about a chemical, companies face serious pressure to find a replacement without slowing or stopping production and losing profits. If manufacturers do not apply the precautionary principle when choosing an alternative, the replacement chemical could be as hazardous as the original. It will merely appear safer to consumers because the product will typically carry a label declaring the product to be free of the original dangerous compound.

There are several cases of these "regrettable substitutions" where replacement chemicals posed similar (and sometimes more serious) environmental health problems as their predecessors.[13] This is the case for replacements for perfluorooctanoic acid (PFOA), a compound used to make nonstick coatings for cookware and stain-resistant coatings that can be applied to carpets and other materials. The company Dupont uses PFOA to make its trademarked compound Teflon. Several of the women interviewed for this book avoided Teflon pans, and safe shopping guides typically recommend avoiding Teflon cookware. PFOA is bioaccumulative, meaning that it stays in the human body, and the CDC estimates that it is present in nearly all Americans.[14] Like most other chemicals used in consumer products, PFOA has not been thoroughly tested for its effects on human health. PFOA (sometimes referred to as C8) came under heavy public scrutiny in 2000. Biomonitoring data showed PFOA to be part of the human body burden, and communities in Ohio, West Virginia, Vermont, and New York discovered elevated PFOA levels in their drinking water and found that residents of towns near Dupont factories making perfluorinated compounds had elevated levels in their blood.[15] In 2006, the EPA fined Dupont for failing to disclose what it had known for decades: that PFOA was bioaccumulative, persistent, and toxic. Dupont agreed to phase out PFOA and replace it with another compound. In 2009, Dupont created GenX, a compound that is chemically similar to PFOA and can withstand heat and repel oil and any other compounds that would otherwise stick to a pan or fabric. Yet Dupont's own tests in rats showed that GenX exposure was associated with cancer and abnormal development of the animals' kidneys, livers, and reproductive systems.[16] Although Dupont registered these results with the EPA, the compound was not banned. Just as is the case with many other chemicals registered with the EPA, manufacturers do not have to submit safety data to the agency. They can, in fact, submit very little information to the EPA by claiming such data is confidential business information. Dupont has sold GenX to its spinoff company, Chemours, which now manufactures the compound, and it is not clear how much is being produced and in what products it can be found. GenX has been discovered in the air and water near Chemours's plants in West Virginia and North Carolina.[17]

Replacement chemicals for BPA and PBDEs have run into similar problems. As was the case for PFOA alternatives, replacements for BPA and PBDEs went through the same broken and inadequate regulatory system as their predecessors. PBDEs, for example, were replaced by several compounds, including chlorinated flame retardants like tris(1,3-dichloro-2-propyl) phosphate (TDCPP), which has been suspected to be toxic since the 1970s.[18] TDCPP was selected as a replacement because it was a reliable compound that industry knew could slow the spread of flames. Compounds replacing BPA in plastic have the same practical utility as BPA, but like BPA, they are also endocrine disruptors.[19] In short, when something is marketed as being free of Teflon, BPA, or PBDEs, consumers should not assume that the product is made with safer chemicals. These compounds fall under the provisions of the TSCA, meaning that the companies that produce them are not required to test new compounds for safety. Consequently, the simple swap is sometimes a *toxic swap,* and this is one of several reasons precautionary consumption, on its own, cannot protect us from exposure to toxic chemicals.

The simple swap approach, furthermore, operates on a product-by-product basis. While BPA is no longer used in baby bottles and most water bottles, it is still used in myriad other products, such as thermal paper receipts, where it is easily absorbed by the skin. Retail workers who handle receipts have high levels of exposure, as do workers who manufacture plastics that use the compound or dismantle electronics and other consumer goods containing BPA.[20] Consequently, when we view environmental contamination through the limited lens of consumer exposure, we fail to see the multiple pathways through which environmental chemicals enter our bodies.[21]

Finally, when a product stops using a problematic compound like PFOA or BPA, those chemicals have not disappeared. Persistent toxic chemicals (those that take years or decades to break down into more harmless components) circulate in our air and waterways and settle in our soil. One study by the World Health Organization (WHO) and the United Nations Environment Programme (UNEP), for instance, found that human and wildlife exposure to endocrine disruptors is much more widespread than previously believed owing to the extensive global circulation and transportation of endocrine disrupting compounds. The only evidence of population-level decreases in human body burdens, this report argues, is in cases where a substance was banned by government. Phthalate bans by European governments in the 1990s, for instance, resulted in lower burdens of those compounds in the European population, just as the blood lead levels of Americans decreased in the late 1970s after the U.S. government banned lead in paint and gasoline. Declines in body burdens for other banned or restricted compounds have been observed for brominated flame retardants, organochlorine pesticides, PCBs, and dioxins.[22] According to the WHO/UNEP report:

> There are good examples where bans or reductions in chemical use have resulted in reduced levels in humans and wildlife. Indeed, human and animal tissue concentrations of many POPs [persistent organic pollutants] have declined because the chemicals are being phased out following global bans on their use. In contrast, EDCs [endocrine disrupting compounds] that are being used more now are found at higher levels in humans and wildlife. It is notable how well production and exposure mirror each other.[23]

Certainly, precautionary consumption creates market pressure for the production of greener goods, but it remains to be seen whether this pressure slows down or stops the production of potentially harmful chemicals. From my observations of the marketplace, the expansion of precautionary consumer goods has resulted in an overall increase in choice, with the conventional and organic varieties of consumer goods for sale alongside one another. For precautionary consumption to make a difference to environmental health, the manufacturing of toxic products must be discontinued and green products must become more affordable and widely available.

TOWARD ENVIRONMENTAL JUSTICE

In the case of universal risks—risks that affect us all—individual consumer options represent temporary stopgaps to a growing problem and provide marginal protection to a privileged few who can afford to cobble together a comprehensive strategy to avoid toxics. As more and more precautionary consumer commodities appear on store shelves—at Whole Foods Market, Walmart, and Target—the outcome may be greater public complacency arising from a false sense that the retail landscape has changed in fundamental ways and is no longer toxic. The trend of shopping our way to safety, as Andrew Szasz powerfully argues, may undercut public support for precautionary chemical regulation at the governmental level while allowing industry to cash in on the sale of green products.[24] The research presented in this book reveals how consumers are skeptical that precautionary consumption provides reasonable protection from chemical exposures, yet it remains their only option.

As a strategy for addressing chemical pollution, precautionary consumption represents an unfair burden for mothers. Fixing the problem of toxics in food and consumer products is not going to happen by fixing what women do as individual shoppers. Addressing this problem will require broad reforms to the regulatory system. As long as precautionary consumption continues to be the major response to widespread chemical pollution, women will do the bulk of the work and feel accountable for doing it well.

Precautionary consumption exacerbates inequalities related to gender, race, class, occupation, and geographic differences in severity of chemical exposure. Workers who manufacture our consumer products and grow our food, and the people living near the factories that produce these products or residing in the spaces where we dispose of our old consumer goods, experience chemical contamination in fundamentally more severe ways than shoppers who are exposed to toxics through their everyday purchases. In other words, the problem of environmental chemicals in our food and consumer products is, at its very core, an *environmental justice* issue. If we believe that all people and communities should have equal access to environmental health protections, then we must confront the rise of precautionary consumption by asking how this practice addresses environmental inequalities and injustices.[25]

The very fact that precautionary consumption depends on consumer agency means that it cannot deliver equitable protection from exposure to toxic substances. For individuals with time and money to shop strategically, it can provide temporary protection. For too many people, however, the ability to engage in precautionary consumption is limited by income, neighborhood, consumer literacy, and whether individuals have flexible time or are coping with chronic stress that makes tasks like reading labels feel overwhelming. Precautionary consumption, furthermore, will not clean up contaminated communities, protect indigenous communities in the far north from further toxic exposures, protect workers who handle chemicals as part of their job, or reverse the most egregious cases of contamination of human bodies. Environmental justice must be the end goal, and this requires thinking beyond individual consumer action as a solution to chemical body burdens.

HOW TO MOVE PAST PRECAUTIONARY CONSUMPTION

I see five steps that would move us in the direction of environmental justice and away from individualized and piecemeal responses. What I provide here is not a list of "five easy things you can do now" or a "list of the top five chemicals to avoid." Rather, the options I recommend will be difficult to implement because they require a fundamentally different approach to thinking about how to prioritize chemical innovation and commerce in relation to environmental protection and human health. They will require us to make a shift from seeing the government as a stumbling block to innovation and progress to seeing it as a democratic institution that can and should provide collective protection from environmental health risks.

First, the government must adopt the strong precautionary principle as the primary operating principle for environmental health law and policy. The Wingspread Statement remains, in my view, the clearest articulation of a strong precautionary principle. This goal will require major reforms to existing regulatory frameworks. Such an approach may appear unattainable at a time of unprecedented rollbacks of environmental regulation and oversight in the United States. Even so, we must not lose sight of this as the gold standard of environmental policymaking. To be clear, this is a structural change that must consider environmental health as a long-term priority. This approach will require existing chemicals, particularly those known to interfere with fetal development and children's health, to be re-evaluated using the precautionary principle to prioritize environmental health rather than the chemical industry's bottom line. Such a shift would place the onus of responsibility to prove a compound is safe on industry and regulatory bodies like the EPA, rather than pregnant women, breastfeeding mothers, and women in their preconception years. While the amended TSCA is a promising step forward in improving how the government reviews chemical safety, the act's provisions are currently being dismantled by the Trump administration.

Second, there must be greater transparency of the mechanisms involved in assessing risk from compounds used in agriculture, food processing, and the manufacturing of consumer products. The public has little view inside the complex and deliberately opaque bureaucracy that controls decisions about chemical hazards. As part of providing more transparency, it is especially critical to reveal who is at the negotiating table when agencies are weighing the risks and benefits of a chemical, and tracking the influence of these actors in defining the acceptable level of scientific uncertainty during evaluations of chemical safety. This information should be not only publicly available but also easy for the public to find. For this to happen, the fractured and confusing regulatory framework that is currently in place will require a major overhaul, one that is beyond what is set out in the amended TSCA. The evaluation of risk from chemicals must be coordinated under one agency or through a cooperative approach involving the EPA, FDA, OSHA, and USDA, as the current system of multiple agencies with different agendas and testing criteria for establishing safety, distinct funding mechanisms, and different organizational structures has proven to be ineffective at protecting the public from exposure to harmful chemicals.

Third, there must be sustained funding and institutional support for precautionary reviews of new and existing chemicals. Given the history of chronic underfunding of government agencies like the FDA and EPA, there is good reason to worry that even if reviews are legislated, their implementation will be inhibited if there is not sufficient government funding to allow agencies to carry out their responsibilities, especially as chemical reviews take time and money, and industry becomes impatient at any delays in bringing new products to market. While a precautionary review of existing chemicals may seem expensive and time-consuming, the EPA does not need to start all reviews from scratch. It could work to gain access to existing substance reviews that are already required by states like California, batch chemical assessments that have been completed in Canada, and chemical evaluations completed under European Union regulations. In fact, U.S. chemical producers that sell their products in the European Union are already required to develop hazard and exposure information for the European Union Chemicals Agency, and this information should be shared with the EPA.

Fourth, there must be greater transparency of industry science and lobbying activities within the U.S. government agencies that oversee chemical safety and the food supply. This transparency goes further than reporting donations or tracking "revolving door" politics.[26] Industry-funded studies that inform government decision-making should be subject to peer review and debate about acceptable risk. Thus far, any real public view into industry science and government evaluation of that science has been the consequence of litigation against a corporation that has forced it to disclose private communications and internal research reports. As part of increased transparency, overseas lobbying activities of American-owned companies and U.S.-based industry groups should be tracked and monitored. If U.S. lobbyists undo reforms in the European Union, as they are currently trying to do, they will remove one of the strongest incentives for precautionary policy: a need for regulatory harmonization to facilitate international trade.[27]

Fifth, and perhaps most obviously, manufacturers must stop producing toxic substances. Industry is quick to remind consumers that chemicals in use today are critical to providing modern conveniences and that restricting chemical innovation would mean losing those conveniences. This assessment fails to consider the promise of green chemistry. Green chemistry refers to an approach to chemistry and technological innovation that prioritizes developing the least toxic materials that will break down easily into nontoxic byproducts, do not interfere with the endocrine system (even at low doses), and do not bioaccumulate.[28] American academic and private research institutions have made investments in green chemistry, but there is opportunity to invest even more in this field.

In short, precautionary logics should be incorporated across political institutions at all levels of government, as well as in science and corporate research and development. Action to reduce environmental pollution must incorporate the goal of environmental justice and demand a return to the precautionary principle as a central organizing logic for designing more equitable approaches to prevent further contamination of environments and bodies and to improve environmental health for all people. These actions will protect not only individual consumers but, more importantly, also workers who must come into contact with chemical substances as part of their jobs and vulnerable communities located near manufacturing hubs or in geographic regions where toxics accumulate in the environment. Reform of this kind requires deep, structural change; it will take time, patience, and a sustained political will. It will not be easy, but we must act now, for the sake of our health and for the sake of our environment.

METHODOLOGICAL APPENDIX

Better Safe Than Sorry represents research on chemical body burdens, eco-shopping trends, and modern motherhood that I conducted in the United States and, to some extent, Canada. While I do not discuss it here, my dissertation project at the University of Toronto was the first phase of this research. In it, I identified precautionary consumption as an individualized lifestyle practice and learned that motherhood marked a moment in a woman's life course when she felt personally responsible for controlling her family's exposure to chemicals. In my research in Canada, I investigated the framing of chemical body burdens and the lived experience of precautionary consumption among mothers in Toronto.[1] After relocating to the United States, I saw more clearly how commonplace precautionary consumption has become: it is present in the marketplace, in the discourse of healthy eating and infant feeding, and in how mothers talk of managing their pregnancies and feeding children. It is also prominent in campaigns of major environmental health advocacy groups. This realization inspired the second phase of my research, documented in this book, which offers a more in-depth exploration of how precautionary consumption has become the dominant approach to addressing environmental toxics in food and consumer products.

This book tells the story of the rise of precautionary consumption, tracing the major political, economic, social, and cultural shifts in the United States that helped to redefine collectively experienced health threats from environmental pollution and toxic chemicals in the food supply and the retail marketplace into a personal consumer problem. The book reviews the history of chemical regulation in the United States and then investigates three domains where precautionary consumption is produced: the environmental health movement; the retail market for certified-organic, "green," and eco-friendly goods; and the work of mothering and shopping for children. The research for this book uses a combination of qualitative methods, namely qualitative content and discourse analysis, case study methods, in-depth interviewing, and grounded theory. This appendix provides more detail about the specific methods I used for each chapter of the book.

HISTORICAL ANALYSIS

For chapter 2, which provides an overview of the history of regulation of synthetic chemicals used in food production and consumer product manufacturing, I draw from the research of environmental historians, namely Nancy Langston's *Toxic Bodies* (2010), which tells the tragic story of DES; Sarah Vogel's *Is It Safe?* (2013), which reviews contested regulation of endocrine disruptors such as BPA; and Frederick Rowe Davis's *Banned* (2014), which chronicles the history of toxicology and pesticide production. These books deftly outline key developments from the early 1900s through to the early 2000s.

My overview of the contemporary regulatory system—the laws and rules in place at the time of writing—draws from policy analyses and critiques provided by legal and political science scholars, Government Accountability Office reports, and my own research into the U.S. regulatory framework. For my research into the specific rules governing food, personal care products, and consumer products, I used information provided on the websites of the EPA, FDA, USDA, and Consumer Product Safety Commission. To track debates surrounding new and ongoing policy changes (including changes made to the Toxic Substances Control Act in 2016), I collected news articles and op-eds on environmental health published in the *Washington Post, Los Angeles Times,* and *New York Times* from 2009 to late 2017.

ENVIRONMENTAL HEALTH MOVEMENT CAMPAIGNS

To conduct research on the environmental health campaigns surrounding chemical body burdens, I reviewed materials produced by a total of thirty-four American environmental health advocacy groups to piece together how these groups have framed the significance of environmental pollution in human bodies. I collected advocacy biomonitoring reports as well as safe shopping and healthy lifestyle materials produced by key organizations.

To identify advocacy biomonitoring reports produced by major environmental health movement organizations, I looked to the work of sociologist Rebecca Altman, who first identified the personalization of body burdens as a major social movement framing strategy.[2] Using her research as a guide, I collected twenty-seven advocacy biomonitoring reports produced by eighteen organizations between 2003 and 2015. Note that of these eighteen organizations, some were coauthors on reports (see table 1 in chapter 3). Although I included 2015 in my search, I did not find any advocacy biomonitoring studies published during that year. I was interested in how organizations framed environmental pollution as a problem, how they measured chemical body burdens (using, e.g., urine, blood, or breast milk), which subjects they studied (infants or adults; mothers or fathers), and which solutions they proposed. I read through each biomonitoring report, paying attention to the methods used in each study and how results were presented. I made notes about the phrases and language that invoked risk, fear, anxiety, or health and all proposed solutions to the problem of environmental chemicals. I also noted the content of all photographs and other visuals.

I then collected all reports, guides, fact sheets, and webpages related to safe shopping that had been published by major environmental health movement organizations or were available on organization websites. I focused only on major organizations, which I defined as organizations that conducted or collaborated with groups that produced advocacy biomonitoring reports or had a national presence (e.g., Breast Cancer Fund, Greenpeace, NRDC, Toxic Free Future). I collected 365 documents produced by twenty-seven organizations. Documents were published between 1992 and 2015. Some of the organizations that I studied, such as the EWG and Silent Spring Institute, publish biomonitoring reports as well as safe shopping guides. Other organizations, like the Campaign for Safe Cosmetics and Breast Cancer Prevention Partners (formerly the Breast Cancer Fund), produce only lifestyle and shopping guides and do not lead advocacy biomonitoring initiatives, but they reference advocacy biomonitoring in their work and occasionally collaborate with major groups, such as EWG. Environmental health movement organizations operate in a close-knit network. They often refer visitors to one another's websites, and there are many coalitions of environmental health advocacy organizations (e.g., the Coming Clean Collaborative and Safer Chemicals, Healthy Families).

I downloaded all materials from the websites of the organizations included in my sample; table A1 lists the number of safe shopping publications by organization. Most materials were published between 2003 and 2014, and of all groups, the EWG and its subsidiary Healthy Child Healthy World produced the most materials: 12 biomonitoring reports and 188 safe shopping documents and webpages. I coded shopping and lifestyle documents using similar criteria to the analysis of advocacy biomonitoring reports, paying special attention to where recommended actions take place (at work, at home, outside the home, etc.). I also documented any lifestyle changes and shopping strategies recommended in these materials. I list these shopping and lifestyle actions in table 2 (see chapter 3). Altogether, I found that environmental health movement organizations recommended nearly sixty actions. The types of recommended actions were very similar across organizations, and many organizations recommended the same precautionary behaviors (e.g., avoiding microwaving plastic, choosing certified-organic food when possible, avoiding fish high in mercury).

While most of the organizations I studied produced safe shopping advice, this was not their sole mandate. Some, like the EWG, featured links on their home pages that helped visitors send letters to their congressperson to demand policy change to

TABLE A1. Key Environmental Health Advocacy Organizations Publishing Precautionary Consumption Advice

Organization	Number of reports examined	Examples of titles
Black Women for Wellness	2	*Black Going Green: A Guide on Avoiding Toxic Chemicals in Your Everyday Life* (2013)
Breast Cancer Fund	23	*What Labels Don't Tell Us: Getting BPA out of Our Food* (2010) *Chemicals in Plastics* (2010)
Campaign for Safe Cosmetics	9	*Pretty Scary: Heavy Metals in Face Paints* (2009) *Not So Sexy: The Health Risks of Secret Chemicals in Fragrance* (2010)
Center for Environmental Health	6	*Kicking Toxic Chemicals Out of the Office: An Easy Guide to Going Flame Retardant-Free* (n.d.)
Children's Environmental Health Network	17	*FAQ: Fragrances* (n.d.) *FAQs: BPA and Phthalates* (n.d.)
Coalition for a Safe and Healthy Connecticut	1	*Top 10 Tips to Reduce Toxins in Your Home* (2013)
Ecology Center	2	*Healthy Stuff Database* (2015) *Top 10 Tips to Avoid Toxics at Home* (2015)
Environment and Human Health	1	*Plastics That May Be Harmful to Children and Reproductive Health* (2008)
Environmental Working Group	173	*Skin Deep Database* (2004–2015) *Food Scores Database* (2014–2015) *Dirty Dozen* (2002–2015)
Greenpeace (USA)	7	*This Vinyl House* (2001) *Guide to Greener Electronics* (2010)
Healthy Child, Healthy World (EWG)	15	*Easy Steps to a Safer Pregnancy* (2014) *Postpartum Pitfalls: Don't Let Your Guard Down* (2015)
Healthy Legacy/IATP	7	*Plastics Tips* (n.d.) *Non-toxic Cleaning Product Recipes* (n.d.) *Smart Plastics Guide: Healthier Food Uses of Plastics* (2008)

Organization		Example Publication
La Leche League	1	Environmental Contaminants and Human Milk (2014)
Making Our Milk Safe	2	Breastfeeding (2012); Preconception (2012)
Moms across America	2	Creating Healthy Communities by Eliminating Exposure to Toxins (n.d.)
Mom's Clean Air Force	14	Mattress Detective: My Hunt for a Chemical-Free Crib Mattress (2013)
Natural Resources Defense Council	13	Food Storage Containers (2011); The 5 Stupidest Chemicals That Shouldn't Be in Your House (2013)
New York State Breast Cancer Network	2	Cancer and the Environment: A Case for the Precautionary Principle (n.d.)
Oregon Environmental Council	6	First, Do No Harm: Strategies to Protect Oregonians from Environmental Health Threats (2003); Eco-Healthy Homes Checkup Kit (2014)
Physicians for Social Responsibility	10	Out of Harm's Way: Reducing Toxic Threats to Child Development (2001)
Planned Parenthood	1	Green Choices (2013)
Safer Chemicals, Healthy Families	6	For Father's Day and Every Day: Men's Health and Toxic Chemicals (2013); Non-toxic Shopping Guide (2012)
Sierra Club	9	The Earth Kit: Environmental and Reproductive Toxins and Health (2014)
Silent Spring Institute	10	Safer Alternative Cleaning Products (2014); In Your Parenting (2015); In What You Eat and Drink (2015)
Washington Toxics Coalition	11	Choosing Safer Products: Art and Craft Supplies (n.d.)
Women's Voices for the Earth	14	Dirty Secrets: What's Hiding in Your Cleaning Products? (2011)
Zero Cancer	1	What Are Some Examples of Common Everyday Exposures to Phthalates and Tips to Avoid Exposure? (2007)

NOTE: This list reflects publications released between January 1995 and December 2015.

existing chemical regulation. At the time of this research, many organizations were lobbying to reform the Toxic Substances Control Act of 1976. Aside from these links, safe shopping advice was the most prominent feature of these organizations' websites, especially in the case of the EWG and the Campaign for Safe Cosmetics. These organizations support regulatory reform and encourage safe shopping as an interim approach, setting up a tension between the promise of collective protection through regulatory reform and self-protection, which I address in chapter 3.

WHOLE FOODS MARKET AND PRODUCT ANALYSIS

Though supermarkets are often denigrated as boring, mundane spaces, I see them as rich cultural texts that offer windows into consumer culture.[3] And, of all retail spaces in which to study precautionary consumption, Whole Foods Market is the most logical, given its vast selection of organic food and nontoxic commodities. Moreover, all of my interview subjects shopped at Whole Foods Market at least once a month (although shopping there was not part of my recruitment criteria). As detailed in chapter 4, my case study of Whole Foods Market took stock of the advertising, store layout and decor, product packaging, and promotional materials within the company's stores located in New York City. The store and product packages were central sites for examining and understanding the growth of precautionary consumption in consumer culture.

During the period I was conducting site visits, from January 2014 to December 2016, Whole Foods Market operated 436 stores in 42 states, 9 of them in New York City.[4] In 2017, the company's stock price began to drop (after years of tremendous growth), and Whole Foods Market announced it was closing nine of its older, smaller locations.[5] That same year, activist investors bought shares in the company and sold it to Amazon, generating intense speculation about the power of Whole Foods Market to dominate the grocery sector.

I conducted approximately seventy-five site visits to Whole Foods Market stores in New York City and collected all company news releases, press kit materials, and annual reports, which were available online. I also followed the company's official website and Instagram account. During this period, I collected news articles about Whole Foods Market published in the *New York Times* and *New York Daily News*. I made site visits to all of the nine New York City locations, but I focused data collection on the Upper West Side, Columbus Circle, and Chelsea stores. For comparison, I visited Whole Foods Market locations in New Jersey, Westchester County in New York, Chicago, and Washington, DC. Decor, precautionary consumer messages, and layout were very similar across all stores.

On each site visit, I took notes on the content and physical placement of promotional posters, quality assurance labels, and any other images or posters that promoted the store, its operating practices, or its general mandate. Whole Foods Market stores, I found, were designed in similar ways, although each location differed in size and some had distinctive features, such as a kombucha bar at the Union Square location and a beer garden on the roof of its Brooklyn store. Products were grouped using the same logic (e.g., coffee was sold alongside tea, and breakfast cereals and granola bars were sold together). Most stores had a bakery, hot bar, salad bar, and café. Stores carried the same brands, although the number of items per brand differed depending on the size of the store. All Whole Foods Market stores I visited used the same advertising images and posters.[6]

At the time of my research, Whole Foods Market had nine quality standards (see table A2) that outlined the company's priorities for deciding what brands and items to carry. These standards described, for example, the company's definition of acceptable farming and food production practices, and listed unacceptable ingredients that were not allowed in any of the products it carried. Quality standards were promoted throughout the store, and their details were posted on the company's website.[7]

As part of my research, I studied Whole Foods Market's Values Matter campaign, which launched in fall 2014. The company made the three television commercials and sixteen promotional images produced for the campaign available to the public on its media kit webpage.[8] I watched the television commercials multiple times and took notes on the images and themes demonstrated in the images and videos. The campaign was highly visible inside the store. There were posters displayed in exterior windows, hanging from the ceiling, and posted at the checkout counter, on the digital checkout screen facing the paying customer, and throughout the café.

Product Analysis

In addition to visiting Whole Foods Market stores, I documented the claims made on product labels of items sold in the store. Data collection for this phase took place between January 2014 and May 2016. The purpose of this analysis was to document the numerous precautionary consumer messages on organic foods and nontoxic products sold at Whole Foods Market.

To collect these data, I walked the aisles of each of the Upper West Side, Columbus Circle, and Chelsea Whole Body stores and cataloged products systematically, starting at the top of the shelf and going down to the bottom. If a brand made more than one product, I selected up to three products. I collected samples from various sections: child and baby care; clothing and household goods; personal care; processed food; fresh produce, dairy, meat, and fish; and cleaning products. I chose not to include vitamins and supplements, as these products are typically used for healing or managing a health condition, whereas precautionary consumption is about avoiding contact with chemicals in food and other consumer goods. For each item, I recorded

TABLE A2 Whole Foods Market Quality Standards, 2015

Standard	Purpose	Scale	How sold in store
Food Ingredient Quality Standards	Identifies ingredients that cannot be used in food products sold at the store (e.g., aspartame, BHT)	n/a	Not displayed in-store
Responsibly Grown	Identifies environmental and labor protections on farms	n/a	Rating presented on a tag placed underneath item
Animal Welfare	Rates animal husbandry and management practices	Color-coded steps: 1 (orange; no cages or crates, no crowding) to 5+ (green; animals spend their entire lives on the same farm, farms practice "animal-centered" husbandry)	Color-code displayed next to item or aisle
Seafood Quality Standards	Identifies whether seafood is sustainably caught or responsibly farmed; lists buying standards for farmed fish (e.g., cannot contain antibiotics or added hormones)*	Blue: seafood that meets the Marine Stewardship Council's standards for certified sustainable seafood. Green: seafood from fisheries that cause little harm to habitats or wildlife. Yellow: seafood from fisheries with some concerns about how fish are caught or managed. Red: over-fished species (not carried at Whole Foods Market).	Color-code placed next to item
Body Care Quality Standards	Identifies fifty ingredients that cannot be used in any personal care products sold in the store (e.g., acetone, formaldehyde)	n/a	Not displayed in-store
Organic Body Care Standards	Specifies how and when a product can use the word "organic" on its label	n/a	"Organic" appears on manufacturer's packaging
Premium Body Care Standards	Identifies four hundred ingredients that cannot be used in any personal care products sold in the store (e.g., parabens, sodium lauryl / laureth sulfate)	n/a	"Premium body care" logo appears on item package or next to aisle

Organic Food Standards	Establishes that the company carries some products that meet USDA organic standards	n/a	n/a
Cleaning Product Standards	Establishes an eco-scale rating system that indicates whether item is safe and environmentally friendly	Green: products containing 100-percent natural ingredients. Yellow: products containing no ingredients with moderate environmental or safety concerns. Orange: products containing no ingredients with significant environmental or safety concerns. Red: products not carried at Whole Foods Market.	Rating presented on a tag placed underneath item

NOTE: This list reflects quality standards that were in place in 2015. In 2016, Whole Foods Market updated their Quality Standards, consolidating some of these categories and adding a new standard for eggs. See www.wholefoodsmarket.com/quality-standards.

*Marine Stewardship Council ratings and Monterey Bay Aquarium Seafood Watch systems are used for wild-caught fish the brand name, product description, and any "clean" or precautionary consumer claim visible on the label. To ensure that I had not missed any major brands sold at the store, I compared my list of brands and products with Whole Foods Market product lists available on the company's website and in coupon booklets.[9]

In total, I examined 800 products from 300 brands. I found that many of the safety and health claims on product labels overlapped across brands and types of products, and I also discovered some products that carried few or no claims. I documented a total of 150 claims, seals, and logos related to precautionary consumption, and I document these in tables 3 and 4 (see chapter 4).

IN-DEPTH INTERVIEWS

Chapters 5 and 6 draw from my interviews with thirty mothers living in New York City. These interviews took place between May 2014 and May 2016. This project went through an institutional research board ethics review at Rutgers University in New Brunswick, and it was approved prior to beginning recruitment for interview participants (IRB Protocol 13–435).

I interviewed mothers who resided in New York City and had children living at home. I chose to interview mothers because they are more likely than other individuals to come across precautionary consumer items in their day-to-day shopping, particularly given how the current market for children's food, toys, and personal care products is saturated with precautionary consumer labels. Furthermore, my initial research in Toronto suggested that mothers take an active interest in precautionary consumption beginning during pregnancy or soon after the birth of a child. I was interested in talking to mothers who practiced a range of precautionary consumer routines, from those who occasionally bought certified-organic foods or nontoxic products to those who made a deliberate effort to incorporate as many of these items as possible into their shopping routines. I wanted to speak to mothers with diverse racial and ethnic backgrounds and social class positions. I used a qualitative research approach, and the purpose of the interviews was to get a sense of how precautionary consumption is accomplished as part of everyday life.[10] To be clear, the sample was not meant to be representative of the experiences of all mothers, nor even of all New York City mothers. The interviews were designed to provide a window into the complexities of mothers' routines and to observe how mothers made sense of the imperative to protect children from chemical exposures. The interviews also provided a window into the kinds of resources that mothers invested in precautionary consumption. The women in the sample were, on average, highly educated and middle class, and because they lived in New York City, they had access to multiple supermarkets and other retail outlets for consumer goods.

To recruit mothers, I placed notices on parent listservs for multiple neighborhoods in the city, including Manhattan, the Bronx, and Brooklyn. Most of the participants were recruited through these notices. I also used snowball sampling by asking interview participants and acquaintances in my own network of parents to suggest friends or neighbors who might be interested in participating in the study. To help broaden recruitment beyond these online and social networks, I also placed printed posters in Laundromats, libraries, and grocery stores in neighborhoods across the city, including low-income areas. I also contacted social workers who work with low-income clients to help distribute flyers at community centers and to identify potential interview subjects. All recruitment flyers and listserv postings advertised for a study of family food shopping, and I offered all participants $20 for participating. Using these strategies, I was able to locate mothers of various demographic and social class backgrounds with a range of precautionary consumption routines.

Most of the mothers in the study are middle- and upper-middle class. I had limited success recruiting very low-income mothers—those making under $15,000 a year and relying on social assistance like SNAP or WIC. Speaking with social workers and dieticians, I learned that these women are reticent to talk to professionals about their foodwork because of the constraints their financial situation places on their ability to practice the middle-class norm of preparing fresh, home-cooked, "balanced" meals, an ideal that is readily promoted by SNAP and WIC, dieticians, and community food programs.[11] As a topic of conversation, food shopping can be stressful and emotional for women who rely on food assistance programs and whose family feeding practices are under continual surveillance by doctors, dietitians, and social workers.[12]

The sample includes some low-income women who had qualified for SNAP or WIC in the past, and their interviews spoke to the difficulties of buying organic and nontoxic products on a constrained income. To be clear, all of these women had some paid income and were not living in austere conditions. When they were on federal food assistance, they would not purchase certified-organic food unless it was the same price as conventional food. The low-income women who participated in interviews practiced moderate to comprehensive precautionary consumption routines, as they had nonmaterial resources that they could leverage to compensate for their lower incomes, as I show in chapter 6. In fact, thinking about social class only in terms of income provides a partial picture of the class-based barriers to precautionary consumption. Practicing precautionary consumption requires an individual to have enough time to shop for affordable organic options, the consumer literacy to make sense of complex ingredient lists and clean label claims, and the mental energy to seek out information about best practices and engage in what is ultimately a complex task. In some low-income neighborhoods in New York City (as in the rest of the country), access to stores that sell certified-organic food is limited. According to one recent study, organic food products are not as available in stores in low-income neighborhoods in New York City as they are in middle- and upper-middle-class neighborhoods.[13]

I therefore consider my understanding of the experience of precautionary consumption for low-income women to be preliminary. This is an area of research that desperately requires more attention.

Description of the Sample

Table A3 documents the demographic details for all thirty mothers I interviewed. I have assigned pseudonyms to all participants. Of the women who had partners, all were in heterosexual relationships. Most women worked part-time or were full-time homemakers. These women had sufficient flexibility in their schedules to accommodate an interview, but even so, interviews had to be scheduled around picking up children from school, participating in volunteer work, and juggling the demands of doing most of the unpaid household labor, namely cooking, shopping, laundry, and cleaning. All had some interest in healthy eating and organic food shopping, which likely explains their willingness to participate in the interview. I am grateful to all of these women for volunteering their time to speak with me.

I asked respondents to indicate their race or ethnicity using the categories of non-Hispanic white, Hispanic, Black or African American, Asian, or other (where the participant could write the designation of their choice). Eighteen of my participants identified as white, five as Asian, three as Hispanic, three as Black, and one as Black-Hispanic. In chapters 5 and 6, I refer to women who identified as Asian in the demographic survey as Asian American to reduce confusion and reflect that the Asian respondents were born in the United States. I refer to participants who indicated that they were Hispanic as Latina, since several mentioned family roots originating in Central or South America.

With the exception of one participant, all of the nonwhite participants had moderate to comprehensive precautionary consumption routines, providing a case against the popular trope that organic food shopping is exclusive to whites.[14] In fact, my research suggests that women of color buy organic and natural foods as part of middle-class mothering.[15] Cerena, for instance, considered organic food to be central to her Southern identity. Indeed, in the American South, African American women like Edna Lewis helped establish a movement of whole foods and kitchen gardens—a crucial part of American food history that is overlooked in the literature.[16]

I measured social class for each participant using details they supplied in the demographic survey. There is no single or standard definition of social class, and

TABLE A3 Demographic Characteristics of Interview Respondents

Pseudonym	Age	Own or rent home	Marital status	Children	Education	Employment status	Race/ethnicity*	Household income	Food assistance?	Class	Type of routine
Abby	35	Own	M/Coh	2	BA	Homemaker	White	>$199,001	No	UMC	Moderate
Allison	45	Own	M/Coh	2	PG	Homemaker	Asian	>$199,001	No	UMC	Comprehensive
Arissa	44	Own	M/Coh	2	BA	Homemaker	Asian	$66,000–$199,000	No	MC	Moderate
Bianca	25	Rent	Single	Planning	BA	Employed FT	Black and Hispanic	$66,000–$199,000	No	MC	Moderate
Camila	28	Rent	M/Coh	2	PG	Homemaker	Hispanic	$15,001–$34,999	N/A	LI MC	Moderate
Carol	41	Rent	Single	1	BA	Self-employed	White	$66,000–$199,000	No	MC	Basic
Cecilia	37	Rent	M/Coh	1	PG	Homemaker	White	$66,000–$199,000	No	MC	Basic
Cerena	40	Rent	M/Coh	2	PG	Employed FT	Black / African American	>$199,001	No	UMC	Comprehensive
Chitra	45	Rent	Separated	1	BA	Student/ Employed PT	South Asian	$15,001–$34,999	WIC, SNAP in past two years	LI	Moderate
Christine	30	Rent	M/Coh	2	BA	Employed PT	White	$35,000–$65,999	SNAP in past two years	LI MC	Comprehensive
Dahlia	34	Rent	M/Coh	3	Some PS	Homemaker	White	<$15,000	SNAP	LI	Comprehensive
Ellen	57	Rent	M/Coh	2	Some PS	Employed PT	Black / African American	$35,000–$65,999	No	WC	Basic
Fiona	40	Own	M/Coh	1	PG	Employed FT	White	N/A	N/A	MC	Comprehensive
Gina	37	Own	M/Coh	2	BA	Homemaker	White	N/A	N/A	UMC	Basic

(continued)

TABLE A3 *(continued)*

Pseudonym	Age	Own or rent home	Marital status	Children	Education	Employment status	Race/ ethnicity*	Household income	Food assistance?	Class	Type of routine
Hannah	43	Rent	Single	2	Some PS	Employed PT	Black/ African American	$35,000–$65,999	In past two years	WC	Comprehensive
Helen	41	Rent	Divorced	2	PG	Unemployed	White	N/A	Not reported	LI	Basic
Jennifer	43	Rent	M/Coh	2	PG	Homemaker	White	>$199,001	No	UMC	Basic
Jodi	22	Rent	Single	1	Some PS	Student	White	$66,000–$199,000	No	MC	Basic
Justina	43	Own	M/Coh	2	PG	Homemaker	White	$66,000–$199,000	No	MC	Basic
Kannitha	36	Rent	M/Coh	2	BA	Homemaker	Asian	$66,000–$199,000	No	MC	Moderate
Karen	47	Rent	M/Coh	2	PG	Self-employed	White	>$199,001	No	UMC	Moderate
Kathleen	47	Rent	M/Coh	2	Some PS	Self-employed	White	N/A	No	MC	Comprehensive
Leanne	26	Rent	M/Coh	1	BA	Student/ Employed PT	Hispanic	$35,000–$65,999	In past two years	WC	Moderate
Lilly	44	Rent	M/Coh	1	PG	Self-employed	White	$66,000–$199,000	No	MC	Comprehensive
Marcy	50	Rent	M/Coh	2	BA	Employed FT	White	$66,000–$199,000	No	MC	Comprehensive
Monique	39	Rent	M/Coh	Pregnant	BA	Employed FT	White	>$199,001	No	UMC	Comprehensive
Naomi	39	Own	M/Coh	1	BA	Self-employed	White	$66,000–$199,000	No	MC	Comprehensive
Olivia	36	Rent	M/Coh	3	BA	Homemaker	Hispanic	$35,000–$65,999	No	LI MC	Moderate
Sabina	45	Own	M/Coh	2	PG	Employed FT	White	$66,000–$199,000	No	MC	Moderate
Sarah	57	Rent	Divorced	1	BA	Employed PT	Asian	N/A	N/A	WC	Moderate

ABBREVIATIONS: M/Coh: married or cohabiting. PS: post-secondary. BA: bachelor's degree. PG: post-graduate degree. FT: full-time. PT: part-time. WC: working class. MC: middle class. UMC: upper-middle class. LI MC: low-income middle class. LI: low income. SNAP: Supplemental Nutrition Assistance Program (food stamps). WIC: Women, Infants and Children (food and nutrition benefit).

* Race/ethnicity was chosen by the respondent.

even within sociology, ways of measuring class vary considerably. I understand social class to be a social category defined in relation to other categories of identity—one that takes into account a person's economic and legal position, place in the labor market, ownership of property, formal education, and household income.[17] I determined social class by asking about the participant's education, occupation (of self and partner, if applicable), and total household income.

The stickiest determination in setting class categories was defining a middle-class income for New York City. There is significant social inequality in New York City, and Manhattan has the largest income gap in the United States.[18] What might be a comfortable middle-class income in one part of the country (e.g., $60,000 for a family of four living in Cleveland, Ohio) would not support a family of four living in a market-rate two-bedroom rental apartment in Manhattan.[19] In designing the demographic survey, I therefore set the income categories according to a report published by the New York City Council entitled *The Middle Class Squeeze*.[20] This report defines middle-class income as falling between $66,000 and $199,000. I also referred to the Pew Research Center's income calculator and the New York City Housing Development Corporation's income eligibility guidelines from 2013, which specify income thresholds to qualify for middle- and low-income subsidized housing in the city.[21] Because of the high educational attainment of the women in my interview sample—nearly all had a bachelor's degree or higher—I elected to divide the category middle class into three categories to acknowledge significant household income variations among those with high educational attainment. These categories are: low-income middle class, middle class, and upper-middle class.[22] Participants in all of these categories had a bachelor's degree or a higher level of educational attainment. Low-income middle-class participants had a total household income between $35,000 and $65,999, and either they or their partner was employed in an occupational category that required a bachelor's degree (e.g., a teacher). Middle-class participants had a total household income between $66,000 and $199,000. Upper-middle-class participants had a total household income exceeding $199,000. Three of the women I interviewed were low-income middle class, thirteen were middle class, and seven were upper-middle class.

I defined participants as working-class when they had a household income under $66,000 and either they or their partner was employed in an occupational category requiring less than a bachelor's degree (e.g., retail or restaurant service). Four mothers were working class. Low-income women had an income lower than $35,000 a year and were unemployed or underemployed. Three women in the sample were low income.

Five women did not report their incomes, and I assigned class status based on their occupation, education, and other details of their living conditions that they described in the interview.

I conducted most of the interviews in person in coffee shops or at the participants' homes, and I conducted two interviews over the phone when scheduling was a problem.

Before starting each interview, I explained the ethics protocols and obtained signed consent to record the interview. I used a semistructured interview questionnaire that opened with general questions asking the participant to give me some information about herself, including her occupation, where she lived, how long she had lived in New York City, the age of her children, and her marital status, among other background details. I then asked questions about weekly shopping routines, meal planning, and priorities for food shopping. I asked if the participant was aware of environmental chemicals in foods and consumers products and followed this up with questions to understand what she was concerned about and how this awareness of environmental chemicals developed. I asked what she thought about the permeability of the human body to environmental chemicals and whether she believed it was possible to cleanse or detox the body of these substances. I ended the interview by asking the participant what she thought could be done to address the problem of chemicals in food, the environment, and the home. After the interview, I asked participants to fill out a short survey to collect details about household income, education, employment status, partner's occupation (if applicable), and whether they received SNAP or WIC benefits.

I took notes during and after each interview. These field notes consisted of my observations about the participant's mood and responses to my questions (e.g., if they seemed comfortable or in a rush, what questions generated an open response, what questions seemed to cause confusion), as well as thoughts I had about their responses and ideas for refining and improving the interview questionnaire. Whenever possible, I visited each participant's neighborhood and went inside the grocery stores and other stores they mentioned in their interviews. These visits provided me with a sense of where they shopped for food and how much of the store was dedicated to precautionary consumer items.

Interview Data Analysis

All interviews were digitally recorded and then professionally transcribed. I cleaned each transcript by listening to the interview while reading over the transcription file. I then coded the interviews using the qualitative data analysis software NVivo 10.2.2.

I started with open coding to develop an initial set of themes. Open coding uses an inductive approach, where the researcher lets the themes emerge from the data rather than imposing predefined codes on the transcripts.[23] After reading through the list of open codes and rereading the transcripts multiple times, I began focused coding, which involved collapsing the open codes into a set of themes,[24] which generated the themes that appear in chapters 5 and 6. Using this method, I interpreted the significance of the interview data in relation to the main research questions.

I continued to recruit and interview middle- and upper-middle-class participants until I reached theoretical saturation—when new themes failed to emerge. This saturation point was informed by my previous research in Toronto, where I studied precautionary consumption among fifty individuals, mostly middle-class women.[25] Many of the themes that emerged from my interviews with middle- and upper-middle-class New York mothers overlapped with themes I first encountered in my Toronto study.

LIMITATIONS OF THE RESEARCH

The research I present in this book offers a wide-ranging look at precautionary consumption, with some important limitations. My research is focused primarily on New York City, and my sample is made up of highly educated and affluent mothers. The book does not examine how fathers experience precautionary consumption, as I found that mothers do most of the grocery shopping. Many fathers who said they did go to the supermarket reported that they followed a list made by their wife and made choices based on what was on the list. There are, of course, exceptions to this general pattern; however, I tried to recruit fathers for this study but had very little success finding fathers who were primarily responsible for both planning and executing the grocery shopping. Therefore, the interview data do not reflect the lived experience of precautionary consumption for fathers. Moreover, the data cannot speak to complexities of precautionary consumption in rural areas, suburbs, or small cities. Whole Foods Market is ubiquitous in New York City, but in many parts of the United States there is no easy access to this store, meaning that many Americans have never visited a Whole Foods Market store, so the company's messages of transparency and "good" food do not reach an important and substantial consumer base.

In-depth interviews, instead of, say, ethnographic observations of individuals' actual shopping and foodwork behaviors, represent one-time accounts of what participants were willing to tell me. Their narratives likely reflect a desire to present their mothering and foodwork in a positive light. It is possible that participants overestimated how much organic food they bought and how concerned they were about chemicals, given my interest in the subject and my status as white, a professor, and a fellow mother. As much as possible, I adapted the interview questions to allow participants to push back against or disagree with the idea that chemical exposures are undesirable, or that organic food or "health" food is the "best" choice for children. Participants' accounts of their male partners' involvement in precautionary consumption reflect the participants' perspectives at the time of their interviews, and I did not crosscheck their accounts with their male partners.

As noted above, this book highlights a need for more research on precautionary consumption among low-income women. From the research I present here and my review of the literature on women's foodwork, I believe that low-income mothers are just as concerned about their children's chemical exposures from food and consumer products as are middle-class mothers, but they are limited in what they can do as consumers and caregivers. Precautionary consumption most likely drops off the priority list when individuals are confronted with pressing concerns of managing stressful life conditions. Moreover, depending on where they live, low-income women's daily chemical exposure from food and consumer products may be far less significant than their exposures to contaminants in indoor and outdoor environments.

Finally, while some of the mothers in my sample came to the United States from other countries, they were from Europe or had upper-class backgrounds in their country of origin. All were comfortable reading and conversing in English. The book therefore does not illuminate immigrant women's experiences with precautionary consumption, which is significant, as precautionary consumption in the American retail landscape is aided by fluency in English and familiarity with American brands and popular international brands. Given the complexities of the retail landscape in the United States, it is presumably overwhelming for a newcomer. Indeed, in my own experience of immigrating to the United States from Canada, I found grocery stores challenging to navigate. There were brands that I had never seen and far more precautionary consumer claims than I had encountered in Canadian grocery stores. I encountered a different consumer experience despite the shared brands, mass media, and similarities in the food system between the United States and Canada.

As I learned in my research in Toronto, for some consumers from less developed countries, the U.S. retail landscape can appear "safer" than the one at home. The immigrant shoppers I interviewed in Toronto assumed that foods and other commodities are more carefully monitored in countries such as Canada and the United States. They did, however, observe that the variety of foods were less fresh and more processed, and they worried that consuming too much of these foods might cause health problems for them or their children. They overwhelmingly preferred cooking from scratch with fresh ingredients, and many missed fruits and vegetables that were abundant back home but hard to find in the conventional grocery store. For shoppers with limited English, decoding an ingredient or product label is especially difficult, meaning that many of these consumers do not engage with the minutiae of precautionary consumer labeling. The factors that become most important are price, taste, and whether a food product fits with the shopper's foodways and family members' food preferences. I suspect, however, that these shoppers have concerns about undesirable ingredients in American foods and consumer products. Indeed, some of the women in this study who were from outside the United States felt strongly about the new taste or texture of American foods and expressed skepticism about product packages that claimed products to be natural or healthy. Immigrant shoppers likely manage environmental risks through grocery shopping, but we know little about what this experience is like—meaning that this is a promising direction for future work.

NOTES

1. INTRODUCTION

Epigraphs: "His Philosophy," Chaz Dean Studio, accessed July 11, 2017, www
.chazdean.com/aboutChaz/philosophy; Monsanto, "What Is Glyphosate?" accessed
July 11, 2017, www.monsantoglobal.com/global/au/products/Documents/what_is
_glyphosate.pdf.

1. "The History of WEN® Hair Care and the Process of Perfection," WEN Hair
Care, accessed July 11, 2017, www.wenhaircare.com/en_us/process-of-perfection
.html.

2. Kwa, Welty, and Xu 2017.

3. Kerin Higa, "More Health Problems Reported with Hair and Skin Care
Products," *Your Health* (blog), National Public Radio, June 26, 2017, www.npr.org
/sections/health-shots/2017/06/26/534411597/more-health-problems-reported-with-
hair-and-skin-care-products.

4. "Settlement Agreement and Release of Claims," WEN® Hair Care Class
Action Official Settlement Website, September 13, 2016, https://www.wenclassset-
tlement.com/content/documents/SettlementAgreement.pdf.

5. Associated Press, "California Can Require a Cancer-Warning Label on
Roundup Weed Killer, Judge Rules," *LA Times,* March 14, 2017, www.latimes.com
/business/la-fi-roundup-california-20170314-story.html.

6. Danny Hakim, "Monsanto Weed Killer Roundup Faces New Doubts on
Safety in Unsealed Documents," *New York Times,* March 14, 2017, www.nytimes
.com/2017/03/14/business/monsanto-roundup-safety-lawsuit.html.

7. Glyphosate residues are monitored by the FDA, but the agency temporarily
stopped testing for this compound in 2016. In response, advocacy groups Food
Democracy Now! and the Detox Project tested popular foods for residues (hiring
the same lab that had been used by the FDA for its testing), and results showed
glyphosate residues on nearly all items evaluated, with Cheerios and Stacy's
Pita Chips showing especially high levels. See Food Democracy Now! and the
Detox Project, "Unsafe on Any Plate," March 2016, https://usrtk.org/wp-content

/uploads/2016/11/FDN_Glyphosate_FoodTesting_Report_p2016–3.pdf. For more analysis of glyphosate residues, see Food and Agriculture Organization of the United Nations and the World Health Organization, *Residues in Food, 2004: Evaluations Part II, Toxicological* (World Health Organization: Rome, 2004), http://apps .who.int/iris/bitstream/10665/43624/1/9241665203_eng.pdf. Since "Roundup Ready" genetically engineered crops were introduced in 1996 (crops engineered to withstand herbicides that surrounding weeds cannot), the application of glyphosate has increased fifteen fold; about 70 percent of all glyphosate use from 1974 to 2014 was sprayed in the past ten years (Benbrook 2016, 6).

8. International Agency for Research on Cancer, "IARC Monographs Volume 112: Evaluation of Five Organophosphate Insecticides and Herbicides," March 20, 2015, www.iarc.fr/en/media-centre/iarcnews/pdf/MonographVolume112.pdf. The European Union is facing pressure from environment and health advocacy groups to ban glyphosate. See, e.g., Britt Erikson, "No Consensus on Glyphosate in the EU," *Chemical and Engineering News,* October 25, 2017, https://cen.acs.org/articles/95/i43/consensus-glyphosate-EU.html. At the time of writing, the European Parliament had voted to ban the substance by 2022, while the European Commission was considering renewing approval of glyphosate use until 2023.

9. In July 2017, the Coalition for Safer Food Processing and Packaging, which includes national environmental advocacy organizations like the Natural Resources Defense Council and Environmental Defense Fund, tested ten varieties of instant macaroni and cheese and found that nearly all of them contained phthalates, which are known to interfere with the human endocrine system. See the campaign's website at www.kleanupkraft.org. Results of their tests were released on July 14 to coincide with National Mac 'n' Cheese Day, and the story received national news media coverage.

10. In this book, I use the terms "chemicals," "environmental chemicals," and "toxics" to refer to synthetic chemical substances that are suspected to be harmful to human health.

11. O'Connor and Spunt 2010; Freinkel 2011; Baker 2008; Duke 2011.

12. "Natural & Organic Retail Foods and Beverage Market Hits $69 Billion," Prepared Foods, October 10, 2016, www.preparedfoods.com/articles/118844-natural-organic-retail-foods-and-beverage-market-hits-69-billion.

13. Kowitt 2014.

14. Organic Trade Association 2015.

15. Watson 2013.

16. Precautionary consumption can also be practiced while online shopping. Many retailers, like Amazon Fresh, FreshDirect, Peapod, Vitacost, and Thrive Market, offer shoppers views of product packages and make claims about the healthfulness and transparency of the commodity chain.

17. MacKendrick 2010.

18. By "conventional," I mean food and agricultural products that are not labeled as certified-organic. This food might be grown with synthetic pesticides and may contain synthetic ingredients, such as artificial colors.

19. MacKendrick 2014.

20. See also Ian Urbina, "Think Those Chemicals Have Been Tested?" *New York Times,* April 13, 2013, www.nytimes.com/2013/04/14/sunday-review/think-those-chemicals-have-been-tested.html.

21. Wilson and Schwarzman 2009, 1205; 2014, 744.

22. Schapiro 2007.

23. "International Laws," Campaign for Safe Cosmetics, accessed January 13, 2016, www.safecosmetics.org/get-the-facts/regulations/international-laws/#sthash .VvJYxR6g.dpuf.

24. Entine 2011; see also Schwarcz 2015.

25. American College of Obstetricians and Gynecologists and American Society for Reproductive Medicine 2013; Di Renzo et al. 2015; Zoeller et al. 2012.

26. Di Renzo et al. 2015, 219.

27. Langston 2010, 17.

28. Landrigan and Goldman 2011. Of these, thirty thousand are produced in quantities greater than one metric ton per year (Thornton, McCally, and Houlihan 2002).

29. Sexton, Needham, and Pirkle 2004.

30. Adibi et al. 2008; Caserta et al. 2011; Perera et al. 2003.

31. LaKind et al. 2001; LaKind et al. 2004.

32. Sexton, Needham, and Pirkle 2004; Washburn 2013.

33. Sexton, Needham, and Pirkle 2004; Washburn 2013.

34. The CDC defines an environmental chemical as "a chemical compound or chemical element present in air, water, food, soil, dust, or other environmental media (e.g., consumer products)." Biomonitoring is defined as "the assessment of human exposure to chemicals by measuring the chemicals or their metabolites in such human specimens as blood or urine" (Centers for Disease Control and Prevention 2009, 1).

35. Washburn 2013.

36. Centers for Disease Control and Prevention 2009; 2015; 2017, 1.

37. Birnbaum 2013, A107.

38. Dewailly et al. 1992; Dewailly et al. 2000.

39. Allen 2003; Bullard 1990; Hoover 2017; Taylor 2009; Szasz 1994.

40. Downey 2006; Mohai and Saha 2007; Sze 2007; Taylor 2009, 2014.

41. See, e.g., Boffetta, Jourenkova, and Gustavsson 1997; Brophy et al. 2012; Harrison 2011; Hines et al. 2009; Kroll-Smith, Brown, and Gunter 2000.

42. Robinson 1991.

43. Weschler 2009.

44. Murphy 2006.

45. Pirkle et al. 1998.

46. Bradman et al. 2011; Zota et al. 2008.

47. Bradman et al. 2011; Zota et al. 2008.

48. Conventional disposal protocols divert these products to landfills, where the PBDEs enter air and waterways. Consequently, homes near landfills may experience

higher exposure to PBDEs, and these compounds will eventually migrate into global air and water currents (Betts 2015).

49. Dodson et al. 2012.

50. Adamkiewicz et al. 2011.

51. See, e.g., Harley et al. 2016.

52. Kwan and Trautner 2009.

53. See Branch et al. 2015; Calafat 2010; Myers et al. 2015; and Flint and Adewumi 2016.

54. See Craig 2002; Wingfield 2009; Zota and Shamasunder 2017; and Bhavna Shamasunder and Janet Flint Robinson, "Beauty Myths 2.0: Breaking Toxic Bonds and Creating Cross Racial Alliances," UCLA Center for the Study of Women, December 9, 2016, https://csw.ucla.edu/2016/12/09/beauty-myths-2-0-breaking-toxic-bonds-creating-cross-racial-alliances.

55. Tyrrell et al. 2013.

56. Tyrrell et al. 2013.

57. For a summary of the vast literature on health effects from environmental chemical exposure, see Bennett et al. 2016; Birnbaum 2013; and Landrigan et al. 2002.

58. Diamanti-Kandarakis et al. 2009; Zoeller et al. 2012.

59. Bennett et al. 2016; Birnbaum 2013; Landrigan et al. 2002; Paulson 2011.

60. See, e.g., Egilman and Bohme 2005.

61. Goldman, Carlson, and Zhang 2015, 2.

62. "Endocrine Society Disregards State of Science around Chemical Exposures and Endocrine System," American Chemistry Council, September 28, 2015, p. 1, www.americanchemistry.com/Media/PressReleasesTranscripts/ACC-news-releases/Endocrine-Society-Views-Disregards-State-of-Science-Around-Chemical-Exposures-and-Endocrine-System.html.

63. The American Chemistry Council was a vocal opponent of listing BPA and phthalates under California Proposition 65. The ACC has claimed that environmental organizations and health researchers are stoking consumer fears by calling chemicals possible carcinogens or endocrine disruptors, and has criticized the research of two influential scientists, Phillippe Grandjean and Philip Landrigan, who study endocrine disruptors and fetal development and infant health. Grandjean and Landrigan have launched scientific programs to address the gap in the medical community's understanding of endocrine disruptors and fetal development. See "ACC Comments on New Report on Industrial Chemicals Published in the Lancet Neurology," American Chemistry Council, February 14, 2014, www.americanchemistry.com/Media/PressReleasesTranscripts/ACC-news-releases/ACC-Comments-on-New-Report-on-Industrial-Chemicals-Published-in-the-Lancet-Neurology.html.

64. See, e.g., Cordner 2016; and S. Vogel 2013.

65. Szasz 2007.

66. Harrison 2011.

67. Szasz 2007.

68. T. Rudel 2013.

69. MacKendrick and Stevens 2016.

70. Allen 2003; Szasz 1994.

71. See, e.g., Environmental Working Group 2005.

72. Murphy 2013, 4.

73. Beck 1992, 1995, 1999.

74. Giddens 1990, 1991.

75. Giddens 1999.

76. Altman et al. 2008.

77. Clarke and Short 1993.

78. Schultz 2015; "Qs&As about Triclosan Reregistration Eligibility Decision," Environmental Protection Agency, accessed June 7, 2017, www.epa.gov/ingredients-used-pesticide-products/qsas-about-triclosan-reregistration-eligibility-decision.

79. Environmental Working Group 2014; Beyond Pesticides 2010.

80. "Our Position on Triclosan," Johnson & Johnson, accessed April 30, 2014, http://mc-3701–1440610202.us-east-1.elb.amazonaws.com/sites/default/files/pdf /cs/Our%20Position%20on%20Triclosan_July%202014.pdf (link no longer active).

81. See Nathan Bomey, "Baby Powder Lawsuit: Woman with Ovarian Cancer Awarded $110M from Johnson & Johnson," *USA Today,* May 5, 2017, www.usatoday .com/story/money/2017/05/05/johnson-johnson-talc-verdict/101320524.

82. Funtowicz and Ravetz 1993; Rosa 1998.

83. Scott 2005.

84. Freudenburg, Gramling, and Davidson 2008.

85. Michaels 2008; Jasanoff 2005.

86. Brown and Mikkelsen 1997; Harrison 2011; M. Reich 2000.

87. Shostak 2013.

88. Markowitz and Rosner 2002a, 2013.

89. Markowitz and Rosner 2000, 44.

90. Markowitz and Rosner 2013.

91. Rosner and Markowitz 2005.

92. While blood lead levels are declining overall, higher risk groups still exist. Non-Hispanic Blacks living in poor urban centers are most at risk for high blood lead levels owing to the increased likelihood that members of this group live in older housing, where old layers of lead paint may be peeling and releasing lead into indoor air (Jones et al. 2009).

93. Kessler 2014.

94. For explanations as to why, see Prasad 2006.

95. Harvey 2005; Prasad 2006.

96. Larner 2000.

97. Hacker 2008, 6.

98. Hacker 2008, 20.

99. Bernstein 2000; Slocum 2004.

100. Guthman 2007; Roff 2007.

101. Khanna, Quimio, and Bojilova 1998.

102. Schor 2010; Carfagna et al. 2014.

103. Jennifer Reich (2016) observes that parents see vaccine refusal as another individual choice but often fail to connect it to larger structural issues—particularly the role of population vaccination in protecting vulnerable groups.

104. Scott 2007.

105. Foucault 1997, 224.

106. Rabinow and Rose 2006; Rose 2007.

107. Shostak 2010.

108. Mansfield 2012b.

109. Reuben 2010, iii.

110. Reuben 2010, 98.

111. See, e.g., Faustman 2000; Perera et al. 1999; and Vogt et al. 2012.

112. Kukla 2010; MacKendrick 2014; Mansfield 2012a, 2012b.

113. Almeling and Waggoner 2013; Daniels 2006; Richardson et al. 2014.

114. See Private Label Manufacturers Association 2013, 2.

115. Waggoner 2017; Markens, Browner, and Press 1997.

116. See, e.g., Cawley and Liu 2012.

117. MacKendrick 2014; Cairns and Johnston 2015.

118. The rate at which a mother's chemical load is transferred through breast-feeding is not well understood, but researchers estimate that it is between 20 and 70 percent, depending on the compound (LaKind et al. 2001; LaKind et al. 2004). Breastfeeding advocates reassure mothers that "breast is still best," and argue that the benefits of breastfeeding outweigh the risk of infants ingesting the contaminants in breast milk (Bauchner 2004).

119. Cairns, Johnston and MacKendrick 2013; Cairns and Johnston 2015; MacKendrick 2014.

120. See the appendix for details on method, data, and analytic strategy.

121. Cairns and Johnston 2015; MacKendrick 2014.

122. The phrase "commodity bubble" comes from Szasz (2007, 97).

2. SAFE UNTIL SORRY

Epigraphs: Otto Pohl, "European Environmental Rules Propel Change in U.S.," *New York Times,* July 6, 2004, www.nytimes.com/2004/07/06/science/european-environmental-rules-propel-change-in-us.html; Juliet Eilperin and Darryl Fears, "Congress Is Overhauling an Outdated Law That Affects Nearly Every Product You Own,"*WashingtonPost,*May19,2016,www.washingtonpost.com/politics/congress-poised-to-pass-sweeping-reform-of-chemical-law/2016/05/18/0da5cd22–1d30–11e6–9c81–4be1c14fb8c8_story.html?utm_term=.6018e56b2621.

1. Hanekamp, Vera-Navas, and Verstegen 2005.

2. Harremoës et al 2001.

3. Harremoës et al 2001.

4. European Commission 2000.

5. Harremoës et al. 2001; Whiteside 2006.

6. Raffensperger and Tickner 1999; Ley 2009.

7. United Nations Environment Program 1992, principle 15.

8. The United Nations Framework Convention on Climate Change was the precursor to the Kyoto Protocol (1997) and the Paris Agreement (2016).

9. Linton and Hall 2013; Gareau 2013; Tickner, Raffensperger, and Meyer 1999; Ley 2009.

10. Gareau 2013.

11. See Stockholm Convention Clearing House, "Status of Ratification," United Nations Environment Programme, accessed October 27, 2017, http://chm.pops.int /Countries/StatusofRatifications/PartiesandSignatories/tabid/252/Default.aspx.

12. Schapiro 2007. REACH stands for Registration, Evaluation, Authorization, and Restriction of Chemicals.

13. Elizabeth Grossman, "A Shocking Number of Chemical Products Are Banned in Europe But Safe in the US," *Business Insider,* June 10, 2014, www.businessinsider. com/products-banned-in-europe-but-safe-in-us-2014–6; "Chemicals of Concern," Campaign for Safe Cosmetics, accessed June 20, 2017, www.safecosmetics.org /get-the-facts/chem-of-concern.

14. Snyder 1984.

15. vom Saal and Myers 2008

16. vom Saal and Myers 2008, 1354; Calafat et al. 2008.

17. See, e.g., vom Saal and Myers 2008; Beronius et al. 2010.

18. See, e.g., Gore et al. 2015; Bevacqua 2013; Zoeller et al. 2012; Diamanti-Kandarakis et al. 2009; and Birnbaum and Fenton 2003.

19. American Chemistry Council 2015.

20. American Chemistry Council 2017.

21. Horel 2015; Nielsen 2015.

22. Nielsen 2015.

23. Horel 2015, 2016; Horel and Bienkowski 2013.

24. See Tweedale 2017.

25. Horel and Bienkowski 2013.

26. Tweedale 2017.

27. Hrudey and Leiss 2003; Mayer, Brown, and Linder 2002; Wurzel 2002.

28. United States Government Accountability Office 2005.

29. Langston 2010; Michaels 2008; Oreskes and Conway 2011; Rosner and Markowitz 2002.

30. United States Government Accountability Office 2017.

31. United States Government Accountability Office 2005, 4.

32. See Frank R. Lautenberg Chemical Safety for the 21st Century Act, Pub. L. No. 114–182, 130 Stat. 450 (June 22, 2016).

33. Environmental Working Group, "Environmental Groups Sue Trump Administration over New Rules That Will Make It Harder to Protect against Harm From Toxic Chemicals," press release, August 14, 2017, www.ewg.org/release/envi-ronmental-groups-sue-trump-administration-over-new-rules-will-make-it-harder-protect#.WgMfgIZrzBI.

34. Langston 2010; Whorton 1975.

35. Davis 2014.

36. Haydu 2011.

37. Davis 2014.

38. Langston 2010, 20–21. Note that Wiley did not use the term "precautionary principle"; he did, however, refer to concepts that are closely related to this principle.

39. Langston 2010, 35.

40. Langston 2010, 35.

41. Cited in Whorton 1975, 176.

42. Schlink 1935, cited in Whorton 1975, 193.

43. Davis 2014, 3.

44. See, e.g., United States Food and Drug Administration 2017c.

45. For a detailed history of the controversy surrounding DES, see Langston 2010.

46. Davis 2014.

47. Davis 2014; S. Vogel 2013.

48. S. Vogel 2013.

49. This amendment is sometimes referred to as the Delaney Clause, after James Delaney, a Democratic senator from New York who spearheaded the initial hearings. This clause was added to an already-revised FDCA that had been changed in 1954 to include guidelines regarding pesticide residues on food.

50. Picut and Parker 1992; S. Vogel 2013.

51. Langston 2010, 100–107.

52. American Chemical Society 1979.

53. *Findings, Policy, and Intent,* sec. 2, Toxic Control Substances Act of 2003, 15 U.S.C. § 2601, 40 CFR R.

54. Freudenburg, Gramling, and Davidson 2008; Lynch and Vogel 2001. The hydrocarbon fluorocarbon phaseout was implemented through an action added to the Clean Air Act (1990) called the "Final Rule Accelerating the Phaseout of Ozone-Depleting Substances," 40 CFR Part 82 (1993), and was brought into force in 1994.

55. Becker, Edwards, and Massey 2010.

56. S. Vogel and Roberts 2011, 900.

57. United States Government Accountability Office 2005.

58. S. Vogel and Roberts 2011.

59. United States Government Accountability Office 2005, 16.

60. United States Government Accountability Office 2005, 18.

61. United States Government Accountability Office 2005.

62. Lee 1991.

63. McGarity 2001.

64. Schierow 2002, CRS-1.

65. Neff et al. 2012; United States Government Accountability Office 2014.

66. United States Government Accountability Office 2014.

67. Neff et al. 2012.

68. United States Government Accountability Office 2014.

69. "Dirty Dozen: EWG's 2017 Shopper's Guide to Pesticides in Produce™," Environmental Working Group, accessed June 12, 2017, www.ewg.org/foodnews /dirty_dozen_list.php.

70. "Pesticides + Poison Gases = Cheap, Year-Round Strawberries," Environmental Working Group, accessed June 12, 2017, www.ewg.org/foodnews/strawberries .php.

71. Neltner et al. 2011.

72. Neltner et al. 2013.

73. Neltner and Maffini 2014.

74. M. Warner 2014.

75. M. Warner 2014; Neltner et al. 2013.

76. Neltner et al. 2013.

77. Neltner and Maffini 2014, 2.

78. Center for Food Safety, "Groups Sue FDA for Food Safety," press release, May 22, 2017, www.centerforfoodsafety.org/press-releases/4956/groups-sue-fda-to-protect-food-safety#.

79. See, e.g., Onyango, Hallman, and Bellows 2007.

80. Pollan 2006.

81. United States Department of Agriculture, "About the National Organic Program," Agricultural Marketing Service, November 2016, www.ams.usda.gov /publications/content/about-national-organic-program. Organic certification organizations that existed before the USDA system was implemented, such as the Northeast Organic Farmers Association and Oregon Tilth, were incorporated into the USDA process as third-party accreditors. Exempted from these rules are individuals and companies whose gross sales are under $5000 a year. They may use the term "organic" to sell their products and must follow the USDA standards, but they are not required to apply for USDA certification.

82. See Guthman 2004a, 2004b.

83. United States Department of Agriculture National Organic Program, 65 FR 80637, December 21, 2000 (title 7, subtitle B, chapter I, subchapter M, subpart G, § 205.6).

84. United States Department of Agriculture, "Labeling Organic Products," Agricultural Marketing Service, accessed July 8, 2017, www.ams.usda.gov/sites /default/files/media/Labeling%20Organic%20Products.pdf.

85. United States Department of Agriculture, "National Organic Program: Cosmetics, Body Care Products, and Personal Care Products," Agricultural Marketing Service, April 2008, www.ams.usda.gov/sites/default/files/media/Organic-CosmeticsFactSheet.pdf.

86. Lang and Hallman 2005.

87. Amani (2015) provides a compelling argument as to how GMOs could be treated as chemicals under the law.

88. "GMO Facts," Non-GMO Project, accessed June 20, 2017, www.nongmo-project.org/gmo-facts.

89. For a concise summary of European Union regulation, see "Restrictions on Genetically Modified Organisms: European Union," Library of Congress, March 2015, www.loc.gov/law/help/restrictions-on-gmos/eu.php.

90. "Verification FAQs," Non-GMO Project, accessed June 20, 2017, www.nongmoproject.org/product-verification/verification-faqs.

91. See, e.g., "FAQs about GMOs," *Consumer Reports,* March 2015, https://consumersunion.org/wp-content/uploads/2015/01/FAQs_About_GMOs_CR_0315.pdf.

92. Ted Agres, "USDA Begins Crafting Rules for Mandatory GMO Food Labels," Food Quality and Safety, September 13, 2016, www.foodqualityandsafety.com/article/usda-begins-crafting-rules-mandatory-gmo-food-labels.

93. The PFDA of 1906 was passed to control improperly labeled foods and consumer products. At the time, consumers and the government were concerned about the misleading statements printed on product packaging and in advertising. The PFDA made it illegal for food and drugs to be "labeled or branded as to deceive or mislead the purchaser" and to fail to contain the contents that they purported to contain (United States Food and Drug Administration 2017c). When Congress passed the FDCA in 1938, it required manufacturers to include certain mandatory information on packaging, such as the net weight or volume of the product, ingredients, and the name and address of the manufacturer (Degnan 1997).

94. United States Food and Drug Administration 2017a.

95. This act was first introduced in 1973.

96. Wartella, Lichenstein, and Boon 2010.

97. 21 C.F.R. 101 (2017).

98. The rule was first scheduled to come into effect in 2018, but the deadline was extended to 2020 after complaints from major food manufacturers. See Jim Spencer and Kristen Leigh Painter, "Food Labeling Delay Just Latest Sign of Business Clout in Washington," *Minneapolis Star Tribune.* July 10, 2017, www.startribune.com/food-labeling-delay-just-latest-sign-of-business-clout-in-washington/433179533.

99. Campos, Doxey, and Hammond 2011.

100. Campos, Doxey, and Hammond 2011.

101. Travernise 2015.

102. Stephanie Strom, "Kellogg Agrees to Alter Labeling on Kashi Line," *New York Times,* May 8, 2014, www.nytimes.com/2014/05/09/business/kellogg-agrees-to-change-labeling-on-kashi-line.html.

103. Dan Charles, "'Natural' Food Sounds Good but Doesn't Mean Much," National Public Radio, June 24, 2014, www.npr.org/sections/thesalt/2014/06/24/325189610/natural-food-sounds-good-but-doesnt-mean-much.

104. If a product contains a sunscreen agent or an antimicrobial ingredient, however, it is regulated by the FDA as an over-the-counter drug and is thus subject to different rules.

105. Food and Drug Administration, "FDA Authority over Cosmetics: How Cosmetics Are Not FDA-Approved, but Are FDA-Regulated," Cosmetics,

March 3, 2005, www.fda.gov/Cosmetics/GuidanceRegulation/LawsRegulations/ucm074162.htm#Who_is_responsible.

106. United States Food and Drug Administration 2017a.

107. Parlett, Calafat, and Swan 2013.

108. United States Food and Drug Administration 2017b; A. Martin 2012.

109. Flaherty 2008, 372.

110. M. A. Quattlebaum and B. Rustin, "The CPSIA: Congressional Response to the 'Year of the Recall,'" *Business Law Today* 19, no. 1 (2009), www.americanbar.org/publications/blt/2009/09/05_rustin.html.

111. Flaherty 2008, 381.

112. "Spin Master Recalls Aqua Dots—Children Became Unconscious after Swallowing Beads," Consumer Products Safety Commission, November 7, 2007, www.cpsc.gov/Recalls/2007/spin-master-recalls-aqua-dots-children-became-unconscious-after-swallowing-beads.

113. Kamrin 2009.

114. Flaherty 2008.

115. See, e.g., Pavilonis et al. (2014).

116. "CPSC Status Report on Crumb Rubber," Consumer Products Safety Commission, accessed June 20, 2017, www.cpsc.gov/Safety-Education/Safety-Education-Centers/Crumb-Rubber-Safety-Information-Center.

117. United States Environmental Protection Agency 2017a.

118. See Cordner 2016.

119. United States Environmental Protection Agency 2017b.

120. United States Environmental Protection Agency 2017b.

121. Dooley 2017, 1.

122. Dellavalle 2016, 17.

123. SB 509, State of California (2007), www.leginfo.ca.gov/pub/07–08/bill/sen/sb_0501–0550/sb_509_bill_20080929_chaptered.html.

124. Michaels and Burke 2017.

125. Lauren Coleman-Lochner, "Chemical Defender Put in Charge of EPA Unit Overseeing Toxins," *Bloomberg,* May 24, 2017, www.bloomberg.com/news/articles/2017–05–24/chemical-defender-put-in-charge-of-epa-unit-overseeing-toxins.

126. Eric Lipton, "E.P.A. Chief, Rejecting Agency's Science, Chooses Not to Ban Insecticide," *New York Times,* March 29, 2017, www.nytimes.com/2017/03/29/us/politics/epa-insecticide-chlorpyrifos.html.

127. "A. G. Schneiderman Challenges Trump EPA over Toxic Pesticide," press release, Office of Eric T. Schneiderman, June 6, 2017, https://ag.ny.gov/press-release/ag-schneiderman-challenges-trump-epa-over-toxic-pesticide.

3. PERSONALIZING POLLUTION

Epigraphs: "Dirty Dozen Endocrine Disruptors: 12 Hormone-Altering Chemicals and How to Avoid Them," Environmental Working Group, October 28, 2013, www.ewg.org

/research/dirty-dozen-list-endocrine-disruptors; Healthy Child Healthy World, *Easy Steps to a Safer Pregnancy,* (Beverly Hills, CA: Healthy Child, Healthy World, 2014), 13.

1. Refer to the appendix for an overview of my methodology for selecting and reviewing these documents.

2. Brown 2007; Mayer et al. 2002.

3. Brown 2007, 203.

4. Szasz 1994; Brulle and Pellow 2006.

5. Szasz 1994.

6. Brown et al. 2006; Brown 2007; Hoover et al. 2015.

7. McCormick, Brown, and Zavestoski 2003; Brown et al. 2003.

8. Compared to other branches of the environmental movement, a disproportionate number of these advocacy groups have women in leadership positions, likely because of women's role in maintaining community ties and advocating for children's health, which offers a pathway to community organizing and activism (Brown and Ferguson 1995; Bell 2013; Krauss 1993). In general, mothers are more likely to take part in community activism because community threats encroach on traditionally gendered domains, such as caring for children's well-being and maintaining community ties (Bell 2013; Brown and Ferguson 1995; Krauss 1993). In communities of color, women's status as mothers aids rather than abets their entry into community leadership and activism owing to the status of mothers in keeping families and communities together in face of larger systemic oppressions and inequalities (Collins 2000; Krauss 1993). Environmental health threats implicate networks of organizations that have mothers as active participants in the movement or as a target audience due to their role in the family and community.

9. Krimsky 2000.

10. Krimsky 2000.

11. Colborn and Clement 1992, 2.

12. Colborn and Clement 1992.

13. Bern 1992, 9.

14. Colborn, Dumanoski, and Myers 1996.

15. S. Vogel 2013.

16. Roberts 2009; J. Vogel 2005; S. Vogel 2013.

17. Brown 2007; Krimsky 2000

18. Tickner 2003, xiii.

19. Mayer, Brown, and Linder 2002.

20. Brown 2007; McCormick, Brown, and Zavestoski 2003.

21. Schecter et al. 2003; Betts 2002.

22. For the Swedish data, see Meironyté, Norén, and Bergman 1999; for the American data, see Betts 2002.

23. Hites 2004.

24. Altman et al. 2008; Shamasunder and Morello-Frosch 2015.

25. Depending on the year of testing (as the technology has advanced rapidly from 2001 to 2014) advocacy biomonitoring has revealed biomarkers for hundreds of synthetic chemicals.

26. Carson 2002, 15–16.

27. Sexton, Needham, and Pirkle 2004; Dennis et al. 2017.

28. Altman 2008; Washburn 2013.

29. Brown 2007; Shamasunder and Morello-Frosch 2015. To conduct their famous *BodyBurden* report, the EWG collaborated with researchers at the Mount Sinai School of Medicine in New York City, who led the study and published the results in the journal *Public Health Reports* a year before they were published on the EWG website. See Thornton et al. 2002.

30. Shostak 2010, 243–244.

31. Environmental Working Group 2003; see also Malkan 2007; Washburn 2013.

32. Environmental Working Group 2003, 10.

33. Centers for Disease Control and Prevention 2001, 2003.

34. Malkan 2007, 37.

35. In 2004, the Pesticide Action Network published a report on chemical trespass that summarizes CDC biomonitoring data documenting the U.S. population's exposure to pesticides. See Pesticide Action Network North America 2004.

36. As outlined in table 1, some of these organizations partnered to produce biomonitoring studies. No advocacy biomonitoring reports were produced in 2015, although it is possible smaller organizations produced such reports that were not captured in the data analysis. See the appendix for an overview of the research methodologies used in this chapter.

37. "Polluted Pets: High Levels of Toxic Industrial Chemicals Contaminate Cats and Dogs," Environmental Working Group, April 17, 2008, www.ewg.org /research/polluted-pets.

38. Sexton, Needham, and Pirkle 2004; Washburn 2013. Note that the early 2000s did not mark the beginning of advocacy biomonitoring. One early well-known study is the Tooth Fairy Project of 1958, organized in part by environmentalist Barry Commoner. The Tooth Fairy Project collected the baby teeth of children living in the greater St. Louis area and tested them for strontium-90, a by-product of hydrogen bomb detonations. Tests revealed higher accumulations of strontium-90 in the baby teeth of children born during years with detonations. See Washington University School of Medicine, *St. Louis Baby Tooth Survey, 1959–1970* (Saint Louis, MO: Bernard Becker Medical Library, 2006).

39. Shamasunder and Morello-Frosch 2015.

40. Persistent organic pollutants are stored in human and animal fat deposits. They take a very long time to break down—both in the body and in the general environment. Volatile organic compounds, or VOCs, break down fairly quickly and are released into the air. Concern about "off-gassing" relates to concerns about VOCs in the indoor environment from carpets, adhesives, and paint, among other products. See, e.g., Minnesota Department of Health, "Volatile Organic Compounds (VOCs) in Indoor Air," accessed July 20, 2017, www.health.state.mn.us /divs/eh/indoorair/voc/vocsfactsheet.pdf.

41. Alliance for a Clean and Healthy Maine, *Body of Evidence: A Study of Pollution in Maine People* (Portland, MA: Alliance for a Clean and Healthy Maine, 2007), 9.

42. Commonweal, *Taking It All In: Documenting Chemical Pollution in Californians through Biomonitoring* (Bolinas, CA: Commonweal Biomonitoring Resource Center, 2005), 25.

43. In 1973, feed grain in Michigan was accidentally contaminated with polybrominated biphenyls (PBBs), compounds used as flame retardants. The accidental contamination took a year to detect and contain, and in the meantime Michigan residents unknowingly consumed contaminated beef and milk. Subsequent breast milk biomonitoring studies confirmed that PBBs were transferred to children through breast milk, which may explain twelve-year-old-Bryan Brown's PBB burden. See, e.g., Brilliant et al. 1978.

44. Altman 2008, 8.

45. Altman 2008.

46. See Shamasunder and Morello-Frosch 2015.

47. Daniels 2006; Richardson 2015.

48. Bloom et al. 2007; Foster et al. 2011.

49. Environmental Working Group 2005, 16.

50. In 2005, Greenpeace International published a report that measured umbilical cord blood for chemical biomarkers. See Greenpeace International, Greenpeace Nederland, and WWF-UK, *A Present for Life: Hazardous Chemicals in Umbilical Cord Blood* (Amsterdam: Greenpeace, September 8, 2005) www.greenpeace.org /eu-unit/en/Publications/2009-and-earlier/a-present-for-life.

51. Waggoner 2017.

52. Environmental Working Group 2006, 10.

53. Environmental Working Group 2006, 4.

54. Schreder 2009. Note that the Washington Toxics Coalition became Toxic Free Future in 2016.

55. Schreder 2009.

56. Almeling and Waggoner 2013.

57. Pesticide Action Network North America 2004, 16.

58. Daniels 2006.

59. See, e.g., Kong et al. 2012; and Anway et al. 2005.

60. Boyle 2016.

61. Boyle 2016.

62. Cf. Daniels 2006.

63. I am grateful to Kate Cairns for helping me identify and articulate this point.

64. See, e.g., Anway et al. 2005; and Daniels 2006.

65. Anway et al. 2005; and Daniels 2006.

66. Gonzales 2010, 21.

67. Gonzales 2010, 21.

68. There are overlaps between DOHaD and postgenomic medicine, namely maternal-fetal epigenetic programming. For a summary of these overlaps, refer to Richardson 2015.

69. Birnbaum and Fenton 2003; Heindel and Vandenberg 2015; Fox et al. 2012.

70. Heindel and Vandenberg 2015.

71. Manikkam et al. 2013. Findings from transgenerational studies of animals are often extended to understand transgenerational effects in humans. Human studies of this kind are costly, complicated, and ideally involve following research subjects from birth to adulthood, meaning that they take decades to complete.

72. Pryor et al. 2000.

73. Grandjean et al. 2015; Mannikam et al. 2013; Richardson et al. 2014.

74. Daniels 2006; Richardson et al. 2014, 221.

75. Markens, Browner, and Press 1997, 352.

76. Healthy Child Healthy World, *Easy Steps to a Safer Pregnancy* (Beverly Hills, CA: Healthy Child Healthy World, 2014), 4–5.

77. Healthy Child Healthy World, "When Looking Good Is Bad for Baby," accessed June 28, 2017, www.healthychild.org/when-looking-good-is-bad-for-baby.

78. See also MacKendrick and Cairns, forthcoming.

79. Breast Cancer Fund 2013, 5.

80. Breast Cancer Fund 2013, 12. Men are rarely included in this clinical interaction. In practice, reproductive health professionals rarely advise women to practice precautionary consumption behaviors, rationalizing that personal avoidance is impossible given the ubiquity of environmental contaminants and that it would be another burden for women to take on as they prepare for a healthy pregnancy. See Stevens 2016.

81. Rudel et al. 2003.

82. Environmental Working Group, "EWG Skin Deep Cosmetics Database," accessed November 12, 2017, www.ewg.org/skindeep.

83. Szasz 2007.

84. Willis and Schor 2012.

85. Breast Cancer Fund 2011, 2.

86. Breast Cancer Fund 2011, 6.

87. Coalition for a Safe and Healthy Connecticut, "Top Ten Tips to Reduce Toxins in Your Home," accessed January 13, 2016, www.safehealthyct.org.

88. Greater Boston Chapter of Physicians for Social Responsibility 2001, 1.

89. Environmental Working Group, "Consumer Tips to Avoid Bisphenol A," March 5, 2007, www.ewg.org/research/bisphenol/consumer-tips-avoid-bpa-exposure.

90. Brulle 2000.

91. Brulle 2000, 225.

92. Brulle 2000.

93. Micheletti 2004.

94. Shamasunder and Morello-Frosch 2015, 11.

95. Micheletti 2003; Barnett et al. 2005.

96. Micheletti 2003, 35.

97. See, e.g., Johnston 2008.

98. Gabriel and Lang 2006.

99. Elkington and Hailes 1988.

100. Elkington and Hailes 1988, 2–3.

101. Colborn, Dumanoski and Myers 1996, 210.

102. Colborn, Dumanoski and Myers 1996, 218.

103. "Ken Cook on EWG's 20th Anniversary," YouTube video, 2:53, posted by "Environmental Working Group (EWG)," October 28, 2013, www.youtube.com /watch?v=HbBoHVS6h64.

104. Natural Resources Defense Council, *Healthy Milk, Healthy Baby: Chemical Pollution* (New York: Natural Resources Defense Council, 2001).

105. "What You Should Know about Breast Cancer and the Environment," Breast Cancer Action, 2014, www.bcaction.org/our-take-on-breast-cancer/environment /#sthash.kkLwx4n5.dpufIn.

4. BE A SUPER SHOPPER!

Epigraphs: Whole Foods Market, *The Whole Deal,* coupon book available in-store and online, January/February 2015; Whole Foods Market, "Quality Standards," accessed June 23, 2017, www.wholefoodsmarket.com/quality-standards.

1. In October 2012, Stonyfield Farm, a large U.S. organic yogurt producer, ran a contest and marketing campaign called "I Will Know My Food". Visitors to the company's website could create their own superhero profile. Food superheroes, according to the company, "Know that ingredients and production processes matter. Know that good food is tasty, nutritious and sustainable. Support family farms." Information from www.iwillknowmyfood.com, accessed October 15, 2012 (website no longer active).

2. Craig Levitt, "U.S. Organic Foods Market Poised to Surpass $45 Billion," *Grocery Headquarters,* April 7, 2015, www.groceryheadquarters.com/April-2015 /US-Organic-Foods-Market-Poised-to-Surpass-45-Billion.

3. Private Label Manufacturers Association, *Today's Primary Shopper* (New York: Private Label Manufacturers Association, 2013), http://plma.com /2013PLMA_GfK_Study.pdf.

4. "Table A–A6: Time spent in primary activities and the percent of married mothers and fathers who did the activities on an average day by employment status, average for the combined years 2011–15, own household child under age 18," *American Time Use Survey, 2011–2015*, Bureau of Labor Statistics, last modified September 19, 2016, www.bls.gov/tus/tables/a6_1115.htm.

5. Deutsch 2010.

6. Kroger, "Kroger Introduces Simple Truth™ and Simple Truth Organic® Brands; Available Exclusively at Kroger's Family of Stores," press release, September 24, 2012, www.prnewswire.com/news-releases/kroger-introduces-simple-truth-and-simple-truth-organic-brands-available-exclusively-at-krogers-family-of-stores-170985811.html.

7. Whole Foods Market 2017.

8. In 2003, Whole Foods Market was authorized by the California Certified Organic Farmers to be an independent certifier—that is, it has been entrusted by the organization to verify the organic claims on all of its merchandise and ensure

that the products meet the United States Department of Agriculture organic guidelines (described in chapter 2).

9. Whole Foods Market 2017, 5.

10. Whole Foods Market 2017, 14.

11. Abha Bhattarai, "Amazon to Buy Whole Foods Market in Deal Valued at $13.7 Billion," *Washington Post,* June 16, 2017, www.washingtonpost.com/news /business/wp/2017/06/16/amazon-to-buy-whole-foods-market-in-deal-valued-at-13-7-billion-2.

12. By mid-2017, the company had a total of twelve locations in New York City: Tribeca, Union Square, Chelsea, Bowery, Williamsburg, Third and 3rd in Brooklyn, Bryant Park, Midtown East, Columbus Circle, Harlem, the Upper East Side, and the Upper West Side.

13. Whole Foods Market 2017, 2.

14. "About Our Products," Whole Foods Market, accessed May 7, 2015, www .wholefoodsmarket.com/about-our-products/quality-standards.

15. Johnston 2008, 230. Sociologists Josée Johnston and Michelle Szabo observed the workings of Whole Foods Market for three years and documented the company's unparalleled ability to market the message "shopping for change" while limiting the potential for actual consumer citizenship—where the good of the planet would be prioritized over consumer desires. They observed Whole Foods Market in Toronto from 2004 to 2007 (Johnston and Szabo 2011).

16. Johnston and Szabo 2011, 307.

17. Whole Foods Market, "Whole Foods Market Values Matter Anthem," accessed November 17, 2017, www.wholefoodsmarket.com/values-matter/values-matter-anthem.

18. Whole Foods Market, "Eco-Scale™: Giving New Meaning to Cleaning," accessed November 17, 2017, www.wholefoodsmarket.com/eco-scale-our-commitment.

19. Feldmann and Hamm 2015; Long 2011.

20. Jim Slama, "Whole Foods' New Produce Ratings: Transparency Bears Fruit," Civil Eats, October 29, 2013, http://civileats.com/2013/10/29/whole-foods-new-produce-ratings-transparency-bears-fruit.

21. Fairway Market operates twelve stores in the Northeast, six of which are in New York City. Trader Joe's is a notoriously secretive company, and one must dig through the FAQ section of its website to find a short list of unacceptable ingredients that are banned from its private label foods. For an overview of Trader Joe's practices, see Beth Kowitt, "Inside the Secret World of Trader Joe's," *Fortune,* August 23, 2010, http://archive.fortune.com/2010/08/20/news/companies/inside _trader_joes_full_version.fortune/index.htm. Independent stores, of course, do not have the economic capital of Whole Foods to invest in decor, marketing campaigns, and the development of quality standards.

22. Observed during a site visit to Honest Chops in 2015.

23. Mackey and Sisodia 2014, 224. Up until 2016, John Mackey and Walter Robb were co-CEOs of Whole Foods Market. A few months prior to an aggressive

takeover by activist shareholders, Walter Robb stepped down as co-CEO, but he remains involved in the company's charitable foundations. John Mackey has remained CEO.

24. Alison Fox, Arina Cuevas, John Ambrosio, "Hundreds of Supermarkets, Grocery Stores Cited for Violations throughout NYC," AMNewYork, June 24, 2015, www.amny.com/news/nyc-supermarket-grocery-store-violations-1.10576055. Every year, New York City newspapers collect public data on health department violations and customer complaints for grocery store violations. Ironically, Whole Foods Market was identified as violating health code rules as part of a scandal where product weights were consistently overestimated. See Justin Moyer, "Whole Foods under Investigation for Overcharging in NYC," *Washington Post,* June 25, 2015, www.washingtonpost.com/news/morning-mix/wp/2015/06/25/whole-foods-under-investigation-for-overcharging-in-nyc.

25. Similar to other middle- and upper-middle-class retail spaces that move into low-income neighborhoods, Whole Food Market drives up rents for local residents as property values increase. See Zukin 2008; and Adam Bonislawski, "The Whole Foods Effect Is Coming to Harlem," *New York Post,* July 28, 2016, http://nypost.com/2016/07/28/the-whole-foods-effect-is-coming-to-harlem.

26. DuPuis 2000; Johnston, Biro, and MacKendrick 2009.

27. Pollan 2006, 136.

28. Busken 2015; L. A. Williams 2015.

29. Simone Baroke, "Today's Consumers Demand Natural, Functional Products with Clean Labels," Euromonitor International (blog). October 22, 2013, http://blog.euromonitor.com/2013/10/todays-consumers-demand-natural-functional-products-with-clean-labels.html; L. A. Williams 2015.

30. Deutsch 2010, 208–209.

31. Wartella, Lichenstein, and Boon 2010, 21. In 1990, the agency released the Nutrition Labeling and Education Act. This act demands comprehensive and standardized nutrition labeling. The FDA regulates the design, layout, and content of these labels.

32. Liaukonyte et al. 2013.

33. Guilabert and Wood 2012.

34. Consumer Reports, *Food Labels Survey: 2014 Nationally-Representative Phone Survey* (Yonkers, NY: Consumer Reports National Research Center, 2014).

35. Buttel 2000; DuPuis 2000.

36. Stephen Daniells, "HFCS-Free: The Trend Stalled by Consumer Indifference?" Food Navigator-USA, September 27, 2013, www.foodnavigator-usa.com/Markets/HFCS-free-The-trend-stalled-by-consumer-indifference.

37. For a discussion of the contested legitimacy of certification systems and labeling schemes, see Fromartz 2006; Guthman 2004a, 2004b; Lockie 2006; and Johnston, Biro, and MacKendrick 2009.

38. Since 2014, Kind bars have become ubiquitous in grocery stores. That year, the company's products were in 150,000 stores in the United States, and its sales had tripled relative to previous years. See Benjamin Snyder, "Kind Bars Don't Deserve a

'Healthy' Label, FDA Says," *Fortune,* April 14, 2015, http://fortune.com/2015/04/14/kind-bars-dont-deserve-a-healthy-label-fda-says.

39. Lavin 2015; Beck 1999.

40. Beck 1999, 6.

41. For a comprehensive history of the natural foods industry and movement, see Miller 2017.

42. Guthman 2007, 473.

43. April Fulton, "Whole Foods Founder John Mackey on Fascism and 'Conscious Capitalism,'" National Public Radio, January 16, 2013, www.npr.org/sections/thesalt/2013/01/16/169413848/whole-foods-founder-john-mackey-on-fascism-and-conscious-capitalism; John Mackey, "The Whole Foods Alternative to Obamacare," *Wall Street Journal* August 11, 2009, www.wsj.com/articles/SB10001424052970204251404574342170072865070.

44. Tom Foster, "The Shelf Life of John Mackey," *Texas Monthly,* June 2016, http://features.texasmonthly.com/editorial/shelf-life-john-mackey.

45. Refer to table A2 for an overview of the quality standards in place at the time of my research.

46. Dodson et al. 2012.

47. Peter Whoriskey, "The Labels Said 'Organic.' But These Massive Imports of Corn and Soybeans Weren't," *Washington Post,* May 12, 2017, www.washingtonpost.com/business/economy/the-labels-said-organic-but-these-massive-imports-of-corn-and-soybeans-werent/2017/05/12/6d165984–2b76–11e7-a616-d7c8a68c1a66_story.html.

48. Belasco 1989.

49. See Howard 2016. For a list of allowed and prohibited substances, see "CFR Title 7, Subtitle B, Chapter I, Subchapter M, Part 205, Subpart G: The National List of Allowed and Prohibited Substances," U.S. Government Publishing Office, accessed July 7, 2017, www.ecfr.gov/cgi-bin/text-idx?c=ecfr&SID=9874504b6f1025eb0e6b67cadf9d3b40&rgn=div6&view=text&node=7:3.1.1.9.32.7&idno=7#sg7.3.205.g.sg0. See also Kimberley Kindy and Lyndsey Layton, "Integrity of Federal 'Organic' Label Is Questioned," *Washington Post,* July 3, 2009, www.washingtonpost.com/wp-dyn/content/article/2009/07/02/AR2009070203365.html.

50. Giddens 1991.

51. Cairns and Johnston 2015; Koch 2013.

52. Nestle 2006, 3.

53. Moisander 2007, 407.

54. Eden, Bear, and Walker 2008.

55. Bauer et al. 2012; Jabs et al. 2007.

5. THE HIGH STAKES OF SHOPPING

1. Richardson et al. 2014, 131.

2. Almeling and Waggoner 2013; Daniels 1997, 583; Wolf 2011.

3. MacKendrick 2014.

4. In the eyes of U.S. health agencies, this abstemious lifestyle should begin before pregnancy. As of 2016, the CDC began instructing all women in their reproductive years who are sexually active but not using birth control to avoid alcoholic beverages (Centers for Disease Control and Prevention 2016).

5. American College of Obstetricians and Gynecologists and American Society for Reproductive Medicine 2013, 9.

6. Cairns, Johnston, and MacKendrick 2013; MacKendrick 2014.

7. "Eight in Ten U.S. Parents Report They Purchase Organic Products," press release, Organic Trade Association, April 4, 2013, http://prn.to/XSInTV.

8. Craig Levitt, "U.S. Organic Foods Market Poised to Surpass $45 Billion," *Grocery Headquarters,* April 7, 2015, www.groceryheadquarters.com/April-2015/US-Organic-Foods-Market-Poised-to-Surpass-45-Billion.

9. Neither I nor any of the women I spoke with used the term "precautionary consumption" during my interviews. Rather, I referred to "shopping to avoid synthetic chemicals in food and other consumer products."

10. The "natural" label is, of course, highly problematic. By "natural," I refer to products labeled as being free of synthetic chemicals or as being made from certified-organic ingredients. At the time of writing, the FDA was reviewing whether to institute a formal definition of the term.

11. Cairns, Johnston, and MacKendrick 2013, 98.

12. Hays 1996; Wolf 2011.

13. Haggerty 2003, 193.

14. Bordo 1993; West and Zimmerman 1987.

15. Bartky 1988; Bordo 1993; Saguy 2013.

16. Cairns and Johnston 2015.

17. Bordo 1993; Bell, McNaughton, and Salmon 2009; Markens, Browner and Press 1997; Whitehead 2016.

18. Germov and Williams 1996.

19. Kukla 2005.

20. Coveney 2000.

21. Carney 2015.

22. Cf. Markens, Browner, and Press 1997.

23. The early to mid-twenties is an age when many university-educated women express an interest in healthy eating, particularly when they have the ability to cook for themselves and do not have to rely on foods provided by a residence cafeteria (Deliens, Clarys, De Bourdeauhuij, and Deforche 2014).

24. Thinness is not always voiced using a language of health. Women associate dieting and thinness with beauty and an acceptable feminine appearance (Germov and Williams 1996). Thinness is also about exerting control over the feminine body (Bordo 1993) and expressing perfection (C. Martin 2007).

25. Bordo 1993; Moore 2010.

26. Bartky 1988.

27. Waggoner 2013, 345.

28. Waggoner 2015, 2017.

29. Indichova 2001. Julia Indichova is an alternative health practitioner based in New York City. She published *Inconceivable* in 2001, chronicling a long struggle with infertility. Trying every possible intervention, Indichova only became pregnant after completely reforming her diet and lifestyle. She now runs an online fertility community and program called Fertile Heart. The website recommends preconception detoxing and cleansing, and cites the Environmental Working Group's research on chemicals and children's health. See www.fertileheart .com.

30. Almeling and Waggoner 2013.

31. MacKendrick and Cairns, forthcoming.

32. Clarke 2004; Cook 1995; Szabo 2014.

33. See, e.g., J. Warner 2005; and Erica Jong, "Mother Madness," *Wall Street Journal,* November 6, 2010, www.wsj.com/articles/SB10001424052748704462704 57559060355367429 6.

34. Kwan and Trautner 2009; Kwan 2009.

35. MacKendrick and Pristavec 2016.

36. I also find this theme in another study of precautionary consumption. See MacKendrick 2014.

37. See Cairns and Johnston 2015; MacKendrick 2014; and Fielding-Singh 2017.

38. Garey 1999.

39. Hochschild 1989.

40. Waggoner and Uller 2015; Mansfield and Guthman 2015.

41. Grandjean et al. 2015.

42. Barouki et al. 2012.

43. Lappé 2016.

44. Mansfield and Guthman 2015; Waggoner and Uller 2015; Richardson 2015; Shostak 2004, 2013.

45. Petersen and Lupton 1996, ix; Lupton 1995.

46. Nettleton and Bunton 2005, 47. One of the first government documents to place the onus on individuals to adopt healthy lifestyles to prevent health problems, rather than relying on medical treatment, was *A New Perspective on the Health of Canadians,* written in 1974 by the health minister of the Canadian federal government. See Lalonde 1974.

47. "Miscarriage," March of Dimes, last modified July 2012, www.marchofdimes .org/complications/miscarriage.aspx.

48. Dolan and Zissu 2006.

49. Dolan and Zissu 2006, 7.

50. Formerly the Breast Cancer Fund; see chapter 3.

51. Rose 1999, 65.

52. Rose 1999, 65; see also O'Malley 2000.

Epigraph: Caroline Tell, "The Nanny Recipes: Skip the Microwave," *New York Times,* November 13, 2013, https://nyti.ms/2uO9odJ.

1. Ladd-Taylor and Umansky 1998.

2. Brenton 2017; Chen 2016.

3. Wolfe Research, *Food Goes Back to the Future: The Pure Foods Trend, One Year Later* (New York: Wolfe Research, 2015), 5, www.wolferesearch.com/sample/x20150427_SM_Audio_Brief.pdf.

4. Jaenicke and Carlson 2016.

5. According to national WIC standards, organic frozen and fresh fruits and vegetables are allowed, but states can make their own rules about the eligibility of other foods. In New York State, for instance, organic yogurt is allowed, but organic milk, peanut butter, and baby food, among many other items, are not eligible for purchase with WIC benefits. See New York State Department of Health, "Current WIC Acceptable Foods Card," last modified April 2017, www.health.ny.gov/publications/4099.

6. See, e.g., Larson, Story, and Nelson 2009.

7. Leggat et al. 2012.

8. Diane Cardwell, "A Plan to Add Supermarkets to Poor Areas, with Healthy Results," *New York Times,* September 23, 2009, www.nytimes.com/2009/09/24/nyregion/24super.html.

9. Dimitri, Geoghegan, and Rogus 2016; Mirsch and Dimitri 2012.

10. See Daniel 2016.

11. Laraia et al. 2017.

12. See J. Reich 2016 for a fascinating examination of how time is central to the project of middle-class parenting. Reich studies parents who refuse to have their children vaccinated. I did not ask parents about vaccinations, and it did not come up in the interviews; however, according to Reich, vaccines are viewed by "antivax" parents as a threat to their children's purity because of the chemical preservatives they contain.

13. MacKendrick 2014; MacKendrick and Stevens 2016.

14. Research in psychology and economics establishes that chronic stress from poverty, racism, and time poverty drains cognitive resources, leading individuals to make worse consumer decisions that cost them time or money or lead them into traps of debt, job loss, and chronic poverty. See Mullainathan and Shafir 2013.

15. See Offer and Schneider 2011.

16. MacKendrick 2014.

17. Avishai 2007.

18. Hays 1996.

19. Alkon et al. 2013.

20. See Wall 2005; Eliot 2000.

21. Collins 2000, 80.

22. Brenton 2017.

23. Lareau 2003.

Epigraph: Bennett et al. 2016, A119.

1. Nestle 2016.

2. Pray and Robinson 2007.

3. The website www.opensecrets.org tracks lobbying disclosure forms (forms asking lobbyists to disclose what bills or agencies they have been lobbying for). In the lead-up to the final 2014 Farm Bill, the site recorded nearly 370 lobbyists who registered to lobby on the bill. Most of these lobbyists represented agricultural or food processing sectors, such as Pepsi, Monsanto, and the American Sugar Alliance. See "Clients Lobbying on S.954: Agriculture Reform, Food, and Jobs Act of 2013," Center for Responsive Politics, accessed October 9, 2017, www.opensecrets.org/lobby/billsum.php?id=s954–113. Note that the website records lobbying activities related to Senate bill S.954, the Agriculture Reform, Food, and Jobs Act of 2013. This passed a Senate vote and received presidential support, but it did not pass the House. It was then incorporated into the final compromise bill, called the Agricultural Act of 2014. See Michael A. Memoli, "Compromise Farm Bill on Verge of Clearing Congress," *Los Angeles Times,* January 27, 2014, http://articles.latimes.com/2014/jan/27/news/la-pn-farm-bill-deal-20140127.

4. Kathryn Vasel, "The Honest Company Gets Sued . . . Again," CNNMoney.com, April 27, 2016, http://money.cnn.com/2016/04/27/news/companies/honest-company-lawsuit-organic-baby-formula.

5. Willis and Schor 2012.

6. Eliasoph 1997, 605.

7. Connolly and Prothero 2008.

8. The environmental health advocacy group Safer Chemicals, Healthy Families operates a Mind the Store program that lobbies major retailers to stop carrying products containing endocrine-disrupting compounds and suspected carcinogens. For a list of companies who are participating in the program, see Safer Chemicals, Healthy Families, "Are Your Favorite Retailers Taking Action on Toxics?" Mind the Store, accessed November 21, 2017, http://retailerreportcard.com/retailers.

9. Lu et al. 2006.

10. Harley et al. 2016.

11. Curtis and Wilding 2017, 4.

12. Barrett et al. 2015, 1941.

13. Zimmerman and Anastas 2015.

14. Centers for Disease Control and Prevention 2009.

15. Sharon Lerner, "The Teflon Toxin: How Dupont Slipped Past the EPA," Intercept, August 20, 2015, https://theintercept.com/2015/08/20/teflon-toxin-dupont-slipped-past-epa.

16. Sharon Lerner, "A Chemical Shell Game: How Dupont Concealed the Dangers of the New Teflon Toxin," Intercept, March 3, 2016, https://theintercept.com/2016/03/03/how-dupont-concealed-the-dangers-of-the-new-teflon-toxin.

17. Sharon Lerner, "Citizen Groups Will Sue DuPont and Chemours for Contaminating Drinking Water in North Carolina," Intercept, August 8, 2017, https://theintercept.com/2017/08/08/citizen-groups-will-sue-dupont-and-chemours-for-contaminating-drinking-water-in-north-carolina.

18. Cordner 2016, 44–45.

19. Kinch et al. 2015.

20. Thayer et al. 2016; Zhang et al. 2016.

21. For a thoughtful overview of this argument, see Scott, Haw, and Lee 2017.

22. Solomon and Weiss 2002.

23. World Health Organization and United Nations Environment Programme 2012, 16.

24. See, e.g., Szasz 2007.

25. For an overview of environmental justice and its significance in the environmental health movement, see Bullard 1990; Mohai, Pellow, and Roberts 2009; Pellow 2016.

26. The revolving door refers to the movement of industry employees into key government positions and government employees into industry jobs, such that these two sectors operate more as a network of current and former colleagues, compromising the independence of government regulators and giving industry key insights into legislative loopholes and the blind spots in government regulation and oversight.

27. Horel 2015; Schapiro 2007

28. Wilson and Schwarzman 2009; and Valerie Brown, "Meet the Green Chemist Who Is Out to Make Chemicals Less Toxic for Humans and the Environment," November 13, 2015, In These Times, http://inthesetimes.com/article/18577/its-not-easy-being-a-green-chemist.

APPENDIX

1. MacKendrick 2010; MacKendrick 2014; MacKendrick and Stevens 2016.

2. Altman 2008.

3. Maxwell and DeSoucey 2016.

4. In mid-2017, Whole Foods Market operated a total of 467 stores: 455 in the United States (12 in New York City), 13 in Canada, and 9 in the United Kingdom.

5. Caitlin Dewey, "Analysis: Why Whole Foods Is Now Struggling," *Washington Post,* February 9, 2017, www.washingtonpost.com/news/wonk/wp/2017/02/09/why-whole-foods-is-now-struggling.

6. For images of the interiors of Whole Foods Market stores across the country, refer to the company's Image Library, http://media.wholefoodsmarket.com/image-library.

7. See Whole Foods Market, "Quality Standards," accessed July 10, 2017, www.wholefoodsmarket.com/quality-standards.

8. See Whole Foods Market, "Values Matter," accessed July 10, 2017, http://media.wholefoodsmarket.com/press/values-matter-brand-campaign (link no longer active).

9. See, e.g., Whole Foods Market, "Non-GMO Project Verified Products List," accessed October 9, 2017, www.wholefoodsmarket.com/service/non-gmo-project-verified-products-list.

10. See, e.g., Charmaz 2006.

11. See also Minkoff-Zern and Carney 2015.

12. Elliott and Bowen 2015; Brenton 2017; Carney 2015.

13. Dimitri, Geoghegan, and Rogus 2016.

14. There is, for example, Christian Lander's tongue-in-cheek book *Stuff White People Like,* which lists shopping at Whole Foods Market and eating organic food as musts for white people. See Lander 2008.

15. See also Brenton 2017.

16. See, for example, Francis Lam, "Edna Lewis and the Black Roots of American Cooking," *New York Times Magazine,* October 28, 2015, www.nytimes.com /2015/11/01/magazine/edna-lewis-and-the-black-roots-of-american-cooking.html; and Tipton-Martin 2015.

17. Krieger, Williams, and Moss 1997, 345–346.

18. Sam Roberts, "Gap between Manhattan's Rich and Poor Is Greatest in U.S., Census Finds," *New York Times,* September 17, 2014, www.nytimes.com/2014/09/18 /nyregion/gap-between-manhattans-rich-and-poor-is-greatest-in-us-census-finds .html.

19. The median rent for a market-rate two-bedroom apartment in Manhattan in 2011 was $2,851.69. Most market-rate rentals in Manhattan require that renters provide proof of income of at least $60,000 per year to be eligible to rent a two-bedroom apartment. In 2012, the national rent-to-income ratio was 17.1 for households making $60,000–$80,000 per year, compared to 22.7 percent for New Yorkers in that income category. Office of the New York City Comptroller, *The Growing Gap: New York City's Housing Affordability Challenge* (New York: City of New York, 2014), 11, 24.

20. Quinn 2013.

21. Fry and Kochhar 2016; New York City Housing Development Corporation, *Income Eligibility* (New York: New York City Housing Development Corporation, 2013). See www.nychdc.com for the most recent guidelines; 2013 guidelines are no longer available online.

22. I did not consider any of the mothers that I interviewed to be upper class, so it does not appear as a class category. Upper class, by New York City standards, is a highly wealthy class of individuals who make well over $199,000 per year, own multiple properties, and live in high-end neighborhoods.

23. Charmaz 2006.

24. Miles and Huberman 1994.

25. See MacKendrick 2014; and Cairns, Johnston, and MacKendrick 2013.

REFERENCE LIST

Adamkiewicz, Gary, Ami R. Zota, M. Patricia Fabian, Teresa Chahine, Rhona Julien, John D. Spengler et al. 2011. "Moving Environmental Justice Indoors: Understanding Structural Influences on Residential Exposure Patterns in Low-Income Communities." *American Journal of Public Health* 101 (S1): S238–S245. doi: 10.2105/AJPH.2011.300119.

Adibi, Jennifer J., Robin M. Whyatt, Antonia M. Calafat, David Camann, Heather Nelson, Hari K. Bhat et al. 2008. "Characterization of Phthalate Exposure among Pregnant Women Assessed by Repeat Air and Urine Samples." *Environmental Health Perspectives* 116 (4): 467–473. doi: 10.1289/ehp.10749.

Alkon, Alison Hope, Daniel Block, Kelly Moore, Catherine Gillis, Nicole DiNuccio, and Noel Chavez. 2013. "Foodways of the Urban Poor." *Geoforum* 48: 126–135. doi: 10.1016/j.geoforum.2013.04.021.

Alkon, Alison Hope, and Christie Grace McCullen. 2011. "Whiteness and Farmers Markets: Performances, Perpetuations ... Contestations?" *Antipode* 43 (4): 937–959. doi: 10.1111/j.1467–8330.2010.00818.x.

Allen, Barbara L. 2003. *Uneasy Alchemy: Citizens and Experts in Louisiana's Chemical Corridor Disputes.* Cambridge, MA: MIT Press.

Allen, P., M. FitzSimmons, M. Goodman, and K. Warner. 2003. "Shifting Plates in the Agrifood Landscape: The Tectonics of Alternative Agrifood Initiatives in California." *Journal of Rural Studies* 19 (1): 61–75.

Almeling, Rene, and Miranda R. Waggoner. 2013. "More and Less Than Equal: How Men Factor in the Reproductive Equation." *Gender and Society* 27 (6): 821–842.

Altman, Rebecca Gasior. 2008. "Chemical Body Burden and Place-Based Struggles for Environmental Health and Justice (A Multi-Site Ethnography of Biomonitoring Science)." PhD dissertation, Brown University, Providence, RI.

Altman, Rebecca Gasior, Rachel Morello-Frosch, Julia Green Brody, Ruthann Rudel, Phil Brown, and Mara Averick. 2008. "Pollution Comes Home and Gets Personal: Women's Experience of Household Chemical Exposure." *Journal of Health and Social Behavior,* 49 (4): 417–435.

Amani, Bita. 2015. "Consuming 'DNA as Chemicals' and Chemicals as Food." In *Our Chemical Selves: Gender, Toxics, and Environmental Health,* edited by Dayna Nadine Scott, 142–187. Vancouver: University of British Columbia Press.

American Chemical Society. 1979. "FDA Bans Livestock Growth Promoter." *Chemical and Engineering News Archive* 57 (28): 7. doi: 10.1021/cen-v057n028.p007a.

American Chemistry Council. 2015. "Endocrine Society Disregards State of Science Around Chemical Exposures and Endocrine System." Press release, September 28, 2015. www.americanchemistry.com/Media/PressReleasesTranscripts/ACC-news-releases/Endocrine-Society-Views-Disregards-State-of-Science-Around-Chemical-Exposures-and-Endocrine-System.html.

———. 2017. "U.S. Chemicals Trade By The Numbers." Fact Sheet, August 2017. https://www.americanchemistry.com/Policy/Trade/US-Chemicals-Trade-by-the-Numbers.pdf.

American College of Obstetricians and Gynecologists and American Society for Reproductive Medicine. 2013. *Exposure to Toxic Environmental Agents.* Washington, DC: American College of Obstetricians and Gynecologists.

Anway, Matthew D., Andrea S. Cupp, Mehmet Uzumcu, and Michael K. Skinner. 2005. "Epigenetic Transgenerational Actions of Endocrine Disruptors and Male Fertility." *Science* 308 (5727): 1466–1469.

Anzman, S.L., B.Y. Rollins, and L.L. Birch. 2010. "Parental Influence on Children's Early Eating Environments and Obesity Risk: Implications for Prevention." *International Journal of Obesity* 34 (7): 1116–1124.

Avishai, Orit. 2007. "Managing the Lactating Body: The Breast-Feeding Project and Privileged Motherhood." *Qualitative Sociology* 30 (2): 135–152.

Baker, Nena. 2008. *The Body Toxic: How the Hazardous Chemistry of Everyday Things Threatens Our Health and Well-Being.* New York: North Point Press.

Barnett, Clive, Paul Cloke, Nick Clarke, and Alice Malpass. 2005. "Consuming Ethics: Articulating the Subjects and Spaces of Ethical Consumption." *Antipode* 37 (1): 23–45.

Barouki, Robert, Peter D. Gluckman, Philippe Grandjean, Mark Hanson, and Jerrold J. Heindel. 2012. "Developmental Origins of Non-Communicable Disease: Implications for Research and Public Health." *Environmental Health* 11 (42): 1–9.

Barrett, Emily S., Marissa Velez, Xing Qiu, and Shaw-Ree Chen. 2015. "Reducing Prenatal Phthalate Exposure through Maternal Dietary Changes: Results from a Pilot Study." *Maternal and Child Health Journal* 19 (9): 1936–1942.

Bartky Sandra. 1988. "Foucault, Feminism, and Patriarchal Power." In *Feminism and Foucault: Reflections On Resistance,* edited by Irene Diamond and Lee Quinby, 61–86. Boston: Northeastern University Press.

Bauchner, Elizabeth. 2004. "Environmental Contaminants and Human Milk." *LEAVEN* 39, no. 6 (December–January): 123–125

Bauer, K.W., M.O. Hearst, K. Escoto, J.M. Berge, and D. Neumark-Sztainer. 2012. "Parental Employment and Work-Family Stress: Associations with Family Food Environments." *Social Science and Medicine* 75 (3): 496–504. doi: 10.1016/j.socscimed.2012.03.026.

Beck, Ulrich. 1992. *Risk Society: Towards a New Modernity.* London: SAGE Publications.

———. 1995. *Ecological Politics in an Age of Risk.* Cambridge: Polity Press.

———. 1999. *World Risk Society.* Malden, MA: Polity Press.

Becker, Monica, Sally Edwards, and Rachel I. Massey. 2010. "Toxic Chemicals in Toys and Children's Products: Limitations of Current Responses and Recommendations for Government and Industry." *Environmental Science and Technology* 44 (21): 7986–7991. doi: 10.1021/es1009407.

Belasco, Warren James. 1989. *Appetite for Change: How the Counterculture Took on the Food Industry, 1966–1988.* New York: Pantheon Books.

Bell, Kirsten, Darlene McNaughton, and Amy Salmon. 2009. "Medicine, Morality and Mothering: Public Health Discourses on Foetal Alcohol Exposure, Smoking around Children and Childhood Overnutrition." *Critical Public Health* 19 (2): 155–170.

Bell, Shannon Elizabeth. 2013. *Our Roots Run Deep as Ironweed: Appalachian Women and the Fight for Environmental Justice.* Urbana, IL: University of Illinois Press.

Bennett, D., D.C. Bellinger, L.S. Birnbaum, A. Bradman, A. Chen, D.A. Cory-Slechta et al. 2016. "Project Tendr: Targeting Environmental Neuro-Developmental Risks; The Tendr Consensus Statement." *Environmental Health Perspectives* 124: A118–A122. doi: 10.1289/EHP358.

Bern, Howard. 1992. "The Fragile Fetus." In *Chemically Induced Alterations in Sexual and Functional Development: The Wildlife/Human Connection,* vol. 21, edited by Theo Colborn and Coralie Clement, 9–15. Princeton, NJ: Princeton Scientific Publishing.

Bernstein, Steven. 2000. "Ideas, Social Structure and the Compromise of Liberal Environmentalism." *European Journal of International Relations* 6 (4): 464–512.

Beronius, Anna, Christina Rudén, Helen Håkansson, and Annika Hanberg. 2010. "Risk to All or None? A Comparative Analysis of Controversies in the Health Risk Assessment of Bisphenol A." *Reproductive Toxicology* 29 (2): 132–146.

Betts, Kellyn S. 2002. "Rapidly Rising PBDE levels in North America." *Environmental Science and Technology* 36 (3): 50A–52A.

———. 2015. "Hand-Me-Down Hazard: Flame Retardants in Discarded Foam Products." *Environmental Health Perspectives* 123 (3): A56–A63. doi: 10.1289/ehp.123-A56.

Bevacqua, Jennifer. 2013. "Manufactured Environmental Toxins and Children's Health: An Evidence-Based Review and Anticipatory Guidance." *Journal of Pediatric Health Care* 27 (1): 13–22. doi: 10.1016/j.pedhc.2011.03.006.

Beyond Pesticides. 2010. "Triclosan Linked to Increased Risk of Allergies." Beyond Pesticides, Daily News Blog, November 30, 2010. http://beyondpesticides.org/dailynewsblog/2010/11/triclosan-linked-to-increased-risk-of-allergies-bpa-linked-to-immune-problems.

Biesterbos, Jacqueline W.H., Tatsiana Dudzina, Christiaan J.E. Delmaar, Martine I. Bakker, Frans G.M. Russel, Natalie von Goetz et al. 2013. "Usage Patterns of

Personal Care Products: Important Factors for Exposure Assessment." *Food and Chemical Toxicology* 55: 8–17. http://dx.doi.org/10.1016/j.fct.2012.11.014.

Birnbaum, Linda S. 2013. "State of the Science of Endocrine Disruptors." *Environmental Health Perspectives* 121 (4): A107.

Birnbaum, Linda S., and Suzanne E. Fenton. 2003. "Cancer and Developmental Exposure to Endocrine Disruptors." *Environmental Health Perspectives* 111 (4): 389–394.

Bloom, Michael S., Germaine M. Buck Louis, Enrique F. Schisterman, Aiyi Liu, and Paul J. Kostyniak. 2007. "Maternal Serum Polychlorinated Biphenyl Concentrations across Critical Windows of Human Development." *Environmental Health Perspectives* 115 (9): 1320–1324. doi: 10.1289/ehp.10086.

Boffetta, Paolo, Nadia Jourenkova, and Per Gustavsson. 1997. "Cancer Risk from Occupational and Environmental Exposure to Polycyclic Aromatic Hydrocarbons." *Cancer Causes and Control* 8 (3): 444–472. doi: 10.1023/A:1018465507029.

Bordo, Susan. 1993. *Unbearable Weight: Feminism, Western Culture, and the Body.* Berkeley, CA: University of California Press.

Boyle, Megan. "Male Exposure to Chemicals Linked to Longer Time to Conceive." HealthyChildHealthyWorld,May31,2016.www.healthychild.org/male-exposure-to-chemicals-linked-to-longer-time-to-conceive.

Bradman, Asa, Lesliam Quirós-Alcalá, Marcia Nishioka, Martha E. Harnly, Alan Hubbard, Thomas E. McKone et al. 2011. "Concentrations and Loadings of Polybrominated Diphenyl Ethers in Dust from Low-Income Households in California." *Environment International* 37 (3): 592–596. doi: 10.1016/j.envint.2010.12.003.

Breast Cancer Fund. 2011. *BPA in Thanksgiving Canned Food.* San Francisco, CA: Breast Cancer Fund. www.bcpp.org/resource/bpa-in-thanksgiving-canned-food.

———. 2013. *Disrupted Development: The Dangers of Prenatal BPA Exposure.* San Francisco, CA: Breast Cancer Fund, September 2013. www.bcpp.org/resource /disrupted-development-report.

Brenton, Joslyn. 2017. "The Limits of Intensive Feeding: Maternal Foodwork at the Intersections of Race, Class, and Gender." *Sociology of Health and Illness* 39 (6): 863–877. doi: 10.1111/1467–9566.12547.

Brilliant, Lawrence, George Van Amburg, John Isbister, Harold Humphrey, Kenneth Wilcox, Janet Eyster et al. 1978. "Breast-Milk Monitoring to Measure Michigan's Contamination with Polybrominated Biphenyls." *Lancet* 312 (8091): 643–646. doi: 10.1016/S0140–6736(78)92758–7.

Brophy, James T., Margaret M. Keith, Andrew Watterson, Robert Park, Michael Gilbertson, Eleanor Maticka-Tyndale et al. 2012. "Breast Cancer Risk in Relation to Occupations with Exposure to Carcinogens and Endocrine Disruptors: A Canadian Case–Control Study." *Environmental Health* 11: 87–104. doi: 10.1186 /1476–069X-11–87.

Brown, Phil. 2007. *Toxic Exposures: Contested Illnesses and the Environmental Health Movement.* New York: Columbia University Press.

Brown, Phil, and Faith I. T. Ferguson. 1995. "'Making a Big Stink': Women's Work, Women's Relationships, and Toxic Waste Activism." *Gender and Society* 9 (2): 145–172.

Brown, Phil, Sabrina McCormick, Brian Mayer, Stephen Zavestoski, Rachel Morello-Frosch, Rebecca Gasior Altman et al. 2006. "'A Lab of Our Own': Environmental Causation of Breast Cancer and Challenges to the Dominant Epidemiological Paradigm." *Science, Technology, and Human Values* 31 (5): 499–536. doi: 10.1177/0162243906289610.

Brown, P., B. Mayer, S. Zavestoski, T. Luebke, J. Mandelbaum, and S. McCormick. 2003. "The Health Politics of Asthma: Environmental Justice and Collective Illness Experience in the United States." *Social Science and Medicine* 57 (3): 453–464.

Brown, P., and E. J. Mikkelsen. 1997. *No Safe Place: Toxic Waste, Leukemia, and Community Action.* Berkeley, CA: University of California Press.

Brown, P., S. Zavestoski, S. McCormick, M. Linder, J. Mandelbaum, and T. Luebke. 2001. "A Gulf of Difference: Disputes over Gulf War-Related Illnesses." *Journal of Health and Social Behavior* 42 (3): 235–257.

Brulle, Robert J. 2000. *Agency, Democracy, and Nature: The U.S. Environmental Movement from a Critical Theory Perspective.* Cambridge, MA: MIT Press.

Brulle, Robert J., and David. N. Pellow. 2006. "Environmental Justice: Human Health and Environmental Inequalities." *Annual Review of Public Health* 27: 103–124.

Bullard, Robert D. 1990. *Dumping in Dixie: Race, Class, and Environmental Quality.* Boulder, CO: Westview Press.

Busken, David F. 2015. "Cleaning It Up: What Is a Clean Label Ingredient?" *Cereal Foods World* 60 (2): 112–113.

Buttel, Frederick H. 2000. "The Recombinant BGH Controversy in the United States: Toward a New Consumption Politics of Food?" *Agriculture and Human Values* 17 (1): 5–20.

Cairns, Kate, and Josée Johnston. 2015. *Food and Femininity.* London: Bloomsbury Academic.

Cairns, Kate, Josée Johnston, and Norah MacKendrick. 2013. "Feeding the 'Organic Child': Mothering through Ethical Consumption." *Journal of Consumer Culture* 13 (2): 97–118. doi: 10.1177/1469540513480162.

Campos, Sarah, Juliana Doxey, and David Hammond. 2011. "Nutrition Labels on Pre-Packaged Foods: A Systematic Review." *Public Health Nutrition* 14 (8): 1496–1506. doi: 10.1017/S1368980010003290.

Carfagna, Lindsey B., Emilie A. Dubois, Connor Fitzmaurice, Monique Y. Ouimette, Juliet B. Schor, Margaret Willis et al. 2014. "An Emerging Eco-Habitus: The Reconfiguration of High Cultural Capital Practices among Ethical Consumers." *Journal Of Consumer Culture* 14 (2): 158–178. doi: 10.1177/1469540514526227.

Carney, Megan A. 2015. *The Unending Hunger: Tracing Women and Food Insecurity across Borders.* Oakland, CA: University of California Press.

Carson, Rachel. 2002. *Silent Spring.* Boston: Houghton Mifflin.

Caserta, D., A. Mantovani, R. Marci, A. Fazi, F. Ciardo, C. La Rocca et al. 2011. "Environment and Women's Reproductive Health." *Human Reproduction Update* 17 (3): 418–433.

Cawley, John, and Feng Liu. 2012. "Maternal Employment and Childhood Obesity: A Search for Mechanisms in Time Use Data." *Economics and Human Biology* 10 (4): 352–364. http://dx.doi.org/10.1016/j.ehb.2012.04.009.

Centers for Disease Control and Prevention. 2001. *National Report on Human Exposure to Environmental Chemicals*. Atlanta, GA: Centers for Disease Control.

———. 2003. *Second National Report on Human Exposure to Environmental Chemicals*. Atlanta, GA: Centers for Disease Control and Prevention.

———. 2009. *Fourth National Report on Human Exposure to Environmental Chemicals*. Atlanta, GA: Centers for Disease Control and Prevention, National Center for Environmental Health.

———. 2016. "Alcohol and Pregnancy." Last modified February 2, 2016. www.cdc.gov/vitalsigns/fasd/index.html.

———. 2017. *Fourth National Report on Human Exposure to Environmental Chemicals, Updated Tables, February 2017*. Atlanta, GA: Centers for Disease Control and Prevention, National Center for Environmental Health.

Chafen, J. J. S., S. Newberry, M. Riedl, D. M. Bravata, M. A. Maglione, and M. Suttorp. 2010. "Prevalence, Natural History, Diagnosis, and Treatment of Food Allergy: A Systematic Review of the Evidence." Rand Health working paper series, WR-757-1, Santa Monica, CA. www.rand.org/content/dam/rand/pubs/working_papers/2010/RAND_WR757-1.pdf.

Chafen, J., S. J. Newberry, M. A. Riedl, D. M. Bravata, M. Maglione, M. J. Suttorp et al. 2010. "Diagnosing and Managing Common Food Allergies: A Systematic Review." *JAMA* 303 (18): 1848–1856. doi: 10.1001/jama.2010.582.

Charmaz, Kathy. 2006. *Constructing Grounded Theory: A Practical Guide through Qualitative Research*. London: SAGE Publications.

Chen, Wei-ting. 2016. "From 'Junk Food' to 'Treats.'" *Food, Culture and Society* 19 (1): 151–170. doi: 10.1080/15528014.2016.1145008.

Clarke, Alison J. 2004. "Maternity and Materiality: Becoming a Mother in Consumer Culture." In *Consuming Motherhood*, edited by Janelle S. Taylor, Linda L. Layne, and Danielle F. Wozniak, 55–71. New Brunswick, NJ: Rutgers University Press.

Clarke, L., and J. F. Short. 1993. "Social-Organization and Risk: Some Current Controversies." *Annual Review of Sociology* 19: 375–399.

Colborn, Theo, and Coralie Clement, eds. 1992. *Chemically Induced Alterations in Sexual and Functional Development: The Wildlife/Human Connection*. Vol. 21. Princeton, NJ: Princeton Scientific Publishing.

Colborn, Theo, Dianne Dumanoski, and John Peterson Myers. 1996. *Our Stolen Future: Are We Threatening Our Fertility, Intelligence, and Survival? A Scientific Detective Story*. New York: Dutton.

Colborn, T., F. S. vom Saal, and A. M. Soto. 1993. "Developmental Effects of Endocrine-Disrupting Chemicals in Wildlife and Humans." *Environmental Health Perspectives* 101 (5): 378–384.

Coleman-Jensen, Alishia, Matthew P. Rabbitt, Christian Gregory, and Anita Singh. 2015. *Household Food Security in the United States in 2014, Err-194.* Washington, DC: United States Department of Agriculture Economic Research Service.

Collins, Patricia Hill. 2000. *Black Feminist Thought: Knowledge, Consciousness, and the Politics of Empowerment.* New York: Routledge.

Coming Clean Work Group for Safe Markets. 2014. *The Market Shift to Safer Chemicals and Materials through Public Disclosure and Informed Substitution of Hazardous Chemicals: Five Essential Practices for Retailers, Brand Owners and Suppliers.* Brattleboro, VT: National Workgroup for Safe Markets.

Connolly, John, and Andrea Prothero. 2008. "Green Consumption: Life Politics, Risk and Contradictions." *Journal of Consumer Culture* 8 (1): 117–145.

Cook, Daniel Thomas. 1995. "The Mother as Consumer: Insights from the Children's Wear Industry, 1917–1929." *Sociological Quarterly* 36 (3): 505–522.

———. 2009. "Semantic Provisioning of Children's Food: Commerce, Care and Maternal Practice." *Childhood* 16 (3): 317–334.

Cordner, Alissa. 2016. *Toxic Safety: Flame Retardants, Chemical Controversies, and Environmental Health.* New York: Columbia University Press.

Coveney, John. 2000. *Food, Morals, and Meaning: The Pleasure and Anxiety of Eating.* New York: Routledge.

Craig, Maxine Leeds. 2002. *Ain't I a Beauty Queen? Black Women, Beauty, and the Politics of Race.* New York: Oxford University Press.

Cranor, Carl. 2008. "Do You Want to Bet Your Children's Health on Post-Market Harm Principles? An Argument for a Trespass or Permission Model for Regulating Toxicants." *Villanova Environmental Law Journal* 19 (2): 251–314.

Curl, Cynthia L., Shirley A. A. Beresford, Anjum Hajat, Joel D. Kaufman, Kari Moore, Jennifer A. Nettleton et al. 2013. "Associations of Organic Produce Consumption with Socioeconomic Status and the Local Food Environment: Multi-Ethnic Study of Atherosclerosis (Mesa)." *PLoS ONE* 8 (7): e69778. doi: 10.1371/journal.pone.0069778.

Curtis, Kathleen, and Bobbi Chase Wilding. 2017. *Is It in Us? Chemical Contamination in Our Bodies.* Body Burden Work Group and Commonweal Biomonitoring Resource Center. http://www.isitinus.org/documents/Is%20It%20In%20Us%20Report.pdf.

Daniel, Caitlin. 2016. "Economic Constraints on Taste Formation and the True Cost of Healthy Eating." *Social Science and Medicine* 148: 34–41. doi: 10.1016/j.socscimed.2015.11.025.

Daniels, Cynthia R. 1997. "Between Fathers and Fetuses: The Social Construction of Male Reproduction and the Politics of Fetal Harm." *Signs: Journal of Women and Culture in Society* 22 (3): 579–616.

———. 2006. *Exposing Men: The Science and Politics of Male Reproduction.* New York: Oxford University Press.

Davis, Frederick Rowe. 2014. *Banned: A History of Pesticides and the Science of Toxicology.* New Haven, CT: Yale University Press.

Degnan, Frederick H. 1997. "The Food Label and the Right-to-Know." *Food and Drug Law Journal* 52: 49–60.

Deliens, Tom, Peter Clarys, Ilse De Bourdeaudhuij, and Benedicte Deforche. 2014. "Determinants of Eating Behaviour in University Students: A Qualitative Study Using Focus Group Discussions." *BMC Public Health* 14 (1): 53.

Dellavalle, Curtis. 2016. *The Pollution in People: Cancer-Causing Chemicals in Americans' Bodies.* Washington, DC: Environmental Working Group.

Dennis, Kristine K., Elizabeth Marder, David M. Balshaw, Yuxia Cui, Michael A. Lynes, Gary J. Patti et al. 2017. "Biomonitoring in the Era of the Exposome." *Environmental Health Perspectives* 125 (4): 502.

Deutsch, Tracey. 2010. *Building a Housewife's Paradise: Gender, Politics, and American Grocery Stores in the Twentieth Century.* Raleigh, NC: University of North Carolina Press.

Dewailly, E., P. Ayotte, S. Bruneau, S. Gingras, M. Belles-Isles, and R. Roy. 2000. "Susceptibility to Infections and Immune Status in Inuit Infants Exposed to Organochlorines." *Environmental Health Perspectives* 108 (3): 205–211.

Dewailly, E., A. Nantel, S. Bruneau, C. Laliberte, L. Ferron, and S. Gingras. 1992. "Breast-Milk Contamination by PCDDs, PCDFs and PCBs in Arctic Quebec: A Preliminary Assessment." *Chemosphere* 25 (7–10): 1245–1249.

Diamanti-Kandarakis, Evanthia, Jean-Pierre Bourguignon, Linda C. Giudice, Russ Hauser, Gail S. Prins, Ana M. Soto et al. 2009. "Endocrine-Disrupting Chemicals: An Endocrine Society Scientific Statement." *Endocrine Reviews* 30 (4): 293–342. doi: 10.1210/er.2009–0002.

Dimitri, Carolyn, Jacqueline Geoghegan, and Stephanie Rogus. 2016. "Two-Stage Determinants of the Organic Food Retailing Landscape: The Case of Manhattan, New York." *Journal of Food Products Marketing* 23 (2): 221–238.

Di Renzo, Gian Carlo, Jeanne A. Conry, Jennifer Blake, Mark S. DeFrancesco, Nathaniel DeNicola, James N. Martin et al. 2015. "International Federation of Gynecology and Obstetrics Opinion on Reproductive Health Impacts of Exposure to Toxic Environmental Chemicals." *International Journal of Gynecology and Obstetrics* 131 (3): 219–225. doi: 10.1016/j.ijgo.2015.09.002.

Dodson, Robin E., Marcia Nishioka, Laurel J. Standley, Laura J. Perovich, Julia Green Brody, and Ruthann A Rudel. 2012. "Endocrine Disruptors and Asthma-Associated Chemicals in Consumer Products." *Environmental Health Perspectives* 120 (7): 935–943. doi: 10.1289/ehp.1104052.

Dolan, Deirdre, and Alexandra Zissu. 2006. *The Complete Organic Pregnancy.* New York: HarperCollins.

Dooley, Cal. 2017. "Practitioner's Insights: Putting Government to Work for Innovation." Bloomberg Bureau of National Affairs, Daily Environment Report, 65 DEN B-1, April 6, 1–2.

Downey, L. 2006. "Environmental Racial Inequality in Detroit." *Social Forces* 85 (2): 771–796.

Duke, Deanna. 2011. *The Non-Toxic Avenger: What You Don't Know Can Hurt You.* Gabriola Island, BC: New Society Publishers.

DuPuis, E. Melanie. 2000. "Not in My Body: rBGH and the Rise of Organic Milk." *Agriculture and Human Values* 17 (3): 285–295.

Eden, Sally, Christopher Bear, and Gordon Walker. 2008. "Mucky Carrots and Other Proxies: Problematising the Knowledge-Fix for Sustainable and Ethical Consumption." *Geoforum* 39 (2): 1044–1057. doi: 10.1016/j.geoforum.2007.11.001.

Edin, Kathryn, and Maria Kefalas. 2005. *Promises I Can Keep: Why Poor Women Put Motherhood before Marriage.* Berkeley, CA: University of California Press.

Egilman, David S., and Rankin Bohme. 2005. "Over a Barrel: Corporate Corruption of Science and Its Effects on Workers and the Environment." *International Journal of Occupational and Environmental Health* 11 (4): 331–337. doi: 10.1179/oeh.2005.11.4.331.

Eliasoph, Nina. 1997. "'Close to Home': The Work of Avoiding Politics." *Theory and Society* 26 (5): 605–647.

Eliot, Lise. 2000. *What's Going on in There? How the Brain and Mind Develop in the First Five Years of Life.* New York: Bantam.

Elkington, J., and J. Hailes. 1988. *The Green Consumer Guide.* London: Gollancz.

Elliott, Sinikka, and Sarah Bowen. 2015. "Risky Feeding: Low-Income Mothers and Children's Bodies under Surveillance." Paper presented at the Annual Meeting of the Eastern Sociological Society, March 1, 2015, New York, NY.

Elliott, Sinikka, Rachel Powell, and Joslyn Brenton. 2013. "Being a Good Mom: Low-Income, Black Single Mothers Negotiate Intensive Mothering." *Journal of Family Issues* 36 (3): 351–370. doi: 10.1177/0192513x13490279.

Entine, Jon. 2011. *Scared to Death: How Chemophobia Threatens Public Health.* New York: American Council on Science and Health.

Environmental Working Group. 2003. *BodyBurden: The Pollution in People.* Washington, DC: Environmental Working Group.

———. 2005. *BodyBurden: The Pollution in Newborns.* Washington, DC: Environmental Working Group.

———. 2006. *Across Generations: Mothers and Daughters.* Washington, DC: Environmental Working Group.

———. 2014. "Triclosan-Containing Antibacterial Soaps Neither Safe Nor Effective." June 16, 2014. www.ewg.org/testimony-official-correspondence/triclosan-containing-antibacterial-soaps-neither-safe-nor#.We-NJYZrzBI.

European Commission. 2000. *Communication from the Commission on the Precautionary Principle.* Brussels: Commission of the European Communities.

Faustman, E. M. 2000. "Mechanisms Underlying Children's Susceptibility to Environmental Toxicants." *Environmental Health Perspectives* 108: 13–21.

Feldmann, Corinna, and Ulrich Hamm. 2015. "Consumers' Perceptions and Preferences for Local Food: A Review." *Food Quality and Preference* 40: 152–164. doi: 10.1016/j.foodqual.2014.09.014.

Fielding-Singh, Priya. 2017. "Dining with Dad: Fathers' Influences on Family Food Practices." *Appetite* 117: 98–108. doi: 10.1016/j.appet.2017.06.013.

Flaherty, Eileen. 2009. "Safety First: The Consumer Product Safety Improvement Act of 2008." *Loyola Consumer Law Review* 21 (3): 372–391.

Flint, Nourbese N., and Teniope Adewumi. *Natural Evolutions: One Hair Story.* Edited by Meridith Merchant and Janette Robinson Flint. Los Angeles, CA: Black Women for Wellness. www.bwwla.org/wp-content/uploads/2016/03/One-Hair-Story-Final-small-file-size-3142016.pdf.

Foster, Warren G., Sandra Gregorovich, Katherine M. Morrison, Stephanie A. Atkinson, Cariton Kubwabo, Brian Stewart et al. 2011. "Human Maternal and Umbilical Cord Blood Concentrations of Polybrominated Diphenyl Ethers." *Chemosphere* 84 (10): 1301–1309. doi: 10.1016/j.chemosphere.2011.05.028.

Foucault, Michel. 1997. "Technologies of the Self." In *Ethics, Subjectivity and Truth: Essential Works of Michel Foucault,* edited by Paul Rabinow, 223–251. New York: New Press.

Fox, Donald A., Philippe Grandjean, Didima de Groot, and Merle G. Paule. 2012. "Developmental Origins of Adult Diseases and Neurotoxicity: Epidemiological and Experimental Studies." *NeuroToxicology* 33 (4): 810–816. http://dx.doi.org/10.1016/j.neuro.2011.12.016.

Franck, Caroline, Sonia M. Grandi, and Mark J. Eisenberg. 2013. "Agricultural Subsidies and the American Obesity Epidemic." *American Journal of Preventive Medicine* 45 (3): 327–333. doi: 10.1016/j.amepre.2013.04.010.

Freinkel, Susan. 2011. *Plastic: A Toxic Love Story.* Boston: Houghton Mifflin Harcourt.

Freudenburg, William R., Robert Gramling, and Debra J. Davidson. 2008. "Scientific Certainty Argumentation Methods (SCAMs): Science and the Politics of Doubt." *Sociological Inquiry* 78 (1): 2–38.

Fromartz, S. 2006. *Organic, Inc.: Natural Foods and How They Grew.* Orlando, FL: Harcourt Books.

Fry, Richard, and Rakesh Kochhar. 2016. *Are You in the American Middle Class? Find Out with Our Income Calculator.* Washington, DC: Pew Research Center.

Funtowicz, Silvio O., and Jerome R. Ravetz. 1990. *Uncertainty and Quality in Science for Policy.* Norwell, MA: Kluwer Academic Publishers.

———. 1993. "Science for the Post-Normal Age." *Futures* 25 (7): 739–755.

Gabriel, Yiannis, and Tim Lang. 2006. *The Unmanageable Consumer.* London: SAGE Publications.

Gareau, Brian J. 2013. *From Precaution to Profit: Contemporary Challenges to Environmental Protection in the Montreal Protocol.* New Haven, CT: Yale University Press.

Garey, Anita Ilta. 1999. *Weaving Work and Motherhood.* Vol. 104. Philadelphia: Temple University Press.

Germov, John, and Lauren Williams. 1996. "The Sexual Division of Dieting: Women's Voices." *Sociological Review* 44 (4): 630–647. doi: 10.1111/1467-954X.ep9703202980.

Giddens, Anthony. 1990. *The Consequences of Modernity.* Stanford, CA: Stanford University Press.

———. 1991. *Modernity and Self-Identity: Self and Society in the Late Modern Age.* Cambridge: Polity Press.

———. 1999. *Runaway World: How Globalisation Is Reshaping Our Lives*. London: Profile Books.

Goldman, Gretchen, Christina Carlson, and Yixuan Zhang. 2015. "Bad Chemistry: How the Chemical Industry's Trade Association Undermines the Policies That Protect Us." Cambridge, MA: Union of Concerned Scientists. www.ucsusa.org /badchemistry.

Gonzales, Shelley. *Mind, Disrupted*. Bolinas, CA: Collaborative on Health and the Environment, 2010. www.minddisrupted.org.

Gore, A. C., V. A. Chappell, S. E. Fenton, J. A. Flaws, A. Nadal, G. S. Prins et al. 2015. "EDC-2: The Endocrine Society's Second Scientific Statement on Endocrine-Disrupting Chemicals." *Endocrine Reviews* 36 (6): E1–E150. doi:10.1210/er.2015–1010.

Gottlieb, Robert. 2005. *Forcing the Spring: The Transformation of the American Environmental Movement*. Washington, DC: Island Press.

Grandjean, Philippe, Robert Barouki, David C. Bellinger, Ludwine Casteleyn, Lisa H. Chadwick, Sylvaine Cordier et al. 2015. "Life-Long Implications of Developmental Exposure to Environmental Stressors: New Perspectives." *Endocrinology* 156 (10): 3408–3415. doi: 10.1210/EN.2015–1350.

Greater Boston Chapter of Physicians for Social Responsibility. 2001. *Out of Harm's Way: Reducing Toxic Threats to Child Development*. Boston, MA: Greater Boston Chapter of Physicians for Social Responsibility.

Guilabert, Margarita, and John Andy Wood. 2012. "USDA Certification of Food as Organic: An Investigation of Consumer Beliefs about the Health Benefits of Organic Food." *Journal of Food Products Marketing* 18 (5): 353–368. doi: 10.1080 /10454446.2012.685028.

Guthman, Julie. 2004a. *Agrarian Dreams: The Paradox of Organic Farming in California*. Berkeley, CA: University of California Press.

———. 2004b. "The Trouble with 'Organic Lite' in California: A Rejoinder to the 'Conventionalisation' Debate." *Sociologia Ruralis* 44 (3): 301–316.

———. 2007. "The Polanyian Way? Voluntary Food Labels as Neoliberal Governance." *Antipode* 39 (3): 456–478. doi: 10.1111/j.1467–8330.2007.00535.x.

Guthman, J., and E. M. DuPuis. 2006. "Embodying Neoliberalism: Economy, Culture, and the Politics of Fat." *Environment and Planning D: Society and Space* 24 (3): 427–448.

Hacker, Jacob S. 2008. *The Great Risk Shift: The New Economic Insecurity and the Decline of the American Dream*. Oxford: Oxford University Press.

Haggerty, Kevin. 2003. "From Risk to Precaution: The Rationalities of Personal Crime Prevention." In *Risk and Morality*, edited by Richard V. Ericson and Aaron Doyle, 193–215. Toronto: University of Toronto Press.

Hanekamp, J. C., G. Vera-Navas, and S. W. Verstegen. 2005. "The Historical Roots of Precautionary Thinking: The Cultural Ecological Critique and 'the Limits to Growth.'" *Journal of Risk Research* 8 (4): 295–310.

Hanser, Amy, and Jialin Camille Li. 2015. "Opting Out? Gated Consumption, Infant Formula and China's Affluent Urban Consumers." *China Journal*, no. 74: 110–128.

Harley, Kim G., Katherine Kogut, Daniel S. Madrigal, Maritza Cardenas, Irene A. Vera, Gonzalo Meza-Alfaro et al. 2016. "Reducing Phthalate, Paraben, and Phenol Exposure from Personal Care Products in Adolescent Girls: Findings from the Hermosa Intervention Study." *Environmental Health Perspectives* 124 (10): 1600–1607. doi: 10.1289/ehp.1510514.

Harremoës, Poul, David Gee, Malcolm MacGarvin, Andy Stirling, Jane Keys, Brian Wynne et al. 2001. *Late Lessons from Early Warnings: The Precautionary Principle 1896–2000.* Copenhagen: European Environment Agency.

Harrison, Jill Lindsey. 2011. *Pesticide Drift and the Pursuit of Environmental Justice.* Cambridge, MA: MIT Press.

Harvey, David. 2005. *A Brief History of Neoliberalism.* Oxford: Oxford University Press.

Haydu, Jeffrey. 2012. "Frame Brokerage in the Pure Food Movement, 1879–1906." *Social Movement Studies* 11 (1): 97–112.

Hays, Sharon. 1996. *The Cultural Contradictions of Motherhood.* New Haven, CT: Yale University Press.

He, Yonghua, Maohua Miao, Chunhua Wu, Wei Yuan, Ersheng Gao, Zhijun Zhou et al. 2009. "Occupational Exposure Levels of Bisphenol A among Chinese Workers." *Journal of Occupational Health* 51 (5): 432–436. doi: 10.1539/joh. O9006.

Heindel, Jerrold J., and Laura N. Vandenberg. 2015. "Developmental Origins of Health and Disease: A Paradigm for Understanding Disease Etiology and Prevention." *Current Opinion in Pediatrics* 27 (2): 248–253.

Hines, Cynthia J., Nancy B. Nilsen Hopf, James A. Deddens, Antonia M. Calafat, Manori J. Silva, Ardith A. Grote et al. 2009. "Urinary Phthalate Metabolite Concentrations among Workers in Selected Industries: A Pilot Biomonitoring Study." *Annals of Occupational Hygiene* 53 (1): 1–17. doi: 10.1093/annhyg/meno66.

Hites, R. A. 2004. "Polybrominated Diphenyl Ethers in the Environment and in People: A Meta-Analysis of Concentrations." *Environmental Science and Technology* 38 (4): 945–956.

Hochschild, Arlie Russell. 1989. *The Second Shift: Working Parents and the Revolution at Home.* New York: Viking.

Hoover, Elizabeth. 2017. "Environmental Reproductive Justice: Intersections in an American Indian Community Impacted by Environmental Contamination." *Environmental Sociology.* Published ahead of print, July 3, 2017. doi:10.1080/2325 1042.2017.1381898.

Hoover, Elizabeth, Mia Renauld, Michael R. Edelstein, and Phil Brown. 2015. "Social Science Collaboration with Environmental Health." *Environmental Health Perspectives* 123 (11): 1100–1106. doi: 10.1289/ehp.1409283.

Horel, Stéphane. 2015. "A Toxic Affair: How the Chemical Lobby Blocked Action on Hormone Disrupting Chemicals." *Corporate Europe Observatory,* May 19, 2015.

———. 2016. "Perturbateurs endocriniens: l'ingérence des États-Unis." *Le Monde,* November 29, 2016. www.lemonde.fr/sante/article/2016/11/29/perturbateurs-endocriniens-l-ingerence-des-etats-unis_5040055_1651302.html.

Horel, Stéphane, and Brian Bienkowski. 2013. "Special Report: Scientists Critical of EU Chemical Policy Have Industry Ties." *Environmental Health News,* September 23, 2013. www.environmentalhealthnews.org/ehs/news/2013/eu-conflict.

Howard, Phil H. 2016. *Concentration and Power in the Food System: Who Controls What We Eat?* London: Bloomsbury Academic.

Hrudey, Steve E., and William Leiss. 2003. "Risk Management and Precaution: Insights on the Cautious Use of Evidence." *Environmental Health Perspectives* 111 (13): 1577.

Indichova, Julia. 2001. *Inconceivable: A Woman's Triumph over Despair and Statistics.* New York: Broadway Books.

Jabs, Jennifer, Carol M. Devine, Carole A. Bisogni, Tracy J. Farrell, Margaret Jastran, and Elaine Wethington. 2007. "Trying to Find the Quickest Way: Employed Mothers' Constructions of Time for Food." *Journal of Nutrition Education and Behavior* 39 (1): 18–25.

Jaenicke, Edward C., and Andrea C. Carlson. 2015. "Estimating and Investigating Organic Premiums for Retail-Level Food Products." *Agribusiness* 31: 453–471. doi: 10.1002/agr.21413.

Jasanoff, Sheila. 2005. *Designs on Nature: Science and Democracy in Europe and the United States.* Princeton, NJ: Princeton University Press.

Johnston, Josée. 2008. "The Citizen-Consumer Hybrid: Ideological Tensions and the Case of Whole Foods Market." *Theory and Society* 37 (3): 229–270.

Johnston, J., A. Biro, and N. A. MacKendrick. 2009. "Lost in the Supermarket: The Corporate-Organic Foodscape and the Struggle for Food Democracy." *Antipode* 41 (3): 509–532.

Johnston, Josée, and Michelle Szabo. 2011. "Reflexivity and the Whole Foods Market Consumer: The Lived Experience of Shopping for Change." *Agriculture and Human Values* 28 (3): 303–319. doi: 10.1007/s10460-010-9283-9.

Jones, Robert L., David M. Homa, Pamela A. Meyer, Debra J. Brody, Kathleen L. Caldwell, James L. Pirkle et al. 2009. "Trends in Blood Lead Levels and Blood Lead Testing among US Children Aged 1 to 5 Years, 1988–2004." *Pediatrics* 123 (3): e376–e385.

Kamrin, Michael A. 2009. "Phthalate Risks, Phthalate Regulation, and Public Health: A Review." *Journal of Toxicology and Environmental Health* 12 (2): 157–174. doi: 10.1080/10937400902729226.

Keep a Breast Foundation and Environmental Working Group. 2013. *Dirty Dozen: List of Endocrine Disruptors.* Washington DC: Environmental Working Group. http://static.ewg.org/pdf/kab_dirty_dozen_endocrine_disruptors.pdf.

Kessler, Rebecca. 2014. "Lead-Based Decorative Paints: Where Are They Still Sold—and Why?" *Environmental Health Perspectives* 122 (4): A96–A103.

Khanna, Madhu, Wilma Rose H. Quimio, and Dora Bojilova. 1998. "Toxics Release Information: A Policy Tool for Environmental Protection." *Journal of Environmental Economics and Management* 36 (3): 243–266. doi: 10.1006/jeem.1998.1048.

Kinch, Cassandra D., Kingsley Ibhazehiebo, Joo-Hyun Jeong, Hamid R. Habibi, and Deborah M. Kurrasch. 2015. "Low-Dose Exposure to Bisphenol A and Replacement Bisphenol S Induces Precocious Hypothalamic Neurogenesis in Embryonic Zebrafish." *Proceedings of the National Academy of Sciences* 112 (5): 1475–1480. doi: 10.1073/pnas.1417731112.

Koch, Shelley L. 2013. *A Theory of Grocery Shopping.* New York: Berg.

Kong, Augustine, Michael L. Frigge, Gisli Masson, Soren Besenbacher, Patrick Sulem, Gisli Magnusson et al. 2012. "Rate of De Novo Mutations and the Importance of Father's Age to Disease Risk." *Nature* 488: 471–475.

Kowitt, Beth. 2014. "Whole Foods Takes over America." *Fortune Magazine,* April 10, 2014. http://fortune.com/2014/04/10/whole-foods-takes-over-america.

Krauss, Celene. 1993. "Women and Toxic Waste Protests: Race, Class and Gender as Resources of Resistance." *Qualitative Sociology* 16 (3): 247–262.

Krieger, Nancy, David R. Williams, and Nancy E. Moss. 1997. "Measuring Social Class in US Public Health Research: Concepts, Methodologies, and Guidelines." *Annual Review of Public Health* 18 (1): 341–378.

Krimsky, Sheldon. 2000. *Hormonal Chaos: The Scientific and Social Origins of the Environmental Endocrine Hypothesis.* Baltimore, MD: Johns Hopkins University Press.

Kroll-Smith, J. Stephen, Phil Brown, and Valerie J. Gunter. 2000. *Illness and the Environment: A Reader in Contested Medicine.* New York: NYU Press.

Kukla, Rebecca. 2005. *Mass Hysteria: Medicine, Culture, and Mothers' Bodies.* Lanham, MD: Rowman and Littlefield Publishers.

———. 2010. "The Ethics and Cultural Politics of Reproductive Risk Warnings: A Case Study of California's Proposition 65." *Health, Risk and Society* 12 (4): 323–334.

Kwa, M., L. J. Welty, and S. Xu. 2017. "Adverse Events Reported to the US Food and Drug Administration for Cosmetics and Personal Care Products." *JAMA Internal Medicine* 177 (8): 1202–1204. doi: 10.1001/jamainternmed.2017.2762.

Kwan, Samantha. 2009. "Competing Motivational Discourses for Weight Loss: Means to Ends and the Nexus of Beauty and Health." *Qualitative Health Research* 19 (9): 1223–1233. doi: 10.1177/1049732309343952.

Kwan, Samantha, and Mary Nell Trautner. 2009. "Beauty Work: Individual and Institutional Rewards, the Reproduction of Gender, and Questions of Agency." *Sociology Compass* 3 (1): 49–71.

Lachance-Grzela, Mylène, and Geneviève Bouchard. 2010. "Why Do Women Do the Lion's Share of Housework? A Decade of Research." *Sex Roles* 63: 767–780.

Ladd-Taylor, M., and L. Umansky, eds. 1998. *Bad Mothers: The Politics of Blame in 20th Century America.* New York: NYU Press.

LaKind, Judy S., Cheston M. Berlin, and Daniel Q. Naiman. 2001. "Infant Exposure to Chemicals in Breast Milk in the United States: What We Need to Learn from a Breast Milk Monitoring Program." *Environmental Health Perspectives* 109 (1): 75–88.

LaKind, Judy S., A. Amina Wilkins, and Cheston M. Berlin. 2004. "Environmental Chemicals in Human Milk: A Review of Levels, Infant Exposures and Health, and Guidance for Future Research." *Toxicology and Applied Pharmacology* 198 (2): 184–208.

Lalonde, M. 1974. *A New Perspective on the Health of Canadians*. Ottawa, ON: Department of Supply and Services.

Lander, Christian. 2008. *Stuff White People Like: A Definitive Guide to the Unique Taste of Millions*. New York: Random House.

Landrigan, Philip J., and Lynn R. Goldman. 2011. "Children's Vulnerability to Toxic Chemicals: A Challenge and Opportunity to Strengthen Health and Environmental Policy." *Health Affairs* 30 (5): 842–850.

Landrigan, Philip J., Clyde B. Schechter, Jeffrey M. Lipton, Marianne C. Fahs, and Joel Schwartz. 2002. "Environmental Pollutants and Disease in American Children: Estimates of Morbidity, Mortality, and Costs for Lead Poisoning, Asthma, Cancer, and Developmental Disabilities." *Environmental Health Perspectives* 110 (7): 721.

Lang, John T., and William K. Hallman. 2005. "Who Does the Public Trust? The Case of Genetically Modified Food in the United States." *Risk Analysis* 25 (5): 1241–1252. doi: 10.1111/j.1539–6924.2005.00668.x.

Langston, Nancy. 2010. *Toxic Bodies: Hormone Disruptors and the Legacy of DES*. New Haven, CT: Yale University Press.

Lappé, Martine. 2016. "The Maternal Body as Environment in Autism Science." *Social Studies of Science* 46 (5): 675–700. doi: 10.1177/0306312716659372.

Laraia, Barbara A., Tashara M. Leak, June M. Tester, and Cindy W. Leung. 2017. "Biobehavioral Factors That Shape Nutrition in Low-Income Populations: A Narrative Review." In "The Supplemental Nutrition Assistance Program's Role in Addressing Nutrition-Related Health Issues," edited by Neal D. Barnard and David L. Katz. Supplement, *American Journal of Preventive Medicine* 52 (2, S2): S118–S126. doi: 10.1016/j.amepre.2016.08.003.

Lareau, Annette. 2003. *Unequal Childhoods: Class, Race, and Family Life*. Berkeley, CA: University of California Press.

Larner, W. 2000. "Neo-Liberalism: Policy, Ideology, Governmentality." *Studies in Political Economy* 63 (1): 5–30.

Larsen, Lars Thorup. 2012. "The Leap of Faith from Disease Treatment to Lifestyle Prevention: The Genealogy of a Policy Idea." *Journal of Health Politics, Policy and Law* 37 (2): 227–252.

Larson, Nicole I., Mary T. Story, and Melissa C. Nelson. 2009. "Neighborhood Environments: Disparities in Access to Healthy Foods in the U.S." *American Journal of Preventive Medicine* 36 (1): 74–81. doi: 10.1016/j.amepre.2008.09.025.

Lavin, Chad. 2015. *Eating Anxiety: The Perils of Food Politics*. Minneapolis: University of Minnesota Press.

Lee, Bryan. 1991. "Highlights of the Clean Air Act Amendments of 1990." *Journal of the Air and Waste Management Association* 41 (1): 16–19. doi: 10.1080/10473289.1991.10466820.

Leggat, Margaret, Bonnie Kerker, Cathy Nonas, and Elliott Marcus. 2012. "Pushing Produce: The New York City Green Carts Initiative." *Journal of Urban Health* 89 (6): 937–938.

Ley, Barbara L. 2009. *From Pink to Green: Disease Prevention and the Environmental Breast Cancer Movement*. New Brunswick, NJ: Rutgers University Press.

Liaukonyte, Jura, Nadia A. Streletskaya, Harry M. Kaiser, and Bradley J. Rickard. 2013. "Consumer Response to 'Contains' and 'Free of' Labeling: Evidence from Lab Experiments." *Applied Economic Perspectives and Policy* 35 (3): 476–507. doi: 10.1093/aepp/ppt015.

Linton, Jamie, and Noah Hall. 2013. "The Great Lakes: A Model of Transboundary Cooperation." In *Water without Borders?* edited by Emma S. Norman, Alice Cohen, and Karen Bakker, 221–243. Toronto: University of Toronto Press.

Lockie, S. 2006. "Capturing the Sustainability Agenda: Organic Foods and Media Discourses on Food Scares, Environment, Genetic Engineering, and Health." *Agriculture and Human Values* 23 (3): 313–323.

Long, Joshua. 2011. "Entering the New Conversational Marketplace: Narratives of Sustainability and the Success of Farm Direct Markets." *Food, Culture and Society: An International Journal of Multidisciplinary Research* 14 (1): 49–69. doi: 10. 2752/175174411X12810842291182.

Lu, Chensheng, Kathryn Toepel, Rene Irish, Richard A. Fenske, Dana B. Barr, and Roberto Bravo. 2006. "Organic Diets Significantly Lower Children's Dietary Exposure to Organophosphorus Pesticides." *Environmental Health Perspectives* 114 (2): 260–263.

Lupton, Deborah. 1995. *The Imperative of Health: Public Health and the Regulated Body*. London: SAGE Publications.

———. 1996. *Food, the Body, and the Self*. Thousand Oaks, CA: SAGE Publications.

Lynch, Diahanna, and David Vogel. 2001. *The Regulation of GMOs in Europe and the United States: A Case-Study of Contemporary European Regulatory Politics*. New York: Council on Foreign Relations Press. www.cfr.org/publication/8688 /regulation_of_gmos_in_europe_and_the_united_states.html.

MacKendrick, Norah A. 2010. "Media Framing of Body Burdens: Precautionary Consumption and the Individualization of Risk." *Sociological Inquiry,* 80(1), 126–149. doi: 10.1111/j.1475–682X.2009.00319.x

———. 2014. "More Work for Mother: Chemical Body Burdens as a Maternal Responsibility." *Gender and Society* 28 (5): 705–728. doi: 10.1177/0891243214529842.

———. 2015. "Protecting Ourselves from Chemicals: A Study of Gender and Precautionary Consumption." In Dayna Nadine Scott (Ed.), *Our Chemical Selves: Gender, Toxics, and Environmental Health*, 58–77. Vancouver: University of British Columbia Press.

MacKendrick, Norah A., and Kate Cairns. Forthcoming. "The Polluted Child and Maternal Responsibility in the US Environmental Health Movement." *Signs: Journal of Women and Culture in Society*.

MacKendrick, Norah A., and Teja Pristavec. 2016. "Between Careful and Crazy: Foodwork as a Balancing Act." Paper presented at the Scarborough Fare, ASFS/

AFHVS/CAFS Annual Meeting and Conference, Scarborough, ON, June 22–25.

MacKendrick, Norah A., and Lindsay M. Stevens. 2016. "'Taking Back a Little Bit of Control': Managing the Contaminated Body through Consumption." *Sociological Forum* 31 (2): 310–329. doi: 10.1111/socf.12245.

Mackey, John, and Rajendra Sisodia. 2014. *Conscious Capitalism: Liberating the Heroic Spirit of Business.* Boston: Harvard Business Review Press.

Malkan, Stacy. 2007. *Not Just a Pretty Face: The Ugly Side of the Beauty Industry.* Gabriola Island, BC: New Society Publishers.

Maniates, Michael F. 2001. "Individualization: Plant a Tree, Buy a Bike, Save the World?" *Global Environmental Politics* 1 (3): 31–52. doi: 10.1162/152638001316881395.

———. 2002. "Individualization: Plant a Tree, Buy a Bike, Save the World?" In *Confronting Consumption,* edited by Thomas Princen, Ken Conca, and Michael Maniates, 43–66. Cambridge, MA: MIT Press.

Manikkam, Mohan, Rebecca Tracey, Carlos Guerrero-Bosagna, and Michael K. Skinner. 2013. "Plastics Derived Endocrine Disruptors (BPA, DEHP and DBP) Induce Epigenetic Transgenerational Inheritance of Obesity, Reproductive Disease and Sperm Epimutations." *PLoS ONE* 8 (1): e55387. doi: 10.1371/journal.pone.0055387.

Manners-Bell, John. 2014. *Supply Chain Risk: Understanding Emerging Threats to Global Supply Chains.* London: Kogan Page Publishers.

Mansfield, Becky. 2012a. "Environmental Health as Biosecurity: 'Seafood Choices,' Risk, and the Pregnant Woman as Threshold." *Annals of the Association of American Geographers* 102 (5): 969–976.

———. 2012b. "Gendered Biopolitics of Public Health: Regulation and Discipline in Seafood Consumption Advisories." *Environment and Planning D: Society and Space* 30 (4): 588–602.

Mansfield, Becky, and Julie Guthman. 2015. "Epigenetic Life: Biological Plasticity, Abnormality, and New Configurations of Race and Reproduction." *Cultural Geographies* 22 (1) 3–20. doi: 10.1177/1474474014555659.

Markens, Susan, Carole H. Browner, and Nancy Press. 1997. "Feeding the Fetus: On Interrogating the Notion of Maternal-Fetal Conflict." *Feminist Studies* 23 (2): 351–372.

Markowitz, Gerald, and David Rosner. 2000. "'Cater to the Children': The Role of the Lead Industry in a Public Health Tragedy, 1900–1955." *American Journal of Public Health* 90 (1): 36–46.

———. 2002a. "Corporate Responsibility for Toxins." *Annals of the American Academy of Political and Social Science* 584: 159–174.

———. 2002b. *Deceit and Denial: The Deadly Politics of Industrial Pollution.* Berkeley, CA: University of California Press.

———. 2013. *Lead Wars: The Politics of Science and the Fate of America's Children.* Berkeley, CA: University of California Press.

Martin, Andrew. 2012. "Maker of a Hair-Straightening Product Settles Lawsuit." *New York Times,* March 5, 2012. www.nytimes.com/2012/03/06/business/brazilian-blowout-agrees-to-a-4-5-million-settlement.html.

Martin, Courtney E. 2007. *Perfect Girls, Starving Daughters: The Frightening New Normalcy of Hating Your Body.* New York: Simon and Schuster.

Maxwell, Rahsaan, and Michaela DeSoucey. 2016. "Gastronomic Cosmopolitanism: Supermarket Products in France and the United Kingdom." *Poetics* 56: 85–97. doi: 10.1016/j.poetic.2016.03.001.

Mayer, Brian. 2008. *Blue-Green Coalitions: Fighting for Safe Workplaces and Healthy Communities.* Ithaca: Cornell University Press.

Mayer, Brian, Phil Brown, and Meadow Linder. 2002. "Moving Further Upstream: From Toxics Reduction to the Precautionary Principle." *Public Health Reports* 117 (6): 574–586.

McCormick, Sabrina, Phil Brown, and Stephen Zavestoski. 2003. "The Personal Is Scientific, the Scientific Is Political: The Public Paradigm of the Environmental Breast Cancer Movement." *Sociological Forum* 18 (4): 545–576.

McGarity, Thomas O. 2001. "Politics by Other Means: Law, Science, and Policy in EPA's Implementation of the Food Quality Protection Act." *Administrative Law Review* 53 (1): 103–222. doi: 10.2307/40711949.

Meironyté, Daiva, Koidu Norén, and Ake Bergman. 1999. "Analysis of Polybrominated Diphenyl Ethers in Swedish Human Milk: A Time-Related Trend Study, 1972–1997." *Journal of Toxicology and Environmental Health* 58 (6): 329–341.

Michaels, David. 2008. *Doubt Is Their Product: How Industry's Assault on Science Threatens Your Health.* New York: Oxford University Press.

Michaels, David, and Thomas Burke. 2017. "The Dishonest Honest Act." *Science* 356 (6342): 989.

Micheletti, Michele. 2003. *Political Virtue and Shopping: Individuals, Consumerism, and Collective Action.* New York: Palgrave Macmillan.

———. 2004. "Why More Women? Issues of Gender and Political Consumerism." In *Politics, Products, and Markets: Exploring Political Consumerism Past and Present,* edited by Michele Micheletti, Andreas Follesdal, and Dietlind Stolle, 245–264. New Brunswick, NJ: Transaction Publishers.

Miles, Mathew. B., and Michael Huberman. 1994. *Qualitative Data Analysis.* Thousand Oaks, CA: SAGE Publications.

Miller, Laura. 2017. *Building Nature's Market: The Business and Politics of Natural Foods.* Chicago: University of Chicago Press.

Minkoff-Zern, Laura-Anne, and Megan A. Carney. 2015. "Latino Im/migrants, 'Dietary Health' and Social Exclusion." *Food, Culture and Society* 18 (3): 463–480. doi:10.1080/15528014.2015.1043108.

Mirsch, Laura, and Carolyn Dimitri. 2012. "Access to Sustainably Produced Food: An Investigation of Organic Food Availability in Manhattan, New York." *Journal of Agriculture, Food Systems, and Community Development* 2 (3): 193–209.

Mohai, Paul, David N. Pellow, and J. Timmons Roberts. 2009. "Environmental Justice." *Annual Review of Environment and Resources,* no. 34: 405–430. doi: 10.1146/annurev-environ-082508-094348.

Mohai, Paul, and Robin Saha. 2007. "Racial Inequality in the Distribution of Hazardous Waste: A National-Level Reassessment." *Social Forces* 53 (2): 343–370.

Moisander, Johanna. 2007. "Motivational Complexity of Green Consumerism." *International Journal of Consumer Studies* 31 (4): 404–409.

Moore, Sarah E. H. 2010. "Is the Healthy Body Gendered? Toward a Feminist Critique of the New Paradigm of Health." *Body and Society* 16(2): 95–118. doi: 10.1177/1357034x10364765.

Morse, J. M., M. Barrett, M. Mayan, K. Olson, and J. Spiers. 2008. "Verification Strategies for Establishing Reliability and Validity in Qualitative Research." *International Journal of Qualitative Methods* 1 (2): 13–22.

Muir, Derek C. G., and Philip H. Howard. 2006. "Are There Other Persistent Organic Pollutants? A Challenge for Environmental Chemists." *Environmental Science and Technology* 40 (23): 7157–7166. doi: 10.1021/es061677a.

Mullainathan, Sendhil, and Eldar Shafir. 2013. *Scarcity: Why Having Too Little Means So Much.* New York: Picado.

Murphy, Michelle. 2006. *Sick Building Syndrome and the Problem of Uncertainty: Environmental Politics, Technoscience, and Women Workers.* Durham, NC: Duke University Press.

———. 2013. "Distributed Reproduction, Chemical Violence, and Latency." *Scholar and Feminist Online* 11 (3): 1–8.

Neff, Roni A., Jennifer C. Hartle, Linnea I. Laestadius, Kathleen Dolan, Anne C. Rosenthal, and Keeve E. Nachman. 2012. "A Comparative Study of Allowable Pesticide Residue Levels on Produce in the United States." *Globalization and Health* 8: 2. doi: 10.1186/1744-8603-8-2.

Neltner, Thomas G., Heather M. Alger, Jack E. Leonard, and Maricel V. Maffini. 2013. "Data Gaps in Toxicity Testing of Chemicals Allowed in Food in the United States." *Reproductive Toxicology* 42: 85–94. doi: 10.1016/j.reprotox.2013.07.023.

Neltner, Thomas G., Neesha R. Kulkarni, Heather M. Alger, Maricel V. Maffini, Erin D. Bongard, Neal D. Fortin et al. 2011. "Navigating the U.S. Food Additive Regulatory Program." *Comprehensive Reviews in Food Science and Food Safety* 10 (6): 342–368. doi: 10.1111/j.1541-4337.2011.00166.x.

Neltner, Thomas. G., and Maricel. V, Maffini. 2014. *Generally Recognized as Secret: Chemicals Added to Food in the United States.* New York: Natural Resources Defence Council.

Nestle, Marion. 2006. *What to Eat.* New York: North Point Press.

———. 2016. "Corporate Funding of Food and Nutrition Research: Science or Marketing?" *JAMA Internal Medicine* 176 (1): 13–14. doi: 10.1001/jamainternmed.2015.6667.

Nettleton, S., and Robin Bunton. 2005. "Sociological Critiques of Health Promotion." In *The Sociology of Health Promotion: Critical Analyses of Consumption, Lifestyle and Risk,* edited by Robin Bunton, Roger Burrows, and Sarah Nettleton, 39–55. New York: Routledge.

Nielsen, Nikolaj. 2015. "EU Court Slams EU Officials on Toxic Chemicals Delay." *EU Observer,* December 15, 2015. https://euobserver.com/environment/131550.

O'Connor, Siobhan, and Alexandra Spunt. 2010. *No More Dirty Looks: The Truth About Your Beauty Products—and the Ultimate Guide to Safe and Clean Cosmetics.* New York: Da Capo Lifelong Books.

Offer, Shira, and Barbara Schneider. 2011. "Revisiting the Gender Gap in Time-Use Patterns." *American Sociological Review* 76 (6): 809–833. doi: 10.1177/0003122411425170.

O'Malley, Pat. 2000. "Uncertain Subjects: Risks, Liberalism and Contract." *Economy and Society* 29 (4): 460–484.

Onyango, Benjamin M., William K. Hallman, and Anne C. Bellows. 2007. "Purchasing Organic Food in US Food Systems: A Study of Attitudes And Practice." *British Food Journal* 109 (5): 399–411.

Oreskes, Naomi, and Erik M. Conway. 2011. *Merchants of Doubt: How a Handful of Scientists Obscured the Truth on Issues from Tobacco Smoke to Global Warming.* New York: Bloomsbury Publishing USA.

Organic Trade Association. 2015. "Organic Looks Like America, Shows New Survey." OTA press release. http://ota.com/news/press-releases/17972.

Parlett, Lauren E., Antonia M. Calafat, and Shanna H. Swan. 2013. "Women's Exposure to Phthalates in Relation to Use of Personal Care Products." *Journal of Exposure Science and Environmental Epidemiology* 23 (2): 197–206.

Paulson, Jerome A. 2011. "Chemical-Management Policy: Prioritizing Children's Health." *Pediatrics* 127 (5): 983–990.

Pavilonis, Brian T., Clifford P. Weisel, Brian Buckley, and Paul J. Lioy. 2014. "Bio-Accessibility and Risk of Exposure to Metals and SVOCs in Artificial Turf Field Fill Materials and Fibers." *Risk Analysis: An Official Publication of the Society for Risk Analysis* 34 (1): 44–55. doi: 10.1111/risa.12081.

Pellow, David N. 2016. "Toward a Critical Environmental Justice Studies." *Du Bois Review: Social Science Research on Race* 13: (2): 221–236. doi: 10.1017/S1742058X1600014X.

Perera, Frederica P., Virginia Rauh, Wei-Yann Tsai, Patrick Kinney, David Camann, Dana Barr et al. 2003. "Effects of Transplacental Exposure to Environmental Pollutants on Birth Outcomes in a Multiethnic Population." *Environmental Health Perspectives* 111 (2): 201–205.

Perera, F. P., R. Whyatt, V. A. Rauh, and W. Jedrychowski. 1999. "Molecular Epidemiologic Research on the Effects of Environmental Pollutants on the Fetus." *Environmental Health Perspectives* 107 (S3): 451–460.

Pestano, Paul, Nneka Leiba, and Brit'ny Hawkins. 2016. *Big Market for Black Cosmetics, but Less Hazardous Choices Limited.* Washington, DC: Environmental Working Group.

Pesticide Action Network North America. 2004. *Chemical Trespass: Pesticides in Our Bodies and Corporate Accountability.* San Francisco, CA: Pesticide Action Network.

Petersen, Alan R., and Deborah Lupton. 1996. *The New Public Health: Discourses, Knowledges, Strategies.* London: SAGE Publications.

Picut, Catherine A., and George A. Parker. 1992. "Review Article: Interpreting the Delaney Clause in the 21st Century." *Toxicologic Pathology* 20 (4): 617–627.

Pirkle, J.L., R.B. Kaufmann, D.J. Brody, T. Hickman, E.W. Gunter, and D.C. Paschal. 1998. "Exposure of the U.S. Population to Lead, 1991–1994." *Environmental Health Perspectives* 106 (11): 745–750.

Pollan, Michael. 2006. *The Omnivore's Dilemma: A Natural History of Four Meals.* New York: Penguin.

Prasad, Monica. 2006. *The Politics of Free Markets: The Rise of Neoliberal Economic Policies in Britain, France, Germany, and the United States.* Chicago: University of Chicago Press.

Pray, Leslie, and Sally Robinson. 2007. *Challenges for the FDA: The Future of Drug Safety, Workshop Summary.* Washington, DC: National Academies Press.

Private Label Manufacturers Association. 2013. *Today's Primary Shopper.* New York: Private Label Manufacturers Association. http://plma.com/2013PLMA _GfK_Study.pdf.

Pryor, Jon L., Claude Hughes, Warren Foster, Barbara F. Hales, and Bernard Robaire. 2000. "Critical Windows of Exposure for Children's Health: The Reproductive System in Animals and Humans." *Environmental Health Perspectives* 108 (S3): 491–503.

Quinn, Christine. 2013. *The Middle-Class Squeeze: A Report on the State of the City's Middle-Class.* New York: New York City Council, Finance Division.

Rabinow, Paul, and Nikolas Rose. 2006. "Biopower Today." *BioSocieties* 1 (2): 195–217.

Raffensperger, Carolyn, and Joel A. Tickner, eds. 1999. *Protecting Public Health and the Environment: Implementing the Precautionary Principle.* Washington, DC: Island Press.

Reich, Jennifer A. 2016. *Calling the Shots: Why Parents Refuse Vaccines.* New York: NYU Press.

Reich, Michael. 2000. "Environmental Politics and Science: The Case of PBB Contamination in Michigan." In *Illness and the Environment: A Reader in Contested Medicine,* edited by J. Stephen Kroll-Smith, Phil Brown, and Valerie J. Gunter, 430–452. New York: NYU Press.

Reuben, Suzanne H. 2010. *Reducing Environmental Cancer Risk: What We Can Do Now; President's Cancer Panel 2008–2009 Annual Report.* Bethesda, MA: National Cancer Institute, National Institutes of Health, US Department of Health and Human Services.

Richardson, Sarah S. 2015. "Maternal Bodies in the Postgenomic Order: Gender and the Explanatory Landscape of Epigenetics." In *Postgenomics: Perspectives on Biology after the Genome,* edited by Sarah S. Richardson and Hallam Stevens, 210–231. Durham, NC: Duke University Press.

Richardson, Sarah S., Cynthia R. Daniels, Matthew W. Gillman, Janet Golden, Rebecca Kukla, Christopher Kuzawa et al. 2014. "Society: Don't Blame the Mothers." *Nature* 512 (7513): 131–132.

Roberts, Jody A. 2009. "Collision Course: Science, Law, and Regulation in the Emerging Science of Low Dose Toxicity." *Villanova Environmental Law Journal* 20 (1): 1–22.

Robinson, James. 1991. *Toil and Toxics: Workplace Struggles and Political Strategies for Occupational Health.* Berkeley, CA: University of California Press.

Rodman, Sarah O., Anne M. Palmer, Drew A. Zachary, Laura C. Hopkins, and Pamela J. Surkan. 2014. "'They Just Say Organic Food Is Healthier': Perceptions of Healthy Food among Supermarket Shoppers in Southwest Baltimore." *Culture, Agriculture, Food and Environment* 36 (2): 83–92. doi: 10.1111/cuag.12036.

Roff, Robin Jane. 2007. "Shopping for Change? Neoliberalizing Activism and the Limits to Eating Non-GMO." *Agriculture and Human Values,* 24 (4): 511–522.

Rosa, Eugene A. 1998. "Metatheoretical Foundations for Post-Normal Risk." *Journal of Risk Research* 1 (1): 15–44.

Rose, Nikolas S. 1999. *Powers of Freedom: Reframing Political Thought.* Cambridge: Cambridge University Press.

———. 2007. *The Politics of Life Itself: Biomedicine, Power, and Subjectivity in the Twenty-First Century.* Princeton, NJ: Princeton University Press.

Rosner, David, and Gerald Markowitz. 2002. "Industry Challenges to the Principle of Prevention in Public Health: The Precautionary Principle in Historical Perspective." *Public Health Reports* 117 (6): 501–512.

———. 2005. "Standing up to the Lead Industry: An Interview with Herbert Needleman." *Public Health Reports* 120 (3): 330–337.

Rossi, Mark. 2007. "The Louisville Charter for Safer Chemicals: A Platform for Creating a Safe and Healthy Environment through Innovation." *New Solutions: A Journal of Environmental and Occupational Health Policy* 17 (3): 173–175. doi: 10.2190/NS.17.3.b.

Rudel, Ruthann A., David E. Camann, John D. Spengler, Leo R. Korn, and Julia G. Brody. 2003. "Phthalates, Alkylphenols, Pesticides, Polybrominated Diphenyl Ethers, and Other Endocrine-Disrupting Compounds in Indoor Air and Dust." *Environmental Science and Technology* 37 (20): 4543–4553. doi: 10.1021/es0264596.

Rudel, Thomas K. 2013. *Defensive Environmentalists and the Dynamics of Global Reform.* New York: Cambridge University Press.

Saguy, Abigail Cope. 2013. *What's Wrong with Fat?* New York: Oxford University Press.

Savage, Jennifer S., Jennifer Orlet Fisher, and Leann L. Birch. 2007. "Parental Influence on Eating Behavior: Conception to Adolescence." *Journal of Law, Medicine and Ethics* 35 (1): 22–34. doi: 10.1111/j.1748–720X.2007.00111.x.

Schapiro, Mark. 2007. *Exposed: The Toxic Chemistry of Everyday Products and What's at Stake for American Power.* White River Junction, VT: Chelsea Green Publishing.

Schecter, Arnold, Marian Pavuk, Olaf Päpke, John Jake Ryan, Linda Birnbaum, and Robin Rosen. 2003. "Polybrominated Diphenyl Ethers (PBDEs) in U.S. Mothers' Milk." *Environmental Health Perspectives* 111 (14): 1723–1729.

Schierow, L.J. 2002. *Pesticide Residue Regulation: Analysis of Food Quality Protection Act Implementation*. Vol. RS20043. Washington, DC: Congressional Research Service and the Library of Congress.

Schlink, F.J. 1935. *Eat, Drink and Be Wary*. New York: Covici Friede Publishers.

Schor, Juliet B. 2007. "In Defense of Consumer Critique: Revisiting the Consumption Debates of the Twentieth Century." *Annals of the American Academy of Political and Social Science* 611 (1): 16–30.

———. 2010. *Plenitude: The New Economics of True Wealth*. New York: Penguin.

Schreder, Erika. 2009. *Earliest Exposures*. Seattle, WA: Washington Toxics Coalition, Commonweal Biomonitoring Resource Center, and Toxic-Free Legacy Coalition. https://toxicfreefuture.org/science/research/earliest-exposures.

Schug, Thaddeus T., Anne F. Johnson, Linda S. Birnbaum, Theo Colborn, Louis J. Guillette Jr., David P. Crews et al. 2016. "Minireview: Endocrine Disruptors: Past Lessons and Future Directions." *Molecular Endocrinology* 30 (8): 833–847. doi: 10.1210/me.2016-1096.

Schultz, David. "EPA Denies Request to Ban Triclosan but Will Assess Endangered Species Impacts." *Bloomberg BNA Chemical Reporter,* May 18, 2015.

Schwarcz, Joe. 2015. *Monkeys, Myths, and Molecules: Separating Fact from Fiction, and the Science of Everyday Life*. Toronto: ECW Press.

Scott, Dayna Nadine. 2005. "Shifting the Burden of Proof: The Precautionary Principle and Its Potential for the 'Democratization' of Risk." In *Law and Risk*, edited by Law Commission of Canada, 50–86. Vancouver, BC: University of British Columbia Press.

———. 2007. "Risk as a Technique of Governance in an Era of Biotechnological Innovation: Implications for Democratic Citizenship and Strategies of Resistance." In *Risk and Trust: Including or Excluding Citizens?* edited by Law Commission of Canada, 23–56. Black Point, NS: Fernwood Publications.

Scott, Dayna Nadine, Jennie Haw, and Robyn Lee. 2017. "'Wannabe Toxic-Free?' From Precautionary Consumption to Corporeal Citizenship." *Environmental Politics* 26 (2): 322–342. doi:10.1080/09644016.2016.1232523.

Sexton, Ken, Larry L. Needham, and James L. Pirkle. 2004. "Human Biomonitoring of Environmental Chemicals." *American Scientist* 92 (1): 38–45.

Shamasunder, Bhavna, and Rachel Morello-Frosch. 2015. "Scientific Contestations over 'Toxic Trespass': Health and Regulatory Implications of Chemical Biomonitoring." *Journal of Environmental Studies and Sciences* 6 (3): 556–568. doi: 10.1007/s13412-015-0233-0.

Shostak, Sara. 2004. "Environmental Justice and Genomics: Acting on the Futures of Environmental Health." *Science as Culture* 13 (4): 539–562.

———. 2010. "Marking Populations and Persons at Risk: Molecular Epidemiology and Environmental Health." In *Biomedicalization: Technoscience, Health and Illness in the US,* edited by Adele E. Mamo, Laura Fosket, Jennifer Ruth Fishman, Jennifer R. Shim, Janet K. Riska, and Elianne Clarke, 242–262. Durham, NC: Duke University Press.

————. 2013. *Exposed Science: Genes, the Environment and the Politics of Environmental Health*. Berkeley, CA: University of California Press.

Siegel, K. R., K. McKeever Bullard, G. Imperatore, Henry S. Kahn, Aryeh Stein, Mohammed Ali et al. 2016. "Association of Higher Consumption of Foods Derived from Subsidized Commodities with Adverse Cardiometabolic Risk among US Adults." *JAMA Internal Medicine* 176 (8): 1124–1132. doi: 10.1001/jamainternmed.2016.2410.

Slocum, R. 2004. "Polar Bears and Energy-Efficient Lightbulbs: Strategies to Bring Climate Change Home." *Environment and Planning D: Society and Space* 22 (3): 413–438. doi: 10.1068/d378.

Snyder, Robert. 1984. "Basic Concepts of the Dose-Response Relationship." In *Assessment and Management of Chemical Risks,* vol. 239, edited by Joseph V. Rodricks and Robert G. Tardiff, 37–55. N.p.: American Chemical Society.

Solomon, G. M., and P. M. Weiss. 2002. "Chemical Contaminants in Breast Milk: Time Trends and Regional Variability." *Environmental Health Perspectives* 110 (6): A339–A447.

Stevens, Lindsay M. 2016. "Environmental Contaminants and Reproductive Bodies: Provider Perspectives on Risk, Gender, and Responsibility." *Journal of Health and Social Behavior* 57 (4): 471–485.

Sulik, Gayle A. 2010. *Pink Ribbon Blues: How Breast Cancer Culture Undermines Women's Health*. New York: Oxford University Press.

Szabo, Michelle. 2014. "Men Nurturing through Food: Challenging Gender Dichotomies around Domestic Cooking." *Journal of Gender Studies* 23 (1): 18–31.

Szasz, Andrew. 1994. *Ecopopulism: Toxic Waste and the Movement for Environmental Justice*. Minneapolis: University of Minnesota Press.

————. 2007. *Shopping Our Way to Safety: How We Changed from Protecting the Environment to Protecting Ourselves*. Minneapolis: University of Minnesota Press.

Sze, Julie. 2007. *Noxious New York: The Racial Politics of Urban Health and Environmental Justice*. Cambridge, MA: MIT Press.

Taylor, Dorceta E. 2009. *The Environment and the People in American Cities, 1600s–1900s: Disorder, Inequality, and Social Change*. Durham, NC: Duke University Press.

————. 2014. *Toxic Communities: Environmental Racism, Industrial Pollution, and Residential Mobility*. New York: NYU Press.

Thayer, Kristina A., Kyla W. Taylor, Stavros Garantziotis, Shepherd H. Schurman, Grace E. Kissling, Dawn Hunt et al. 2016. "Bisphenol A, Bisphenol S, and 4-Hydroxyphenyl 4-Isoprooxyphenylsulfone (BPSIP) in Urine and Blood of Cashiers." *Environmental Health Perspectives* 124 (4): 437–444.

Thornton, Joseph W., Michael McCally, and Jane Houlihan. 2002. "Biomonitoring of Industrial Pollutants: Health and Policy Implications of the Chemical Body Burden." *Public Health Reports* 117 (4): 315.

Tickner, Joel A. 2003. Introduction to *Precaution, Environmental Science and Preventive Public Policy,* edited by Joel A. Tickner, xiii–2. Washington, DC: Island Press.

Tickner, Joel A., Carolyn Raffensperger, and Nancy Myers. 1999. *The Precautionary Principle in Action: A Handbook*. Windsor, ND: Science and Environmental Health Network. www.sehn.org/rtfdocs/handbook-rtf.rtf.

Tipton-Martin, Toni. 2015. *The Jemima Code: Two Centuries of African American Cookbooks*. Austin: University of Texas Press.

Trasande, Leonardo, R. Thomas Zoeller, Ulla Hass, Andreas Kortenkamp, Philippe Grandjean, John Peterson Myers et al. 2015. "Estimating Burden and Disease Costs of Exposure to Endocrine-Disrupting Chemicals in the European Union." *Journal of Clinical Endocrinology and Metabolism* 100 (4): 1245–1255.

Travernise, Sabrina. 2015. "FDA Sets 2018 Deadline to Rid Foods of Trans Fats." *New York Times*. June 16, 2015. www.nytimes.com/2015/06/17/health/fda-gives-food-industry-three-years-eliminate-trans-fats.html.

Tronto, Joan C. 1993. *Moral Boundaries: A Political Argument for an Ethic of Care*. London: Routledge.

Tweedale, Anthony C. 2017. "The Inadequacies of Pre-Market Chemical Risk Assessment's Toxicity Studies—The Implications." *Journal of Applied Toxicology* 37 (1): 92–104. doi: 10.1002/jat.3396.

Tyrrell, Jessica, David Melzer, William Henley, Tamara S. Galloway, and Nicholas J. Osborne. 2013. "Associations between Socioeconomic Status and Environmental Toxicant Concentrations in Adults in the USA: NHANES 2001–2010." *Environment International* 59: 328–335. doi: 10.1016/j.envint.2013.06.017.

United Nations Environment Program. 1992. *Rio Declaration on Environment and Development*. Rio de Janeiro: United Nations Environment Program. www.unesco.org/education/pdf/RIO_E.PDF.

United States Environmental Protection Agency. 2017a. "History of Safer Choice and Design for the Environment." Safer Choice. Accessed November 28, 2017. www.epa.gov/saferchoice/history-safer-choice-and-design-environment.

———. 2017b. "What Does the Safer Choice Label Mean?" Safer Choice. Accessed November 28, 2017. www.epa.gov/saferchoice/learn-about-safer-choice-label.

United States Food and Drug Administration. 2017a. "How FDA Evaluates Regulated Products: Cosmetics." FDA Basics. Last modified September 22, 2017. www.fda.gov/aboutfda/transparency/basics/ucm262353.htm.

———. 2017b. "Hair-Smoothing Products That Release Formaldehyde When Heated." Cosmetics. Last modified November 3, 2017. www.fda.gov/Cosmetics/ProductsIngredients/Products/ucm228898.htm.

———. 2017c. "How FDA Evaluates Regulated Products: Drugs." FDA Basics. Last modified November 26, 2017. www.fda.gov/AboutFDA/Transparency/Basics/ucm269834.htm.

United States Government Accountability Office. 2005. *Options Exist to Improve EPA's Ability to Assess Health Risks and Manage Its Chemical Review Program*. Washington, DC: US Government Accountability Office.

———. 2014. *Federal Food Safety Oversight: Additional Actions Needed to Improve Planning and Collaboration*. Washington, DC: US Government Accountability Office.

———. 2017. "About GAO." Washington, DC: US Government Accountability Office. www.gao.gov/about/index.html.

Ventura, Alison K., and John Worobey. 2013. "Early Influences on the Development of Food Preferences." *Current Biology* 23 (9): R401–R408. doi: 10.1016/j.cub.2013.02.037.

Vogel, Jason M. 2005. "Perils of Paradigm: Complexity, Policy Design, and the Endocrine Disruptor Screening Program." *Environmental Health* 4 (1): 1–11. doi: 10.1186/1476–069x-4–2.

Vogel, Sarah A. 2013. *Is It Safe? BPA and the Struggle to Define the Safety of Chemicals.* Berkeley, CA: University of California Press.

Vogel, Sarah A., and Jody A. Roberts. 2011. "Why the Toxic Substances Control Act Needs an Overhaul, and How to Strengthen Oversight of Chemicals in the Interim." *Health Affairs* 30 (5): 898–905.

Vogt, Rainbow, Deborah Bennett, Diana Cassady, Joshua Frost, Beate Ritz, and Irva Hertz-Picciotto. 2012. "Cancer and Non-Cancer Health Effects from Food Contaminant Exposures for Children and Adults in California: A Risk Assessment." *Environmental Health* 11 (1): 83. https://doi.org/10.1186/1476–069X-11–83.

vom Saal, Frederick, and John J. Myers. 2008. "Bisphenol A and Risk of Metabolic Disorders." *JAMA: Journal of the American Medical Association* 300 (11): 1353–1355. doi:10.1001/jama.300.11.1353.

Waggoner, Miranda R. 2013. "Motherhood Preconceived: The Emergence of the Preconception Health and Health Care Initiative." *Journal of Health Politics, Policy and Law* 38 (2): 345–371.

———. 2015. "Cultivating the Maternal Future: Public Health and the Pre-pregnant Self." *Signs* 40 (4): 939–962.

———. 2017. *The Zero Trimester: Pre-pregnancy Care and the Politics of Reproductive Risk.* Oakland, CA: University of California Press.

Waggoner, Miranda R., and Tobias Uller. 2015. "Epigenetic Determinism in Science and Society." *New Genetics and Society* 34 (2): 177–195. doi: 10.1080/14636778.2015.1033052.

Wall, Glenda. 2005. "Is Your Child's Brain Potential Maximized? Mothering in an Age of New Brain Research." *Atlantis* 28 (2): 41–50.

Warner, Judith. 2005. *Perfect Madness: Motherhood in the Age of Anxiety.* New York: Riverhead Books.

Warner, Melanie. 2014. *Pandora's Lunchbox: How Processed Food Took over the American Meal.* New York: Simon and Schuster.

Wartella, Ellen A., Alice H. Lichtenstein, and Caitlin S. Boon. 2010. *Examination of Front-of-Package Nutrition Rating Systems and Symbols: Phase I Report.* Washington, DC: National Academies Press.

Washburn, Rachel. 2013. "The Social Significance of Human Biomonitoring." *Sociology Compass* 7 (2): 162–179. doi: 10.1111/soc4.12012.

Washington University School of Medicine. 2006. *St. Louis Baby Tooth Survey, 1959–1970.* St. Louis, MO: Bernard Becker Medical Library.

Watson, Emily. 2013. "How Clean Is Your Label?" *Food Navigator-USA,* May 24, 2013.

Webber, Laura, Lucy Cooke, Claire Hill, and Jane Wardle. 2010. "Associations between Children's Appetitive Traits and Maternal Feeding Practices." *Journal of the American Dietetic Association* 110 (11): 1718–1722. http://dx.doi.org/10.1016/j.jada.2010.08.007.

Weir, Lorna. 2006. *Pregnancy, Risk and Biopolitics: On the Threshold of the Living Subject.* New York: Routledge.

Weschler, Charles J. 2009. "Changes in Indoor Pollutants since the 1950s." *Atmospheric Environment* 43 (1): 153–169. http://dx.doi.org/10.1016/j.atmosenv.2008.09.044.

West, Candace, and Don H. Zimmerman. 1987. "Doing Gender." *Gender and Society* 1 (2): 125–151. doi: 10.1177/0891243287001002002.

Whitehead, Krista. 2016. "Motherhood as a Gendered Entitlement: Intentionality, 'Othering,' and Homosociality in the Online Infertility Community." *Canadian Review of Sociology/Revue canadienne de sociologie* 53 (1): 94–122.

Whiteside, Kerry H. 2006. *Precautionary Politics: Principle and Practice in Confronting Environmental Risk.* Cambridge, MA: MIT Press.

Whole Foods Market. 2017. *2016 Annual Report.* Austin, TX: Whole Foods Market.

Whorton, James C. 1975. *Before Silent Spring; Pesticides and Public Health in Pre-DDT America.* Princeton, NJ: Princeton University Press.

Wigle, D. T., T. E. Arbuckle, M. Walker, M. G. Wade, S. Liu, and D. Krewski. 2007. "Environmental Hazards: Evidence for Effects on Child Health." *Journal of Toxicology and Environmental Health, Part B* 10 (1–2): 3–39. http://dx.doi.org/10.1080/10937400601034563.

Wiles, Richard, Kenneth Cook, Todd Hettenbach, and Christopher Campbell. 1999. *How 'bout Them Apples: Pesticides in Children's Food Ten Years after Alar.* Washington, DC: Environmental Working Group and Tides Foundation.

Wiles, Richard, Kurt Davies, and Susan Elderkin. 1995. *A Shoppers Guide to Pesticides in Produce.* Washington, DC: Environmental Working Group and Tides Foundation.

Williams, Christine. 2006. *Inside Toyland: Working, Shopping, and Social Inequality.* Berkeley, CA: University of California Press.

Williams, Lu Ann. 2015. "2015 Clean Label Report." Global Food Forums, September 9, 2015. www.globalfoodforums.com/clean-label-a-shifting-global-trend.

Willis, Margaret M., and Juliet B. Schor. 2012. "Does Changing a Light Bulb Lead to Changing the World? Political Action and the Conscious Consumer." *Annals of the American Academy of Political and Social Science* 644 (1): 160–190. doi: 10.1177/0002716212454831.

Wilson, Michael, and Megan Schwarzman. 2009. "Toward a New U.S. Chemicals Policy: Rebuilding the Foundation to Advance New Science, Green Chemistry, and Environmental Health." *Environmental Health Perspectives* 117 (8): 1202–1209. doi: 10.1289/ehp.0800404.

———. 2014. "International Chemicals Policy, Health, and Human Rights." In *Textbook of Occupational and Environmental Medicine,* 5th edition, edited by Robert J. Harrison and Joseph LaDou, 741–747. New York: McGraw-Hill Education.

Wingfield, Adia Harvey. 2009. *Doing Business with Beauty: Black Women, Hair Salons, and the Racial Enclave Economy*. Lanham, MD: Rowman and Littlefield.

Wolf, Joan B. 2011. *Is Breast Best? Taking on the Breastfeeding Experts and the New High Stakes of Motherhood*. New York: NYU Press.

World Health Organization and United Nations Environment Programme. 2012. *State of the Science of Endocrine Disruptors*. Geneva: Inter-Organization Programme for the Sound Management of Chemicals.

Wurzel, Rüdiger. 2002. *Environmental Policy-Making in Britain, Germany and the European Union: The Europeanisation of Air and Water Pollution Control*. Manchester, UK: Manchester University Press.

Zepeda, Lydia, Hui-Shung Chang, and Catherine Leviten-Reid. 2006. "Organic Food Demand: A Focus Group Study Involving Caucasian and African-American Shoppers." *Agriculture and Human Values* 23 (3): 385. doi: 10.1007/s10460-006-9001-9.

Zhang, Tao, Jingchuan Xue, Chuan-zi Gao, Rong-liang Qiu, Yan-xi Li, Xiao Li et al. 2016. "Urinary Concentrations of Bisphenols and Their Association with Biomarkers of Oxidative Stress in People Living near E-Waste Recycling Facilities in China." *Environmental Science and Technology* 50 (7): 4045–4053.

Zimmerman, Julie B., and Paul T. Anastas. 2015. "Toward Substitution with No Regrets." *Science* 347 (6227): 1198–1199.

Zoeller, R. Thomas, T. R. Brown, L. L. Doan, A. C. Gore, N. E. Skakkebaek, A. M. Soto et al. 2012. "Endocrine-Disrupting Chemicals and Public Health Protection: A Statement of Principles from the Endocrine Society." *Endocrinology* 153 (9): 4097–4110. doi: 10.1210/en.2012–1422.

Zota, Ami R., Cassandra A. Phillips, and Susanna D. Mitro. 2016. "Recent Fast Food Consumption and Bisphenol A and Phthalates Exposures among the U.S. Population in NHANES, 2003–2010." *Environmental Health Perspectives* 124 (10): 1521–1528. doi: 10.1289/ehp.1510803.

Zota, Ami R., Ruthann A. Rudel, Rachel A. Morello-Frosch, and Julia Green Brody. 2008. "Elevated House Dust and Serum Concentrations of PBDEs in California: Unintended Consequences of Furniture Flammability Standards?" *Environmental Science and Technology* 42 (21): 8158–8164. doi: 10.1021/es801792z.

Zota, Ami R., and Bhavna Shamasunder. 2017. "The Environmental Injustice of Beauty: Framing Chemical Exposures From Beauty Products as a Health Disparities Concern." *American Journal of Obstetrics and Gynecology* 217 (4): 418. e1–418.e6. doi: 10.1016/j.ajog.2017.07.020.

Zukin, Sharon. 2004. *Point of Purchase: How Shopping Changed American Culture*. New York: Routledge.

———. 2008. "Consuming Authenticity." *Cultural Studies* 22 (5): 724–748. doi: 10.1080/09502380802245985.

INDEX

Page numbers in *italics* denote tables. Abbreviations used in the index and text are listed on pages xv–xvi.

65 cancer warning, 2; and "natural" as term on labels, 46; pesticides and farmworkers in, 17; Proposition 65 requirements, 2, 182n63; reviews of chemicals, requirements for, 157; Toxic Information Clearinghouse, 51

Canada: chemical assessment for, 157; methodology of current study with background in, 159, 175, 176; neoliberalism in, 19; pregnancy and interest of mothers in precautionary consumption, 168

cancer, 9, 11, 119, 121–22. *See also* carcinogens

canned food, BPA and, 56, 76

carcinogens (and potential carcinogens): Alar, 42; baby powder lawsuit, 16; drugs kept on market despite being, 35, 36–37; formaldehyde, 47–48; glyphosate as, 2; labeling laws for, 2; occupational exposure to, 9; postwar period and rise of concerns about, 36; pressure on retailers to curtail use of, 150–51, 201n8; regulation to protect consumers from, 36–37, 40

Carson, Rachel, 61

Center for Science in the Public Interest, 42

Centers for Disease Control and Prevention (CDC): biomonitoring survey of (aggregated results), 8, 62, 64, 181n34, 191n35; definition of "environmental chemical," 181n34; environmental health organizations as alternative to, 56–57; lifestyle recommendations for women, 111, 198n4; on PFOA, ubiquity of, 152

chemical dose. *See* body burden

chemical industry: biomonitoring studies rejected by, 64; as percentage of U.S. economy, 30; postwar boom in, 7, 15; precautionary principle rejected by, 26–27, 29; role in amplifying uncertainty of harm, 31; stalling regulation of chemicals, 6, 18–19, 29, 30, 31, 158. *See also* agribusiness and food processors; consumer citizenship; industry-funded research

chemical industry, relationship of with government regulators: corporations as controlling balance of power in, 32–33; EPA decisions and, 11; evidence of harms ignored by regulators to protect industry, 35, 36–37; glyphosate and, 2; transparency in, need for, 157–58, 202n26; undermining European Union regulations, 30, 144, 158; undermining global environmental agreements, 28. *See also* lobbying of government; regulatory politics

chemicals: "chemophobia," 6, 182n63; defined as term, 180n10, 181n34; environmental justice and precautionary reviews of, 157; fears about, as warranted based on peer-reviewed research, 6–7, 10–11, 182n63; high- or low-priority substances, 51. *See also* biomonitoring; body burden; BPA (bisphenol A); chemical industry; cleaning products; cosmetic chemicals; endocrine disruptors; flame retardants; food additives, synthetic; fragrances, synthetic; pesticides; phthalates; *specific chemicals by name*

chemicals, numbers of: grandfathered in by TSCA, 37; newly introduced per year, 7; reviewed for safety, 6, 38; total registered with EPA, 7, 38

Chemours, 153

children: childcare combined with shopping, 46, 135–36; contaminated, 112; early childhood development, discourse of, 139; fire retardant exposures of, 9; reduction of expenses by reserving organic purchases for, 126; tirecrumb playground material, precautionary measures against, 49; transgenerational effects of chemical exposures, 69–71, 193n71. *See also* fetal development; infants; maternal accountability for children's health; maternal responsibility for precautionary consumption

children and care products, toys, clothing, and furniture: BPA and, 51; labeling and, 91, 96–97, 98, 100; phthalates and, 49; precautionary consumption and, 103, 105, 106; recalls and, 48–49; regulations governing, 48 children, purity of: antivax parents and concerns about, 200n12; as false or elusive ideal, 119, 146; high stakes of child-rearing and, 117–19, 139; and purity of maternal body, 108–13; as symbol, 112

China, 48–49, 100

chlorpyrifos, 52

Chobani (yogurt manufacturer), 46–47

class and precautionary consumption: access to stores and, 124, 127, 128–29, 138, 170; and balance of money, time, and mental labor, 125–26, 133, 142, 145–46, 169–70; childcare and other pressures and, 46, 135–36; comprehensive routines and, 126, 133–38; constrained choices and, 126, 176; definition of categories of, 170, 173, 203nn19,22; as environmental justice issue, 155–56; ideal routines and, 122, 129; illness and, 129–31; income sources and, 126–27, 133–34, 135, 136, 140, 169; and labels, reading, 46; and luxury, organic food as, 129; methodology of study and, 169–70, *171–72*, 173, 203nn19,22; middle-class cultural capital and, 135–36, 137–38; moderate routines and, 126; and normative motherhood, 126–27, 140–41, 142; and prenatal/preconception awareness, 22; shift of class status and lack of ability to practice, 131–33; shopping strategies and, 126, 128–29, 130, 134, 135, 137, 140, 142; status among store clientele, 130; stay-at-home moms and, 137; stress as influencing food choices, 133, 155, 176, 200n14; and time, low-income women and flexible use of, 133–38; and two-tiered marketplace, 82; under conditions of poverty, 127, 135, 142, 169–70, 176, 200n5. *See also* expense of precautionary consumption; income level; poverty

Clean Air Act (1970), 37

Clean Air Act Amendments (1990), 26, 38; fluorocarbons, phaseout of aerosols containing (1994), 37, 53, 186n54

Clean Fifteen (EWG), 72, 107

cleaning products: basic routines and, 105; comprehensive routines and, 106, 134; homemade, 76, 106, 142; labeling of, 87; moderate routines and, 105; Whole Foods quality standards for, 87

Clean Water Act (1972), 37

Colborn, Theo, 58–59, 80

Collins, Patricia Hill, 140

Commoner, Barry, 191n38

Commonweal, 151

complexity of precautionary consumption, 76–77, 101–2, 108

comprehensive precautionary consumption routines: overview of, 106–7; attention to detail required for, 107; factors influencing choice of, 112–13, 120–23; guilt/anxiety about failures in, 106–7; and "intensive mothering/total motherhood" ideologies, 107, 133, 137–38, 141, 149–50; middle- and lower-income women and, 126

Congress, U.S.: House Select Committee to Investigate the Use of Chemicals in Food Products, 36; Office of Chemical Safety and Pollution Prevention, 52. *See also specific laws*

Connecticut, 44, 76

Conscious Capitalism: Liberating the Heroic Spirit of Business (Mackey and Sisodia), 88

consumer citizenship: action opportunities provided on environmental health organizations websites, 81, 161, 164; definition of, 78–79; environmental health movement literature and message of, 79–81; as individualized collective action, 79–80, 81; limitations of, 81, 82; minimal impact of, on precautionary consumption, 86, 149–50; transparency and, 99; Whole Foods marketing message of, 86, 195n15

consumer groups, early twentieth-century, 33–34

consumer literacy: class and cultural capital of, 135; definition of, 46; environmental health movement demanding, 78; and labels, interpretation of, 2–3, 46, 93, 94–96, 101–2; and limits to precautionary consumption, 151; as replacement for regulatory action, 148–49; as requirement of precautionary consumption, 142, 145. *See also* mental labor of precautionary consumption

consumer products: class and ability to purchase, 126; misrepresentation of, by eco-friendly companies, 148; recalls of products, 1, 48–49; risk of chemical exposures from, 10. *See also* children and care products, toys, clothing, and furniture; cosmetic products; furniture; organic food

Consumer Product Safety Act (1972), 48, 49

Consumer Product Safety Commission (CPSC), 48–49, 56

Consumer Product Safety Improvement Act (2008), 49

consumer self-protection. *See* precautionary consumption

"conventional," definition of, 180n18

conventional grocery stores: access to, residential location and lack of, 127; and class, 138; conditions in and distrust for, 88–89, 196n24; immigrants and navigation of, 176–77; labels on food originally simplified for, 93; status in retail landscape of, 84

conventional grocery stores, natural and organic products sold in: generic brands, 84, 127; mainstreaming of precautionary consumption and, 84; percentage of stores carrying, 84; sales and profits in, 3; selection available in, 91

cooking. *See* foodwork

Cook, Ken, 62, 80–81

cosmetic chemicals: disproportionate exposure to, 10; endocrine disruptors in, 47; European Union bans and restrictions on, 6; FDA bans and restrictions on, 6, 47; FDA review of, 5–6; industry-funded research used to review, 47; premarket approval not required for, 47. *See also* cosmetic products

cosmetic products: anticipatory motherhood and, 111; comprehensive precautionary consumption routines and, 106, 113, 121, 134; FDA unable to ban, 47–48; homemade, 106, 142; labeling of, 47–48; maternal-fetal conflict and, 70; misrepresentation of, by eco-friendly companies, 148; moderate precautionary consumption routines and, 105–6; organic ingredients in, 43; over-the-counter drugs as ingredients in, 188n104; regulation of, 47; strict elimination of, resulting in modest reductions in body burden, 151; trust for Whole Foods and, 89. *See also* children and care products, toys, clothing, and furniture

cost-benefit analysis, 26

Costco, 105, 135, 140, 150

CVS (pharmacies), 150

dairy products: affluent household toxic exposures and, 10; allergen labeling for, 45; and labels, interpretation of, 3; PBB contamination of, 192n43; rBGH-free label on, 94; USDA as regulatory agency for, 39; WIC benefits for organic, 131

Daniels, Cynthia, 68

Davis, Frederick Rowe, 160

DBP (dibutyl phthalate), 69

DDT (dichloro-diphenyl-trichloroethane): biomonitoring of, 64; body burden of, 8, 60; endangered species and, 15; persistence in the environment, 28; and postwar chemical boom, 15; precautionary consumption choices and, 107; regulation of, and body burden decline, 60

DEHP (di-2-ethylhexyl phthalate), 29, 69

Delaney Clause (FAA, 1958), 36, 40–41, 53, 186n49

Delaney, James, 186n49

DES (estrogen diethylstilbestrol), 35, 36–37

Design for the Environment program (EPA), 49–50

Deutsch, Tracey, 93

dioxins, 60, 64, 154

Dirty Dozen (EWG), 3, 40, 72, 76, 105, 113

DOHaD (developmental origins of health and disease) model, 69–71, 118–19, 192n68, 193n71

domestic environment. *See* home environment

dose-response model for safety thresholds, 29–30; "the dose makes the poison," 59

drug safety, 35. *See also* Food and Drug Administration (FDA); industry-funded research

Dumanoski, Diane, 59, 80

Dupont, 152–53

Earth Summit (Rio Declaration), 27–28, 59

Easy Steps to a Safer Pregnancy (HCHW), 56, 70

Eat, Drink and Be Wary, 35

eco and "green" labels, neoliberalism and growth in, 20

eco-friendly companies: accountability constrained by bottom line, 148; green chemistry, investment in, 158; and the two-tiered marketplace, 154

economic growth: chemical export sector, 30; environmental justice and, 156, 157; as industry argument against precautionary principle, 29, 53, 55, 157; as industry argument against regulation, 32–33, 40–41, 50; organic food sector, 3–4, 104; precautionary principle and, 20, 53, 144, 146–48. *See also* consumer citizenship; neoliberalism

educational attainment of consumers: as cultural capital, 136, 137, 142; and labels, reading of, 46, 109; middle-class income gradations and, 173

education of children, importance of, 141

education of consumers. *See* consumer literacy

eggs, 39–40, 91

Eliasoph, Nina, 149

Elixir Sulfanilimide, 35

Endangered Species Act (1973), 37

endocrine disruptors: chemical industry denial of effects of, 11, 30, 59, 182n63; in cosmetics, 47; decline in body burdens resulting from regulation/banning by government, 154; dose-response model as inadequate for evaluation of, 29–30, 59; environmental health movement revealing hazards of, 58–59; European Union and regulation of, 29, 30; "fragile fetus" and susceptibility to, 59, 182n63; green chemistry to avoid, 158; health effects of exposure to, 10–11, 58–59; life-cycle exposures, assessment of, 29; low-dose exposures, assessment of, 29–30, 59; male vulnerability to, 68, 69; occupational exposure to, 9; precautionary principle approach to, 30; pressure on retailers to curtail use of, 150–51, 201n8; replacement chemicals as toxic swap, 152–53; residues found in foods, 3, 180n9; transgeneration effects caused by, 69–70, 193n71; widespread exposure due to global use of, 153–54. *See also* BPA (bisphenol A)

Endocrine Society, 6, 30

endometriosis, 129–30

environmental chemicals: defined by CDC, 181n34; as term, 180n10. *See also* chemicals

Environmental Defense Fund, 180n9

environmental health movement: overview of, 14, 56–57, 144–45; beginnings of, 58, 78; and developmental origins of health and disease (DOHaD) model, 69–71, 118–19, 192n68, 193n71; urban environmental movement (late nineteenth–early twentieth centuries) compared to, 78. *See also* consumer citizenship; environmental health organizations

environmental health organizations: overview of, 56–57; as alternative to government regulators, 42, 56–57; appealing for individual self-protection and regulatory change, 80–81, 82, 119; and endocrine disruptors, revelation of hazards of, 58–59; methodology of study and, 160–64, *162–63*; pressure on retailers to reform product ingredients, 150–51, 201n8; as producers of precautionary consumption advice, 57, 58;

FAA (Food Additives Amendment), 36, 40–41, 53, 186n49

Farm Bill (2014), 201n3

farmers' markets, 106, 126, 137

farmworkers, 12, 17, 52, 67–68, 128

FDA. *See* Food and Drug Administration

federal government. *See* chemical industry, relationship of with government regulators; Congress, U.S.; lobbying of government; regulatory politics; *specific agencies and laws*

Federal Insecticide, Fungicide and Rodenticide Act (FIFRA, 1947), 35–36, 39

femininity, normative: as biopolitical project, 108–9; definition of, 108; invisible and effortless performance expected for, 115; "pure" maternal body as embodiment of, 110–12; thinness, weight control, and health/nutrition discourse, 108–9, 110–11, 112, 123, 198nn23–24; and trajectory of dieting leading to practice of precautionary consumption, 109–12, 123

fetal development: biopolitics and, 21–22; critical windows of vulnerability in, 69; early life exposures of greatest concern, 11; endocrine disruptor effects on ("fragile fetus"), 59, 182n63; male parent body burden, effect of, 67–68; umbilical cord blood revealing body burden in, 62, 66, 192n50. *See also* children; maternal bodies

fish, mercury exposures and, 10, 22

flame retardants: organohalogens, 49; tris(1,3-dichloro-2-propyl) phosphate (TDCPP), 153. *See also* flame retardants (PBDEs and PBBs)

flame retardants (PBDEs and PBBs): beef and milk contamination (Michigan 2007 incident), 17, 65, 192n43; as bioaccumulated in the body, 7; biomonitoring of, 64; body burden of, 8, 60, 62; decline in body burdens resulting from regulation of, 60, 154; furniture replacement following bans and restrictions on, 9, 115, 181–82n48; health effects of exposure to, 10–11, 121–22; landfills and environmental

migration of, 181–82n48; replacement chemicals for, as toxic swap, 9, 153; state bans and restrictions on, 6, 9, 51

fluorocarbons, phaseout of aerosols, 37, 53, 186n54

food: regulatory system for, generally, 38–39. *See also* dairy products; fruits and vegetables; meat; organic food; pesticide residues; processed and packaged foods

food additives, synthetic: evidence of carcinogenic compounds ignored, 36–37; food colorings, rules for, 29, 36, 41, 45; loophole created for (GRAS expansion), 40–41; "natural" label disallowed for, 45, 46; precautionary approach to, 36; premarket approvals, 40, 41; preservatives, 89, 116

Food and Drug Administration (FDA): overview of, 34–35; authority delegated by, 42; cosmetic chemicals and, 5–6, 47–48, 188n104; dose-response model used by, 29; drug harms ignored to protect industry, 35, 36–37; environmental health organizations as alternative to, 56; funding of, 147; GAO report on, 40; labeling authority of, 45, 196n31; "natural" claims and, 45, 198n10; as unable to recall products, 1, 48; as underfunded and understaffed, 41, 157

Food, Drug and Cosmetic Act (FDCA, 1938): overview of, 35, 40; amendment (2002), 39; Food Additives Amendment, aka Delaney Clause (FAA, 1958), 36, 40–41, 53, 186n49; generally recognized as safe (GRAS) category of food additives, expansion of, 40–41; mandatory information required by, 188n93; pesticide residues (1954 revision), 186n49

Food Quality Protection Act (FQPA, 196), 39, 40

Food Safety and Inspection Service (FSIS), 39–40

foodways: of American South, 112–13, 170; precautionary consumption in conflict with, 130 foodwork: classes in cooking and household budgeting, 136; mothers as using to safeguard children's health, 22; normative femininity and development of skills, 108, 109, 198n23; women's responsibility for, 126, 129

formaldehyde, 9, 47–48

Foucault, Michel, 21, 108, 119

fragrances, synthetic, 47, 71, 72, 89

Frank R. Lautenberg Chemical Safety for the 21st Century Act (2016), 11, 32, 38, 50–53, 55, 157

freedom of choice, 99, 123–24

fruits and vegetables: children refusing to eat, 131–32; conventional, 39–40, 180n18; *Dirty Dozen* guide (EWG), 3, 40, 72, 76, 105, 113; "good mothering" as creating children who will eat, 132; pesticide residue monitoring of, 39–40. *See also* organic food

furniture, eco-friendly, 106

furniture, flame retardants in: recommendation against, 49; replacement and disposal of, 9, 115, 181–82n48. *See also* children and care products, toys, clothing, and furniture

Gareau, Brian, 28

Garey, Anita, 116

gender: biomonitoring reports and gendering of body burdens, 66–71; and biopolitics of reproduction, 21–22; and education, importance of, 141; grocery shopping as gendered labor, 84, 97, 117; and labels, reading, 46; and risk of exposure to chemicals, 10; safe-shopping guides and, 77–78. *See also* men; women

gendered labor of precautionary consumption. *See* maternal responsibility for precautionary consumption

General Federation of Women's Clubs, 33–34

genetic mutations, 68–70, 118–19, 193n71

gentrification, and Whole Foods, 90, 196n25

GenX, 152–53

Germany, 27

Gibbs, Lois, 58

Giddens, Anthony, 15–16

glyphosate, 2, 179–80nn7–8

GMOs (genetically modified organisms): absence of (GMO-free claims), 44; as chemicals, 187n87; definition of, 43; distinguished from selective breeding, 43; European Union restrictions on, 43–44; in food, 43–45; and glyphosate application rates, 179–80n7; labeling of, 44–45; USDA as regulatory agency for, 39, 44–45

Government Accountability Office (GAO), 31–32, 40, 41

Grandjean, Phillippe, 182n63

GRAS (generally recognized as safe) category of food additives, expansion of, 40–41

Great Lakes Water Quality Agreement (1972, 1978), 28

great risk shift, 19–20

green chemistry, investment in, 158

Green Consumer Guide, 79

Greenpeace International, 192n50

guilt about failures of precautionary consumption, 106–7, 132

Guthman, Julie, 99

Hacker, Jacob, 19

hair dye, 29

health and chemical exposures: overview of, 10–11; epigenetic mutations and, 118–19; and individual responsibility for health, 123, 129–30, 136; as spatially displaced, 14; as temporally displaced, 14. *See also* health problems; medical care; public health; reproductive health disorders

health code violations, 88–89, 196n24

health problems: "new" public health and lifestyle modifications for, 119–20, 121, 199n46; precautionary consumption as critical to prevention and treatment of, 120–23, 129–31. *See also* health and chemical exposures

Healthy Child, Healthy World (HCHW), 56, 68, 70, 71, 161

heavy metals, 48, 64

and standardized, 188n93, 196n31; misleading statements, protection from, 45, 46, 188n93; "natural" as term on, 45, 46–47, 198n10; nutritional provisions for, 45–46, 93; organic food, 43, 93, 96; "storied food," 90–91; sugar content requirement, 46, 188n98; voluntary, 93, 94. *See also* labels; seals and labels

labels: bait-and-switch of replacement ingredients, 94; for children's products, 91, 96–97, 98, 100; for cleaning products, 87; consumer literacy required to interpret, 2–3, 46, 93, 94–96, 101–2; and consumers, importance to, 93, 96; for cosmetics, 47–48; education level and reading of, 46, 109; English-language proficiency and decoding of, 176; false claims on, 100; gendered labor of precautionary consumption portrayed on, 83, 97; idea of safety promoted via, 2–3, 96–97; and individualization of risk, 99; ingredient lists, 87, 96; as integral to precautionary shopping, 83; multiple messages, navigation of, 101–2; percentage of consumers who read, 46; plastic recycling symbols and safety choices, 77; precautionary claims made on, 91–94, *92*, *95*, 165, 168; priority of reading, and multiple pressures while shopping, 46, 135; priority of reading, stress and poverty as influencing, 133, 155, 176, 200n14; as stoking anxiety, 97–98; tables of precautionary claims on, *92*, *95*; thinness ideal and learning to read, 109

landfills, and chemical exposures, 181–82n48

Landrigan, Philip, 182n63

Langston, Nancy, 34, 160

Latinos/as, as organic consumers, 3–4

Lavin, Chad, 98

lead: American Medical Association warning label for, 18; biomonitoring of, 64; children's exposure to, health effects of, 18–19; in children's toys, 48, 49; continued exposure to, 19; decline in body burdens resulting from ban

of, 18–19, 154; early restrictions on lead paint, 18; families of color and exposure to, 9; health effects of exposure to, 10–11; income levels and exposure to, 9, 19, 183n92; industry stalling of restrictions on, 18–19, 31; phaseout of, 18–19; pregnancy/breastfeeding as passing through to child, 66, 67; removal of, as process, 18; water pipes, 9, 19

Learning and Developmental Disabilities Initiative, 69

Lewis, Edna, 170

lobbying of government: against TSCA, 11, 50; budget of, 11; of European Union to prevent banning and restricting chemicals, 6, 29, 30, 158; and funding of regulatory agencies, 147, 201n3; global environmental agreements undermined by, 28; influence on the EPA, 11; low-dose exposure to endocrine disruptors, denial of health effects of, 11, 30, 59, 182n63; revolving door of lobbyists and government regulators, 157, 202n26; as suppressing or delaying regulation, 144

local food, interest in, 87–88, 100

Louisiana, "Cancer Alley," 15

Love Canal, New York, toxic waste site, 58

low-dose exposures: advocacy biomonitoring reports concerned with, 64–65; denial of validity of, 64–65; endocrine disruptors and, 29–30, 59

low-income, definition of, 173

low-income middle class, definition of, 173

low-income neighborhoods: Whole Foods and rising rents in, 90, 196n25. *See also* residential location

low-priority substances, 51

Lupton, Deborah, 120

Mackey, John, 88, 90, 99, 195–96n23

Maine, 6, 44

makeup. *See* cosmetic products

Mansfield, Becky, 21

marketplace: effecting change through (*see* consumer citizenship); precautionary principle as goal for, 82; as two-tiered, 13, 82, 154. *See also* Whole Foods Market

Markowitz, Harold, 18

Massachusetts, 51, 76

maternal accountability for children's health: biomonitoring reports and focus on, 66–71, 81–82; developmental origins of health and disease (DOHaD) model and, 70–71; internalization of responsibility for, 67, 108; and lower-income mothers, 136; maternal-fetal conflict (maternal selfishness) and, 70–71; new and unfair measures of lifestyle choices and, 71; social and cultural expectation of, 5, 70, 103–4, 107–8, 111, 112, 117, 144, 145, 146. *See also* maternal responsibility for precautionary consumption

maternal bodies: avoidance of alcohol recommended by CDC, 198n4; avoidance of chemicals during, 103, 111; as baby's first environment, 103, 119, 146; biomonitoring and focus on, 66–71, 81–82; biopolitics and, 21–22, 108–9; "pure," normative femininity practices and preparation of, 108–13

maternal responsibility for precautionary consumption: overview of, 4–5, 103–4, 123–24; exhaustion as price of, 116; freedom of choice and, 123–24; judgments of "hysteria" as risk of, 114–15; labels portraying, 83, 97; male partners as supportive bystanders to, 114–17, 123, 175–76; motherhood as consumer project, 121; normative motherhood and, 107–8, 110–12, 123, 144, 149–50; and trajectory of normative femininity as leading to, 109–12, 123. *See also* precautionary consumption routines

meat: affluent household toxic exposures and, 10; DES residues in, 36–37; expense reductions via choices in, 126; GMO feeds for animals, 44; PBB poisoning of (Michigan, 1970s), 17, 65, 192n43; pesticide residue monitoring of, 39–40; USDA as regulatory agency for, 39; Whole Foods quality standards for, 89–90, 100

medical care and caregivers: as encouraged to give precautionary consumption advice, 71; lifestyles of patients as focus of, vs. structural factors, 66; postgenomic medicine, 192n68; precautionary consumption advice as rarely issued by, 193n80; surveillance of women as "vectors for fetal risk," 103. *See also* public health

medical society statements urging regulation, 6, 18

men: biomonitoring reports as largely ignoring, 22, 67, 69, 82; body burden as passed on to children by, 67–69; body burdens of, 66; DOHaD studies as generally ignoring, 70; as grocery shoppers, 84; home environment and, 68; infertility and, 68, 82; methodology of study and, 175; occupational hazards and, 67–68; reproductive equation and, 67–69, 70, 112, 113, 123; and "reproductive masculinity," 68; safe-shopping guide depictions of, 77; as supportive bystanders to practice of precautionary consumption, 114–17, 123, 175–76; surveillance not extended to, 103, 112; transgenerational effects of chemical exposures and, 70

mental labor of precautionary consumption: basic shopping routines and, 107; class and balance of time, expense, and, 125–26, 133, 142, 145–46, 169–70; class and cultural capital of ability to perform, 135–36, 137–38; comprehensive shopping routines and, 107; learning curve as steep for, 126, 134, 135; moderate shopping routines and, 105–6; and multiple pressures while shopping, 46, 135–36; and neoliberalism, 141; price comparisons/unit price calculations, 134, 135; reduction of, by shopping at expensive specialty stores, 126; as requirement for practice of, 125–26, 133; resistance to comprehensive routines and, 116–17. *See also* access to retail spaces for precautionary consumption; expense of precautionary consumption; time as requirement for precautionary consumption

mercury exposure, 10, 22, 67
methodology of text: overview of, 23, 159; demographics of respondents, 170–73, *171–72*, 203nn14,19,22; environmental health movement campaigns, 160–64, *162–63*; history of regulation and, 160; interviews with respondents, 168–75; limitations of research, 169–70, 175–77; and precautionary consumption, as term, 198n9; recruitment of respondents, 169–70; Whole Foods Market and product analysis, 164–68, *166–67*
methyl bromide, 28
methylene glycol, 47–48
Michigan: Flint lead poisoning, 19; PBB contamination of meat, 17, 65, 192n43
middle-class individuals and families: income levels defining, 173, 203n19; normative motherhood coded as, 141, 142; as safe-shopping guide audience, 78. *See also* class and precautionary consumption
Mind the Store program, 201n8
minority communities and families: occupational chemical exposures as disproportionately affecting, 9; stereotypes of, 140; and women in leadership of environmental health organizations, 190n8. *See also* occupation and risk of chemical exposure; race; residential location and risk of chemical exposure
miscarriages, 120–21
Monsanto, 1, 2
Montreal Protocol on Ozone Depleting Substances (1987), 12, 28
Morello-Frosch, Rachel, 79
motherhood, normative: "anticipatory motherhood," 111; and Black single mothers, stereotypes of, 140–41; "calculative rationality" and, 107; coded as white, heterosexual, and middle-class, 141, 142; concerted cultivation (of extracurricular school activities), 141; "good," requiring children to consume organic food, 107; intensive mothering/total motherhood ideologies, 107, 133, 137–38, 141, 150;

and maternal responsibility for precautionary consumption, 107–8, 110–12, 123, 144, 149–50; pathologization of anxious mother, 115; "too perfect mother" label, 141; working-class and low-income mothers and claims to, 126–27, 140–41, 142. *See also* maternal accountability for children's health; maternal bodies; maternal responsibility for precautionary consumption
Moyers, Bill, 62
multiple chemical exposures, 7, 65, 153
Murphy, Michelle, 14
Myers, Pete, 59, 80

National Bioengineered Food Disclosure Law (2016), 44–45
National Environmental Policy Act (1970), 37
National Institute for Environmental Health Sciences (NIEHS), 8
National Organic Product Act, 53
National Organic Program, 42–43. *See also* organic certification
"natural" as claim, 45, 46–47, 198n10
Natural Resources Defense Council (NRDC), 36–37, 81, 180n9
Needleman, Herbert, 18
neoliberalism: overview of, 19–20; fragility of class status and, 132–33; good health as individual imperative in, 119–20; and labor required for precautionary consumption, 141; precautionary principle rejected under, 20; and shift of risk to families and individuals, 19–20, 99–100, 119, 134–35, 146, 149; Trump administration and, 20
Nestle, Marion, 101
neurological development and cognition, 11
New York (state), 58, 152
New York City: and class categories, definitions of, 173, 203nn19,22; programs to improve access to fresh food, 127; rental market-rates in, 203n19; rent-to-income ratio in, 203n19
Non-GMO Project, 44, 96
Nutrition Labeling and Education Act (NLEA, 1990), 45, 53, 196n31

replacement of, with glass or stainless steel, 105, 126

political avoidance, culture of, 149–50

politics, shopping as. *See* consumer citizenship

Pollan, Michael, 91

poverty: defined, 169; lack of representation in study, 169, 176

poverty and stress: and impossibility of practicing precautionary consumption, 127, 135, 142, 169–70, 176, 200n5; as influencing food choices, 133, 134–35, 155, 176, 200n14; and loss of class status blamed on personal choices, 132–33; medical focus on lifestyles of patients vs., 66; as obscured by precautionary consumption, 12–13, 142

precautionary consumption: biopolitics and, 21–22; complexity of, 76–77, 101–2, 108; as defensive environmentalism, 13–14; definition of, 4; and distrust of medical, science, and corporate authority, 20, 146–48, 184n103; English-language proficiency and, 176; environmental health organizations that don't recommend, 81; as expected to appear invisible and effortless, 115; government encouragement of, 35–36, 38, 50; and individualization of risk, 4, 12–14, 21, 81, 98, 99, 108, 113, 145, 146; inverted quarantine concept and, 12, 13, 76; mainstreaming of, 84, 85; as personal standard of safety, 4; precautionary principle distinguished from, 11–12; as replacement for regulations, 143–44, 148–49, 150; stereotype of, 125; structural problems as obscured by, 12–13, 142; as term in methodology, 198n9. *See also* maternal responsibility for precautionary consumption; precautionary consumption advice; precautionary consumption routines

precautionary consumption, limited success of: class differences in feasibility of precautionary consumption and, 151; consumer education of limited help in, 151; inequalities in severity of chemical exposures and, 155–56; infant body

burdens as evidence of, 67; multiple pathways of contamination and, 153; persistent toxics and, 153–54; regulations recommended vs., 151, 155–56; replacement chemicals as equally hazardous, 152–53; strict adherence to regimes no guarantee of success, 151; two-tiered marketplace and, 154. *See also* environmental justice

precautionary consumption advice: overview of, 72; environmental health organizations as producers of, 57, 58; medical caregivers as rarely issuing, 193n80; methodology of study and, 161–64, *162–63*; and simplicity and ease, language of, 76–77; table of actions recommended, *73–75*; women's responsibility as focus of, 70–71

precautionary consumption routines: overview of, 104–5; basic routines, 105; "good enough" precautionary consumption, 106; guilt/anxiety about failures in, 106–7, 132; and high stakes of feeding a child, 117–18; and illness, response to, 120–23; learning curve and building of, 126, 134, 135; and maternal accountability for health of children, 107–8, 114; moderate routines, 105–6, 126. *See also* class and precautionary consumption; comprehensive precautionary consumption routines; maternal responsibility for precautionary consumption; shopping practices

precautionary principle: and burden of proof, 28, 29, 36, 144, 156; chemical industry's rejection of, 26–27, 29; definition of, 11–12, 26, 27, 56; early debates using idea of, 33–34; economic priority used as argument against, 29, 53, 55, 157; endocrine disruptors and, 30; European adoption of, 6, 26, 27, 144; government embrace of, proposal for, 156–58; and government intervention, consensus supporting, 28, 146–47; as guiding logic behind major environmental initiatives, 12, 27–28; hostility toward, as policy ethic in the United States, 12, 17, 29, 52–53,

cautionary policies, 37, 53; timeline of, 53, *54*; Trump administration and weakening of regulations, 11, 32, 38, 51–52, 53, 156. *See also* chemical industry, relationship of with government regulators; lobbying of government; *specific agencies and laws*

regulatory politics, 1990s to present: overview of, 38; chemical regulation, 49–52; consumer products, 48–49; conventional fruits and vegetables, 39–40; food, generally, 38–39; food labeling, 45–47; GMOs in food, 43–45; organic standards, 42–43; personal care products, 47–48; processed foods, 40–42

Reich, Jennifer, 20, 184n103, 200n12

replacement chemicals: as forming new exposure risks (toxic swap), 9, 152–53; product-by-product basis of, 153; safer, need for development of, 82

replacement ingredients, bait-and-switch and, 94

replacement products: advice for, 76; class and ability to purchase, 126; for plastics, 105, 126

reproductive health, biopolitics and, 21–22

reproductive health disorders: endocrine disruptors and, 58–59; gendered responsibility for, 112; increases in incidence of, 11; infertility, 11, 68, 82, 112, 199n29; occupational chemical exposures and, 9; precautionary consumption as solution to, 120–21

"reproductive masculinity," 68

residential location and access. *See* access to retail spaces for precautionary consumption

residential location and risk of chemical exposure: overview of, 8–9, 176; agriculture and pesticide drift, 12; environmental health organizations in fight against, 58; as environmental justice issue, 155–56, 158; as high risk, 12, 152, 153; landfill locations and, 181–82n48; racist zoning ordinances and covenants and, 9

Richards, Ellen Swallow, 78

Richardson, Sarah, 103

Rio Convention ("Earth Summit," 1992), 12, 27–28, 59

risk and risk assessment: "calculative rationality" and, 107; great risk shift to individuals and families, 19–20, 134–35; industry approved models of, 51; "organized irresponsibility" and, 98; and preoccupation with making risk calculable and predictable, 16; purity of children and management of, 118–19; "risk society," 15–16, 98. *See also* individualization of risk

Robb, Walter, 195–96n23

Rose, Nikolas, 21

Roundup, 2, 179–80n7. *See also* glyphosate

Rudel, Thomas, 13

Safe Drinking Water Act (1974), 37

Safer Chemicals, Healthy Families, 81, 201n8

Safer Choices Label, 50

safe-shopping guides: overview of, 3, 72, 76; appealing for individual self-protection and regulatory change, 80–81, 82; language used in, 79; methodology of study and, 161, *162–63*; middle class as target audience for, 78; white women as target audience for, 77–78. *See also* precautionary consumption advice

safety: labels as promising, 97–98; labels as promoting, 2–3, 96–97; Whole Foods merchandising message of, 86

safe-until-sorry model: overview of, 33, 41–42; cosmetics as regulated under, 47; and food industry watchdogs as external to government, 42; precautionary principle rejected in favor of, 26–27; Year of the Recall (2007) and scrutiny of, 48–49

scientific uncertainty: acceptable levels of, 17; chemical industry role in amplifying, 31; precautionary principle and threshold of, 27–28; proof-of-harm model requiring certainty, 31, 144; questions of, as delaying regulation, 17–19; Rio Convention agreement and, 27–28, 59 seals and labels: as branding products as superior to conventional, 96; Non-GMO Project, 96; organic certification, 43, 93, 96; Safer Choices Label, 49–50. *See also* labeling of food; labels

Shamasunder, Bhavna, 79

shopping practices: class and strategies for, 126, 128–29, 130, 134, 135, 137, 140, 142; complexity and, 101–2, 108; consistent choices required for protection, 77; expensive specialty stores as reducing time and effort of, 126, 142; as gendered labor, 84, 97, 117; multiple stores shopped to find bargains and sales, 126, 129–30, 135, 137, 140, 142; price comparisons/unit price calculations, 134, 135; smartphone apps to identify toxics, 77; time required to make choices, 77. *See also* precautionary consumption routines

Shostak, Sara, 21, 61

Silent Spring (Carson), 61

Silent Spring Institute, 71, 100, 122

single mothers, 126–27, 138–41

Sisodia, Rajendra, 88

Skin Deep Cosmetic Database (EWG), 3, 4, 71, 72

smartphone apps for precautionary consumption, 77, 134

SNAP benefits, 134, 135, 136, 137, 169, 174

social media, consumer organizing and, 1

sodium laureth sulfate, 148

sperm, 68–69, 70

stainless steel vs. plastic, 2, 97, 126

state laws: as alternative to weakness of TSCA, 51; bans and restrictions on chemicals, 6; Toxic Information Clearinghouse (California), 51; TSCA revision prohibiting, 51; WIC program limitations on purchase of organic foods, 127, 200n5

states, suing EPA for failing to ban chlorpyrifos, 52

Stockholm Convention on Persistent Organic Pollutants (2001), 12, 28

Stonyfield Farm (yogurt producer), 83, 99, 194n1

strawberries, 28, 40, 71

stress. *See* under poverty

strontium-90, 191n38

sugar: labeling requirement for, 46, 188n98; lower-income mothers and dependence on, 132; and "natural" as term on labels, 46–47; as replacing HFCS, 94

sunscreen, 10, 76, 98, 100, 116–17, 148, 188n104

Supplemental Nutrition Assistance Program (SNAP), 134, 135, 136, 137, 169, 174

surveillance of women: of Black single mothers, 140; and food assistance programs, 169; medical, and fetal risk, 103; and weight, 108, 111

Sweden, 60

Szabo, Michelle, 195n15

Szasz, Andrew, 12, 13, 76, 155

Target, 150

technologies of the self, 119–20

Teflon, 72, 152–53

time as requirement for precautionary consumption: basic routines and, 105; class and balance of expense, mental labor, and, 125–26, 133, 142, 145–46, 169–70; and class privilege, 124, 133; complexity of consumer advice and, 77, 102; comprehensive routines and, 106–7; exhaustion as price of, 116; initial investment of (learning curve), 126, 134, 135; low-income mothers and flexible use of, 133–38, 142; moderate routines and, 105–6; as necessary to practice of, 125; neoliberalism and, 141; reduction of, by shopping at expensive specialty stores, 126, 142. *See also* access to retail spaces for precautionary consumption; expense of precautionary consumption; mental labor of precautionary consumption

tire crumb materials, review for safety of, 49

Tooth Fairy Project (1958), 191n38

Toxic Release Inventory, 20

toxics. *See* chemicals

Toxic Substances Control Act (TSCA, 1976): amendment (2016), 11, 32, 38,

50–53, 55, 157; chemical industry lobbying against, 11, 50; Design for the Environment program/Safer Choices label, 49–50; grandfathered chemicals and burden of proof on EPA, 37–38; industry-approved risk assessment models and, 50–51; lobbying to reform (2017), 164; premarket review and, 51; replacement chemicals (toxic swap) and, 153; review by agency as new requirement of, 50; reviews required by, 50, 51; state laws as option due to weakness of, 51; state laws prohibited by, 51; Trump administration and weakening of, 32, 38, 51–52, 156

toys. *See* children and care products, toys, clothing, and furniture

Trader Joe's, 85, 88, 131, 135, 137, 195n21

trade secrets, protection of fragrances, 47

trans fats, 45, 46

transgenerational effects of chemical exposures, 69–71, 193n71

transparency: consumer empowerment and, 99; environmental justice and, 156–57; and the exercise of precautionary control, 89, 98, 100; as industry trend, 88, 93–94; as stylized representation, 98; as Whole Foods Market marketing message, 87, 88–89, 98–99, 100

triclosan, 6, 8, 16

Trump, Donald, administration of: neoliberalism and, 20; weakening of regulations under, 11, 32, 38, 51–52, 53, 156

TSCA. *See* Toxic Substances Control Act

Udall, Tom, 26

umbilical cord blood, body burden revealed in, 62, 66, 192n50

uncertainty. *See* scientific uncertainty

United Kingdom, neoliberalism and, 19

United Nations Conference on Environment and Development (1992), 27–28

United Nations Environment Programme (UNEP), 153–54

United Nations Framework Convention on Climate Change, 28

upper class, definition of, 203n22

upper-middle class, definition of, 173

urban environmental movement (late nineteenth–early twentieth centuries), 78

USDA (U.S. Department of Agriculture): Agricultural Marketing Service, 40; cosmetics not regulated by, 43; and DES use in livestock, 36–37; Food Safety and Inspection Service (FSIS), 39–40; funding of, 147, 201n3; GAO report on testing methodologies of, 40; rBGH approval, 94; responsibilities of, 39, 44–45. *See also* National Organic Program; organic certification

vaccines and refusal of, 184n103, 200n12

Vermont, 44, 152

vitamins and supplements, as excluded from study, 165

VOCs (volatile organic compounds), 64, 191n40

Vogel, Karl, 34

Vogel, Sarah, 160

Waggoner, Miranda, 111

Walmart, 150

Washington, 6

Washington Toxics Coalition, 67

water bottles, 2, 72, 153

water supply: lead pipes, 9, 19; PFOA contamination of, 152

waterways: and body burden, 8; migration of PBDEs in, 181–82n48

West Virginia, 152, 153

What to Eat (Nestle), 101

whiteness. *See* race

Whole Foods Market: overview of, 84–85, 145; access to (number and locations of stores), 85, 127, 145, 164, 175, 195n12; affordability of, 90, 129, 140; Amazon purchase and ownership of, 85, 145, 164, 195–96n23; avoidance by some shoppers, 89–90; class and shopping strategies in, 129, 130; and consumer citizenship, message of, 86, 195n15; design and merchandising in, 84–86, 164–65; employee practices of, 90,